PALLADIAN STYLE

PALLADIAN STYLE

Steven Parissien

**To my Mother
and in memory of Val**

Phaidon Press Limited
Regent's Wharf
All Saints Street
London N1 9PA

First published 1994
Reprinted in paperback 2000

ISBN 0 7148 4026 2

A CIP catalogue record for
this book is available from the
British Library

Printed in Hong Kong

Endpapers **A floral wallpaper of
c.1730, block-printed with a pat-
tern based on the Indian Tree of
Life. The wallpaper was rescued
by Treve Rosoman and Orde
Solomons from a second-floor
room at 29 Sackville Street,
London, and is now in English
Heritage's Architectural
Study Collection.**
Page 1 **The garden at Hartwell
House, depicted in 1738 by
Balthasar Nebot.**
Frontispiece **The north front of
Roger Morris' Marble Hill House,
built in 1724–9.**
Page 3 (title page) **Part of a John
Sanderson design for the Salon at
Kimberly near Wyndham in
Norfolk, built in 1755–7.**
Opposite **Design for an ornamental
gate from Batty Langley's** *Treasury
of Designs* **of 1740.**

The four decades which followed the establishment of the House of Hanover on the British throne in 1714 represent a time when Britain finally graduated to a commanding position on the world's stage, establishing an economic dominance and a territorial empire that were to last two centuries. Although the new royal family were not, like their predecessors, of central importance in supporting the arts of Georgian Britain, the 40 years after 1714 were years of great artistic achievement: the satires of Swift and Pope, the novels of Richardson and Fielding, the art of Hogarth and the music of Handel. In particular, the early eighteenth century was a time of architectural revolution. Challenging the predominance of the tamed Baroque forms which had become commonplace since the Restoration of Charles II in 1660 was a wholly new architectural style, based on firm rules of proportion and with an impeccable pedigree stretching back through Renaissance Italy to Ancient Rome: a style that became known as Palladianism.

This book, which deals with homes from the succession of George I to the middle of the eighteenth century, completes a trio of architectural and decorative studies of the Georgian period. As with its predecessors *Adam Style* and *Regency Style*, *Palladian Style* does not aim merely to tell the story of the great Palladian architects, but seeks to examine what the 'Palladian' style meant, and how it percolated down to the middle-class homes of the period. There are a number of recent works by John Harris and others which do an excellent job of analysing the buildings designed or financed by the grandees of early Georgian Britain. *Palladian Style*, however, while inevitably charting the development of the Palladian villa – a building type which helped to establish Palladianism in Britain and North America – principally examines the homes of the middling sort, who could not afford designers of the calibre of Campbell or Kent but who adopted Palladian rules and fashions as soon as was practically possible.

This is not yet another 'style' book reproducing suppliers' modern, highly contrived room sets with the aim of convincing you that such approximate 'inspirations' reflect true historical practice. Instead, I have tried to explain exactly what the 'Palladian' fashion signified, how it came about, and how it affected the average homes of the period. I have looked not just at the great buildings of the era but at the theories behind the architecture, at the ways middle-class houses were actually built, and at how modest Palladian interiors were both decorated and used. The result, I hope, is a book which both informs and entertains, and which provides a detailed and vivid impression of how the early Georgian house looked, evolved and worked.

Left **Brick terraced houses of the mid-1720s in Montpelier Row, Twickenham, Middlesex.**

Steven Parissien, October 1993

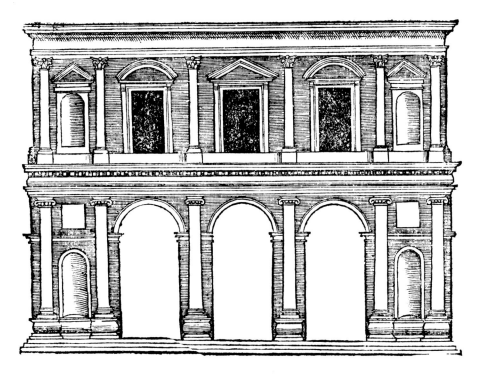

Above Title page from
Sebastiano Serlio's
seven-book *Tutte l'Opere
d'architettura e prospettiva* of
1619. This particular copy
was owned by Inigo Jones,
who passed it to his pupil
John Webb. By 1720 the
book was in the hands of
Sir James Thornhill.

WHEN BRITAIN FIRST AT HEAVEN'S COMMAND,

AROSE FROM OUT THE AZURE MAIN,

THIS WAS THE CHARTER OF THE LAND,

AND GUARDIAN ANGELS SUNG THIS STRAIN –

'RULE, BRITANNIA, RULE THE WAVES;

BRITONS NEVER WILL BE SLAVES.' James Thomson, *Alfred*, 1740

Left Antonio Canaletto's
Old Horse Guards Parade of
c.1749. Inigo Jones' Banqueting House is clearly visible in
the background, the only
survivor of the 1698 fire
which burnt the rest of the
old Palace of Whitehall to
the ground. The shocking
intrusion of Jones' severely
classical proportions into
the comfortable Early Stuart
cityscape is still fully
comprehensible over a
century after the building's
construction.

The accession of King George I to the British throne in 1714 heralded an era of peace, prosperity and relative stability. This tranquil period has earned the epithet 'Augustan', a label employed by modern literary historians to signify the great literary flowering of the late seventeenth and the first half of the eighteenth centuries, but which is additionally used, as social historian Roy Porter has pointed out, 'to evoke [the] majestic imperial calm' of the years which followed the Treaty of Utrecht of 1713, which brought an end to the harrowing War of the Spanish Succession. 'Augustan' was a term also used by the early Georgians themselves. It quickly became the watchword of the fawning and socially ambitious; of these, none was more sycophantic than the androgynous Court wit and gossip Lord Hervey (Pope's 'painted child of dirt that stinks and sings'), who announced the beginning of an 'Augustan age of England' in literature, a golden era to be celebrated 'either for learning, strength of diction, or elegance of style'. For Hervey and his fellow courtiers, the term 'Augustan' also had another, rather fortuitous, connotation: 'Augustus' happened to be the second name of George I's son and heir, Prince George Augustus, whose long reign (1727–60) witnessed the flowering of the Palladian style.

George I was at first glance an unlikely choice as King of England. He was a middle-aged German from Hanover who could barely speak English. His was also a notoriously unattractive personality. In Hanover he had had his wife permanently incarcerated in a castle dungeon for an alleged affair with a Swedish count; at the same time he entertained a succession of legendarily ugly mistresses, the most famous of whom, Baroness von Schulenberg (created Duchess of Kendal by a fawningly enraptured monarch in 1719) was so thin that she came to be nicknamed 'The Maypole' by the irreverent British. Along with his mistresses, George I brought with him to London a vast retinue of Germans, who proceeded to carve up the most rewarding Court posts for themselves.

Unsurprisingly, the new King was soon the subject of ridicule, especially by those disaffected Tories who saw their governmental influence disappear overnight. Even before his arrival, Tory pamphleteers were brusquely informing old Queen Anne that 'if in sense or politicks you fail'd,/ 'Twas when his lousy long succession you entail'd,' and warning of the pernicious effect the new monarch would have:

Behold he comes to make thy people groan,
And with their curses to ascend thy throne;
A clod-pate, base, inhuman, jealous Fool,
The jest of Europe, and the faction's tool.

The bestselling satirical pamphlet *The Blessings Attending George's Accession* went even further in its libellous commentary on the decidedly unheroic new monarch:

Hither be brought the dear Illustrious House:
That is, himself, his pipe, close stool and louse;
Two Turks, three Whores, and a half a dozen nurses,
Five hundred Germans, all with empty purses.

Right King George I and his son Prince George Augustus, later George II, shown in a detail from the Painted Hall at Greenwich Hospital (now the Royal Naval College). This magnificent hall, designed by Sir Christopher Wren, was painted by Sir James Thornhill between 1708 and 1727. George I is shown landing in England in 1714 – a direct counterpoint to the adjacent depiction of William III's landing at Torbay 26 years before. Both monarchs had been invited by Parliament to help safeguard the nation's Protestant liberties.

George I's son and heir was not much more endearing. Prince George Augustus, later George II, could at least speak English, though with a pronounced German accent. Nevertheless, he proved as boorish and philistine as his father. Inheriting the House of Hanover's legendary lack of interest in any form of artistic patronage, his most famous domestic achievement was to continue the dubious family tradition of collecting ungainly mistresses. Notoriously argumentative, George II's bad temper and disinclination to compromise helped to encourage his eldest son, Prince Frederick of Wales, to establish a rival Court and formal Opposition in 1737 – much as George himself had done when heir to the throne in 1716. George II does, it is true, possess the distinction of being the last British monarch to lead an army into battle. However, even this martial success rapidly proved to be a disappointment. Having engineered the defeat of the French by British, Hanoverian and Austrian troops at the Battle of Dettingen in 1743, the King completely neglected to follow up the advantage he had won and let the French escape. This unfortunate lapse did not prevent the victory from being optimistically hailed in Britain as a second Blenheim, the composer Handel actually being commissioned to write a special *Dettingen Te Deum* to mark the event.

Nevertheless, however dull, insensitive and unattractive the new Hanoverians may have been, they were first and foremost Protestant monarchs who could be relied upon to safeguard the Protestant liberties of the people of Britain. Since the death of poor Queen Anne's last surviving son, the 11-year-old Duke of Gloucester, in July 1700, the issue of the royal succession had dominated British politics. The only Stuart heir to the monarchy was the ageing James II – ousted in the bloodless 'revolution' of 1688 – and, after his death in 1702, his son Prince James, soon to earn the dismissive soubriquet of 'The Old Pretender'. The Act of Settlement of 1701 had attempted to solve the problem by offering the throne to Electress Sophia of Hanover and, after her, to her son George, the future Elector. Not that the Hanoverians were by any means the closest in line to the throne; as historian W A Speck has noted, 'As many as fifty-eight people could claim closer kinship with the dead queen than George Lewis, Elector of Hanover.' Yet the Hanoverian dynasty remained the safest and thus the most suitable Protestant candidates; their succession would, it was fervently hoped, preclude the return to Britain of what remained of the Catholic and hopelessly pro-French Stuarts.

The Tories – who had been in power for four years following their landslide victory in the 1710 election – were fatally compromised by the accession of the new King. As the Duke of Newcastle observed in 1721, George I was very conscious that 'the Whig party is the only security he has to depend on'.

Thomas Patch's caricature of c.1755 of Prince George (later George II) whilst on his obligatory Grand Tour shows, in contrast to Thornhill's official version, how the early Hanoverians were popularly regarded. Note the stunning scagliola floor; this type of tessellated, multicoloured design was subsequently mimicked by British and American floorcloths. Even in this grand interior the candles have been placed in front of mirrors, so as to maximize the amount of light in the evening at comparatively little extra cost.

The concept of the Divine Right of Kings, which to many Tories was the bedrock of their beliefs, had already taken a few knocks during the seventeenth century; now, with the arrival of a little-known German prince to claim the throne at Parliament's invitation, it was totally shattered. Those who could not reconcile themselves to the new régime – most famously Lord Bolingbroke, perhaps the most important figure in Anne's last government – fled to the Continent. Others remained in England and kept their heads down, watching from the wings as the Whigs swept to power and proceeded to create what they claimed would be a more tolerant society. The schism between those who cast in their lot with the exiled Stuarts (named 'Jacobites' after the Stuart heir Prince James) and those who, however reluctantly, remained loyal to the Hanoverian succession, effectively kept the Tories out of government for almost 50 years.

The Tories were also excluded from power by clever measures such as the Septennial Act of 1716, which lowered the temperature of politics by stipulating that elections for a Parliament be held at least every seven years, rather than every three years as formerly. At the same time, the economic prosperity which followed the South Sea Company crash of 1720 helped to pacify the powerful trade lobby. While a third of London banks went under during the South Sea débâcle, between 1720 and 1740 the British gross national product rose by an exceedingly healthy 11.5 per cent. The result was that, whereas 217 Tories and 341 Whigs were returned to Parliament by the 1715 election (an election was always necessitated by the accession of a new monarch), by the time of the death of George I in 1727 the number of Tory MPs in the House of Commons had shrunk to a mere 130.

The disintegration of the Tories did not, however, allow the government to relax. Indeed, the first eight years of George I's reign were a time of uninterrupted rumours, threats and rebellions, plotted or actual. In 1715 Prince James Stuart landed in Scotland and attempted to lead an invasion of England, hoping to unite Scottish nationalism with Jacobite predilections on both sides of the border. In the event, however, the rising proved a damp squib. The Jacobite army got as far as Preston in Lancashire, but, contrary to the Old Pretender's expectations, hardly any Englishmen joined the cause. On returning to Scotland, the Earl of Mar's rebel army of 10,000 was held by the Duke of Argyll's government force of 3,300; soon afterwards, Prince James callously abandoned his followers – many of whom were either executed or transported to North America – and returned to France. However, even 20 years later, there were still tangible threats to the Protestant succession. In 1744 the south coast of England awaited invasion by the French, while the following year Prince James' son, Charles Edward Stuart, landed in Scotland with the aim of unseating George II and avenging his father. A royal army was defeated at Prestonpans, and by December 1745 'Bonnie Prince Charlie' had reached Derby in the heart of the English Midlands. However, this proved to be the limit of his progress. Once again a Jacobite army returned to Scotland to be annihilated by government forces – this time under the King's brother, the Duke of Cumberland, whose easy victory at Culloden earned him the name of 'The Butcher'. In 1747 an attempt was made to scotch the Jacobite threat once and for all: the bearing of arms in Scotland, and even the wearing of kilts, was formally abolished.

Despite the Jacobite menace, most Englishmen felt fairly secure and assured in the years following George I's accession. Britain had, after all, successfully weathered two major changes of monarch – in 1689 and in 1714. The result was a detectable growth in national self-confidence. The Constitution of 1689, with its Hanoverian adjustments, was repeatedly hailed by Britons as a masterpiece of reason and moderation – 'a legal limited monarchy' rather than the continental model of 'an arbitrary despotic power', as the Scots claimed in 1689. To the poet James Thomson in 1736, the British Constitution guaranteed 'fame sustained / of British freedom – independent life; / Integrity in office; and, o'er all / Supreme, a passion for the commonweal.'

The years immediately preceding the Hanoverian succession had also seen the foundation of the British Empire. In particular, the impressive

Right **A contemporary engraving showing the principal events of the 1715 Jacobite rising. The grim fate of many of the Jacobite rebels, graphically depicted at the bottom, contrasted markedly with James Stuart's distinctly premature escape to France.**

CHIEF INCIDENTS OF THE JACOBITE
RISING IN SCOTLAND (1715) — THE
MARCH ON PERTH; BATTLE NEAR
DUNBLANE; ATTEMPT UPON THE
CASTLE OF EDINBURGH, ETC.

From " Prints after Louis du Guernier "
(1917-12-8-1151), in the British Museum.

military victories won by the Duke of Marlborough during the War of the Spanish Succession prompted not only general self-congratulation but also substantial territorial aggrandisement. As historian Geoffrey Holmes has written, 'Not since Agincourt had there been military achievements by an English general on continental soil to compare with Marlborough's triumphs of 1704–8.' And although the incoming Tory government had effectively ended the war – dismissing the Whig Marlborough and opening secret negotiations with the enemy, Louis XIV's France – substantial territorial gains were secured in Europe and, most significantly, in the Americas by the Treaty of Utrecht of 1713. Foreigners were increasingly depicted (most famously by William Hogarth) either as victims of political or religious tyranny, or as malevolent enemies of British liberties who sheltered Jacobites and plotted to undermine both the Constitution and the Protestant succession.

Left The latest style of home – the product of the building Acts of 1667 and 1709 – is seen in this revealing view of London's Fish Street Hill by Canaletto of 1755. White or stone-coloured sash joinery can be seen in virtually every house in this scene, which is dominated by Robert Hooke's Monument to the Great Fire.

Illustration from the title page of Richard Bradley's *Experiments in Husbandry and Gardening* of 1724. Described by the publisher as 'Concerning the Order of Nature, and the Use of that Knowledge in the propagation and cultivating of Plants', the book neatly demonstrates the ready equation the early Georgians made between the cosmic Order and every aspect of the natural world.

Such xenophobic stereotypes quickly became associated, as we will see, with the emergent fashion for Palladian design. Inevitably, the political repression and High Baroque architectural excesses of continental Europe were graphically contrasted both with British liberty and with the new, restrained style of English Palladianism. In 1710 the Third Earl of Shaftesbury used his *Soliloquy* to combine a discussion of artistic temperament with an examination of what he loftily declared was the innate British devotion to the principle of political and artistic liberty. In 1712 he took his argument further, calling for a national architectural style based on the essentially British spirit of freedom, as enshrined in the unwritten but celebrated British Constitution. And the years which followed the accession of George I witnessed increasing numbers of literary contrasts between the calm, rational perfection of the English Palladian style and the unhealthy Baroque fancies of the rest of Europe – 'Detested forms!', James Thomson wrote, 'that, on the mind impressed, / Corrupt, confound, and barbarize an age.' Thomson's verse in particular sought to emphasize the relationship between the wise moderation of British politics and the simple and rational – and, of course, easily affordable – façades of English Palladianism: 'Even framed with elegance the plain retreat, / The private dwelling. Certain in his aim, / Taste, never idly working, saves expense.' By the 1730s even the new-style 'English' garden – 'sylvan scenes, where art alone pretends / To dress her mistress and disclose her charms' – was being used as an analogy to the liberty guaranteed by the splendid Constitution of 1689. The naturalism of William Kent's and Charles Bridgeman's revolutionary new landscapes provided an easily comprehended contrast with the rigid formalism of continental garden planning.

The overweening, almost obnoxious self-satisfaction of Augustan Britain found its mirror in the paintings and engravings of William Hogarth. Nothing was more redolent of the arrogant and complacent spirit of John Bull than Hogarth's *Gate of Calais* of 1749, in which the symbols of the old enemy, France – an obese monk, leering soldiers and emaciated peasants – are seen enviously admiring 'the Roast Beef of Old England'. Yet, at the same time

Sir Robert Walpole, Britain's first true Prime Minister, depicted with all the trappings of power in an engraving after Charles Jervas.

that national self-confidence was apparently brimming, England was, oddly enough, also popularly known in Europe as the land of suicides. The Frenchman César de Saussure, having documented this strange disposition whilst on a visit to Britain in the late 1720s, ultimately found himself succumbing to what much of Europe termed 'the English disease':

> Little by little I lost my appetite and my sleep; I suffered from great anxiety and uneasiness, and that without any reason. Finally I fell into the deepest and blackest melancholy, and suffered untold misery... Had I been an Englishman I should certainly have put myself out of my misery.

In many ways, the relative stability of early Georgian Britain was due to the ability of one man: Robert Walpole, Britain's first true Prime Minister. Having reconciled the bickering Prince of Wales with his father the King in 1720, and survived the spectacular financial crash of the South Sea Bubble of the same year with his reputation (if not his personal finances) just about intact, he had by 1721 emerged as the King's chief minister. Even the death of his royal protector in 1727 failed to shake his position, strengthened as it was by his ability to secure all the principal sources of royal and government patronage while doing little to unsettle the status quo of propertied society. Reform was avoided at all costs. 'His great maxim in policy', Lord Hervey wrote later, 'was to keep everything as undisturbed as he could, to bear with some abuses rather than risk reformations and submit to old inconveniences rather than encourage innovations.' No electoral change was initiated after the Septennial Act of 1716, and Walpole's one attempt at economic reform – the new Excise of 1733 – was abandoned in the face of likely electoral defeat. The Church was kept unreformed and wholly subdued under the leadership of Bishop Gibson (Bishop of Winchester 1716–23, and of London 1723–48), who until 1736 was able to provide his master with the requisite cast-iron majority in the House of Lords. (The break of 1736 was prompted by Gibson's obstruction of an uncharacteristic Walpolean reform – a bill designed to halt the imprisonment of Quakers for not paying tithes.) Throughout this period foreign affairs, too, were kept uncannily quiet. This was largely due to Walpole's mould-breaking French alliance, which enabled him to avoid any serious foreign conflicts until 1740. When taunted with his inaction at the time of the War of the Polish Succession of the mid-1730s, the Prime Minister laconically but sensibly replied that ''twas a comfortable reflection that 100,000 men had already perished in the war...and many millions of money spent, yet not one drop of English blood spilt, or one shilling of English money spent on it.'

Right Hogarth's satirical painting *The Gate of Calais* of 1749 – also known, for obvious reasons, as 'Oh! The Roast Beef of Old England' – is a splendid evocation of Britain's self-confidence during this period. Caricature Frenchmen enviously admire the healthy liberties of Britain, symbolized by the joint of beef being paraded before them, while the impoverished Scot in proscribed tartan dress in the right-hand corner is a reminder of the recent defeat of Bonnie Prince Charlie's Jacobite rebellion. Hogarth was fired by more than his usual xenophobic nationalism in devising this picture: while sketching in Calais he had actually been arrested by the suspicious authorities. Thereafter the artist took great delight in denigrating all things French; even the homes of France were to Hogarth 'all gilt and beshit'.

Walpole was, as historian Eveline Cruickshanks has noted, 'the first modern prime minister, introducing a new style of premiership because he chose to stay in the House of Commons'. As George II himself testified, Walpole's reputation as 'the most able man in the kingdom' was largely based on the fact that he 'knew how to manage that formidable and refractory body, the House of Commons, so much better than any other man'. At the same time, his political image was cannily manipulated in a surprisingly modern fashion. Although he was the owner of a large estate in Norfolk, crowned by Colen Campbell's vast new Palladian mansion of Houghton Hall, in London Walpole cultivated the image of a simple, apple-munching country squire – the people's friend, who preferred to live not in an ancient pile but in a modest, new, middle-class terrace on the north side of Downing Street.

In the event, Walpole was brought down more by unforeseeable economic developments than by the backstairs political intrigue at which he was so adept. A general European slump following the outbreak of the War of the Austrian Succession in 1740, allied to appalling harvests and severe winters in 1740–1, raised the political temperature sufficiently to effect his ejection in 1742. Even then, the Opposition had to resort to bringing in 'the sick and the dead' to vote (a 'shocking sight' in Horace Walpole's opinion) in order finally to unseat the premier.

By the time of his fall in 1742, Robert Walpole had helped to deflate national politics to the level of a comparatively harmless joke. True, the scurrilous Opposition newspaper *The Craftsman* had won an astoundingly large readership of half a million, while John Gay's hugely popular satirical play *The Beggar's Opera* of 1728 had caricatured Walpole's government as a set of unprincipled gangsters and highwaymen. Yet neither the contributors to *The Craftsman* nor Gay brought the government any closer to falling. Instead, while the easy and familiar corruption of the hustings provided an obvious target for William Hogarth – most notably in his famous four-part satire *An Election* of 1754 – there was little pressure for either parliamentary or social reform.

To those who were outside the political arena, early Georgian politics were less of a joke. Democracy itself remained proscribed within very narrow limits. This was, after all, an age when even intellectual giants such as Samuel Johnson were complacent in the belief that 'mankind are happier in a state of inequality and subordination'. Only 160,000 voters in the 40 English counties returned the 80 county MPs, while the 409 borough MPs, from 205 boroughs, were returned by an electorate of only 201,000 voters. Walpole's security – and Britain's stability – was founded on the continuing disgrace of bought 'rotten boroughs'.

Right The south front of Houghton Hall in Norfolk, designed by Colen Campbell for Sir Robert Walpole and begun in 1722. *Top*, an engraving made for *Vitruvius Britannicus*, with the towers from Wilton House terminating each end of the façade; *bottom*, as executed, with domed pavilions replacing the original towers. The Wilton towers – which were believed by Campbell and his contemporaries to be by Inigo Jones – represent one of early Palladianism's most often-quoted sources. However, even these celebrated features may not actually have been designed by Jones. John Harris and Gordon Higgott have recently stated that 'There is no doubt that de Caus designed the famous south front at Wilton House long venerated as a masterwork by Jones'; other historians (most notably Timothy Mowl) have in turn questioned this judgement.

The endemic discontent at the lack of government action found its
expression in the traditional manner: violence. In 1734, the year of the
general disturbances surrounding Walpole's attempted introduction of a new
cider excise, Sir Charles Wager barked that 'we must govern the mob, or
they will govern us'. Serious disturbances and widespread violence at the
election of 1715 led to the passing of the Riot Act, by which a crowd of 12

Left **An engraving after Hogarth of a scene from John Gay's hugely successful and daringly subversive** *Beggar's Opera* **of 1728. Hogarth's original paintings of the opera were themselves a notable success, encouraging him to paint the satirical series for which he is perhaps best known.**

A scene from Edinburgh's notorious Porteous Riots of 1736, engraved after a painting by James Drummond.

people or more could be sentenced to death if they did not disperse within one hour of being ordered to do so by the authorities. Nevertheless, only seven years later the Coventry election of 1722 was to be declared void because of the tumultuous rioting which accompanied it. As H T Dickinson has written of the Coventry hustings, 'Over 2,000 men, on horse and foot, with green twigs and leaves in their hats, colours flying, drums beating and trumpets sounding marched to the polls. They attacked their political opponents, damaged property, and cried out, "…No Hanoverians! No seven years Parliament!"'

The most famous outbreak of concerted mob violence, the Porteous Riots of 1736, occurred after a militia officer, Captain Porteous, had ordered his soldiers to fire on an Edinburgh crowd protesting against the hanging of a popular smuggler. (A highly partial and intimidated Edinburgh court subsequently condemned Porteous himself to hanging; before the government could intervene to reverse this judgement, rioters broke into his prison and lynched the unfortunate officer.) The one truly liberal piece of legislation of the period, the Jewish Naturalization Act of 1753, was withdrawn following severe anti-Semitic mob violence. And even the belated decision to adopt the Gregorian calendar in 1752 (two centuries after most of Europe had abandoned the ancient Julian system) met with prolonged mob violence, rioters demanding back the 11 days they had 'lost' when the calendar necessarily leaped from 2 to 14 September overnight.

Georgian society was not a refined tableau of polite parties held in gracious Palladian villas. Violence always lurked beneath the surface, if it was not openly displayed on the streets. In the 1720s the Frenchman de Saussure was shocked to find that favourite English pastimes included beating cockerels to death with clubs and throwing dead cats and dogs, while an observer of 1736 noted that the English were 'very brutish and barbarous, much in the nature of their bull dogs' and 'much addicted to drunkenness'.

This endemic violence not unnaturally provoked a determined reaction amongst the propertied upper and middle classes. The only possible basis to society, as they saw it, was Order. Order was, not entirely by coincidence, the key to the new, rational environment of the Enlightenment philosophers. 'In the Whole of Things (or in the Universe)', declared Francis Hutcheson, 'all is according to a good Order, and the most agreeable to a general Interest.' As early as 1709, the aesthetic philosopher the Earl of Shaftesbury suggested:

> *Nothing surely is more strongly imprinted on our Minds, or more closely interwoven with our Souls, than the Idea or Sense of* Order *and* Proportion...*What a difference there is between* Harmony *and* Discord! Cadency *and* Convulsion!

Shaftesbury's fear of the likely effects of Discord and Convulsion neatly reflected contemporary society's preoccupation with maintaining social order. Arguments demonstrating the primacy of Natural Order in the world were used to excuse a socially discriminating judicial system by which, while the disgraced ex-Chancellor Lord Macclesfield was fined £30,000 (a large sum, but one which he could well afford) for large-scale embezzlement whilst in public office prior to his sacking in 1725, in 1748 17-year-old William Stevens was hanged for stealing half a pound of tobacco and six gallons of brandy. Cases like William Stevens' abound; in 1753, for example, a woman was hanged simply for stealing a pair of stays.

Propertied society had to be defended at all costs, and Natural Order was invoked to buttress this system. Shaftesbury himself held that 'the mere Vulgar of Mankind' might perhaps 'often stand in need of such a rectifying Object as *the Gallows* before their Eyes', and indeed not one of the capital statutes imposed after 1715, which served private property so well, was repealed until 1808. Shaftesbury and his fellow intellectuals were quick to defend their Order against any attempt to undermine it. Thus in 1709 the Earl even denounced the Whig hero John Locke, alleging, ''Twas Mr Lock [sic] that struck at all Fundamentals, threw all *Order* and *Virtue* out of the World, and made the Very Ideas of these...*unnatural* and without foundation

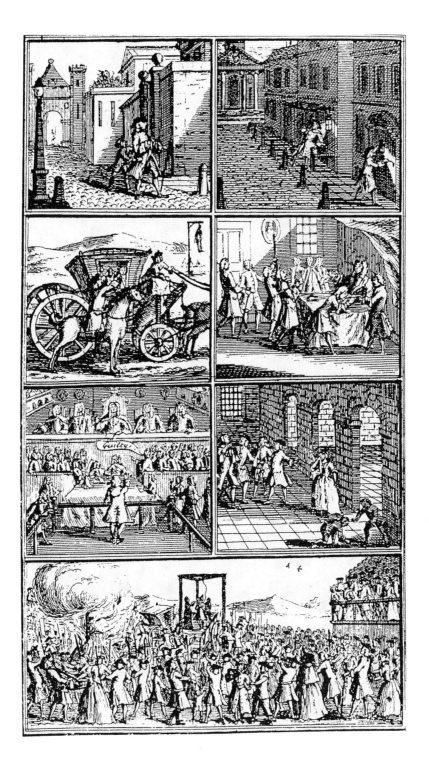

A moral tale from *Select Trials* of 1732. The pickpocket turns highwayman, but is arrested, tried, imprisoned and, inevitably, hanged. Public hangings such as this were a great entertainment in eighteenth-century Britain.

Hogarth's *March of the Guards to Finchley* of 1749–50 exposes the apathetic reaction to the Jacobite invasion of England in 1745 and the dangers inherent in such laxity. Finchley, north of London, was where the government was preparing a second line of defence should Charles Stuart penetrate the Midlands, yet in Hogarth's view the troops on which the country was relying were all too easily distracted by brothels, alcohol and bargains. On the right, prostitutes can be seen leaning from light-coloured sash windows – modern features (the brothel is obviously flourishing) whose relative sophistication is in sharp contrast to the old-fashioned leaded lights seen in the house across the road. Note the external shutters on the King's Head Tavern.

in our Minds.' To Shaftesbury, Order protected a world which needed no social reform or tinkering with the processes of Nature. 'If everything which exists', he confidently declared, 'be according to a good Order, and *for the best*, then of necessity there is no such thing as real ILL in the Universe, nothing ILL with respect to the Whole.' Such sentiments were surely what Voltaire had in mind when, some 40 years later, his celebrated satire *Candide* ridiculed the intellectual pretensions of contemporary philosophers in the form of Dr Pangloss' 'best of all possible worlds': 'It is proved…that things cannot be other than they are, for since everything was made for a purpose, it follows that everything is made for the best purpose…For it is impossible for things not to be where they are, because everything is for the best.'

The most notorious example of the power of statute being invoked to protect private property was the Waltham Black Act of 1723. This measure created 50 new capital offences, including the death penalty for those bearing 'offensive weapons, and having his or their faces blacked' in forests or parks, and for those who poached deer, horses and even fish. As E P Thompson has written, this Act, 'which coincided with the year of Walpole's final political ascendancy, signalled the onset of the flood-tide of eighteenth-century retributive justice'. Nor were the victims always from the rural underclass. Alexander Pope's brother-in-law and nephew were both heavily involved in Black activity in the Windsor Forest in Berkshire.

The Tar's Triumph or Bawdy-House Battery **shows a riot in a Strand brothel of 1749 – almost an everyday occurrence in Palladian England. The rioter leaning from the first floor demonstrates how convenient the sash window could be.**

Georgian capital statutes were invariably interpreted in favour of private property at the expense of the poor, the sick or the vulnerable. Dorothy George has contrasted the 1733 case of John Bennett – a Thames fisherman who killed his 11-year-old apprentice by beating him with a rope and a tiller and then leaving him to die of starvation and exposure, but was acquitted of murder – with the tragic fate a year later of Mary Wotton, 'a little girl of nine, who had been apprenticed fourteen months before by the parish to the wife of a certain John Easton'. Mary 'broke open her mistress's drawers, took twenty-seven guineas, and was found in Rag Fair. She was sentenced to death.' Thankfully, some sought more humane alternatives to introducing yet more capital offences. During the 1740s the novelist Henry Fielding and his blind half-brother Sir John Fielding campaigned for the introduction of an official police service in the capital. Ignored by the authorities, in 1749 they set up their own network of Bow Street Runners, each of whom was paid a guinea a week plus a share of the reward for every criminal successfully prosecuted after capture.

For many of the poor, crime was the only alternative to starvation. An Act of 1723 empowered parishes to set up local workhouses, but this did not betoken a more liberal attitude to the less well-off. One report of the 1720s marvelled that 'the very great numbers of lazy people, rather than submit to the confinement and labour of the workhouse, are content to throw off the mask, and maintain themselves by their own industry'. By 1730 the workhouse system had spread around the country. Yet to many – particularly the young and elderly – the workhouse represented an early grave. As historian Derek Jarrett has written, 'Hogarth's England was an England of landless labourers, many of them totally dependent on daily wages to keep them and their families out of the workhouse.'

By the 1740s most labourers in the capital worked daily hours of 6am to 8pm or even 9pm, shops often remaining open from 7am to 8pm. For those who could not find work, the prospects were far more grim. In 1753 John Wesley was appalled by the condition of the London poor: 'I found some in their cells underground, others in their garrets, but I found not one of them unemployed who was able to crawl about the room. So wickedly, devilishly false is that common objection, they are poor only because they are idle.' Jonathan Swift wrote in 1729 of the prevalence of beggars in Dublin, where every street was 'crowded with Beggars of the female Sex, followed by three, four or six Children, all in Rags, and importuning every Passenger for Alms'. His celebrated, tongue-in-cheek solution was not so far removed from the proposals of those who really did direct the fate of the poor and destitute:

> *I do therefore humbly offer it to publick Consideration, that of the Hundred and Twenty thousand Children, already computed, Twenty thousand may be reserved for Breed...[and] the remaining Hundred thousand may, at a Year old, be offered in Sale to Persons of Quality and Fortune...A Child will make two Dishes at an Entertainment for Friends; and when the family dines alone, the fore and hind Quarter will make a reasonable Dish; and seasoned with a little Pepper or Salt, will be very good Boiled on the fourth Day, especially in Winter.*

It was to provide children with a more hopeful alternative that the philanthropist Thomas Coram established the world's first children's hospital in London. Work began on his Foundling Hospital in 1742; today the foundation survives as the world-famous Great Ormond Street Hospital. By 1742 other, equally celebrated hospitals had already been established: Westminster Hospital was created in 1720 and Guy's Hospital in 1724, while in the provinces the Edinburgh and Bristol Royal Infirmaries were founded in 1729 and 1735 respectively.

The spread of modern hospitals was accompanied by other medical advances. The first properly trained midwives had appeared by the 1740s. In 1716 Lady Mary Wortley Montagu brought back from Turkey the concept of inoculation against the dreaded killer, smallpox, having both her son and her daughter inoculated during the next two years and convincing the

This detail from Hogarth's sympathetic portrait of Captain Coram of 1740 shows the benefactor of the Foundling Hospital in a modest and relaxed setting and with an open, amicable expression. Hogarth's fresh, unpretentious and classless approach represents a complete break with Godfrey Kneller's stiff and formulaic society style of 30 years earlier.

Princess of Wales to support the idea. And some genuine progress was being made in the treatment of that most celebrated of Georgian ailments, gout. In 1720 Dr George Cheyne – all 448 pounds of him – wrote that gout was caused by 'immoderate diet, lack of proper exercise, and an uncertain climate', remarks that presage much of the medical advice we receive from the media today. By the mid-1720s Cheyne was a happily converted vegetarian; his books, immediate best-sellers, continued to be reissued well into the next century.

For many, however, contemporary medicine offered little in the way of hope. Cholera, tuberculosis and diptheria were never far away. As Geoffrey Beard has recently noted, 'In February 1733 nearly sixteen hundred people died in London in one week of violent colds, coughs and fever.' In 1750 the mortality rate in the capital was 1 in 20, a figure which worsened in times of exceptional hardship such as the dismal harvests of 1727–8 and 1740–1, when the price of corn rose from 56 shillings to over 81 shillings a ton. By the early 1740s burials in London were exceeding births; it was only the welcome influx of immigrants from the Continent which kept the population stable.

Although hospitals were becoming increasingly common, the average quack was still in no position to effect a cure for his patients. The legendary incompetence of doctors was neatly revealed by the case of Mary Tofts, an illiterate woman who in 1726 claimed she had borne a litter of rabbits. Not only was the local doctor, John Howard, convinced; so was the royal anatomist, Nathanael St André. Only the royal midwife, Sir Richard Manningham, was suspicious. Once he had locked Tofts up in a sealed room she failed to deliver any more creatures, and, when he threatened to dissect her to discover the gynæcological reason for this miracle, she broke down and confessed that it had all been a hoax. Small wonder that few Georgians had much confidence in the medical profession. Unsurprisingly, when the plague – absent from England since 1665 – reappeared in Mediterranean ports in 1720, the reaction was widespread hysteria. The legislative result was the passing of the draconian Quarantine Act of 1721, by which the government secured the power completely to seal off any affected area.

As for the healthy, not all felt they had to abide by John Wilkes' pessimistic dictum 'Life can little else supply/But a few good fucks and then we die.' For the more ambitious, an advantageous marriage was one way to secure a comfortable life. However, whilst this was an enticing prospect to impoverished males, for women seeking to escape their dismal lot through wedlock the prospects were not always very appealing. Early Georgian court-ships were conducted much in the manner of a cattle-market, with breeding and dowry the most important considerations. Contemporary newspapers, Roy Porter notes, advertised the successful unions, complete with the financial reward the groom was to receive: '25 March 1735, John Parry, Esq. of Carmarthenshire, to a daughter of Walter Lloyd, Esq. member for that county, a fortune of £8,000.' Derek Jarrett similarly records an advertisement in a 1750 issue of the *Daily Advertiser*, requesting a wife who was 'Tall and graceful in her person…[with] good teeth, soft lips, sweet breath…[and] a good understanding without being a wit.' The wife was also to be aged between 7 and 14.

Some brave souls rebelled against such regimentation. In 1712 Lady Pierrepont turned down the chance of £500 a year – and a gift of £20,000 for her father – in rejecting the aptly named Clotworthy Skeffington, preferring instead to marry the relatively impoverished Edward Wortley Montagu. Such rebellions were rare, however. Forty years later, Hardwicke's Marriage Act of 1753 stipulated the proclamation of banns and the issuing of diocesan licences before marriages could be conducted, so as to prevent elopements and any other unions of those aged under 21 which were not conducted in accordance with parental wishes.

Unsurprisingly, early Georgian society attempted to divert itself wherever possible. At Bath, Richard 'Beau' Nash presided over the most

Right Canaletto's 1754 view of the Rotunda at London's Ranelagh Gardens success-fully evokes the grandeur and sumptuousness of this astonishing building. Opened in 1742 (and, alas, demolished in 1805) the Rotunda was the work of the relatively unknown Palladian architect William Jones. Here the most elegant and fashion-conscious – though not necessarily the wealthiest – Londoners gathered to drink tea, listen to music, swap gossip and arrange assignations.

fashionable of watering-holes, dictating dress, arranging the entertainment and regulating gambling. In London the new pleasure gardens at Vauxhall (opened in 1732) and at Ranelagh (inaugurated ten years later) saw aristocrats and the humbler classes mixing in easy familiarity at venues where, as Horace Walpole noted, 'a royal Duke elbowed his shopkeeper'.

The Palladians were also happy to indulge in excess. Geoffrey Beard records an average aristocratic meal of the times, consumed by a dozen guests of the notoriously profligate Duke of Chandos in 1725:

> *First there was a brown and white soup of mushrooms and cream, then a fricassé, pudding, brown ragoût, and collops. Relief was provided by the carrying in of two cooked salmon, lamb and chicken accompanied by artichokes and spinach. A silver épergne in the centre of the table*

Left Hogarth's *Gin Lane* of 1751 shows all the horrors of unrestricted spirit drinking: a flourishing pawnbroker, a neglectful mother, a suicide (the dispirited barber has been unable to find any customers), poverty, death and violence. The eccentric pyramidal spire in the background – topped by a statue of George I – is that of Hawksmoor's church of St George, Bloomsbury, built between 1716 and 1731.

was filled with fruit. In 1733 alone Robert Walpole's Norfolk household guzzled its way through over a thousand bottles of 'White Lisbon wine' and 1,200 pounds of chocolate – still then very much an extravagant luxury.

For the poorer classes, food offered little in the way of variety or excitement, their diet relying heavily on bread, peas and beans. There was, however, always the panacea of gin. The 'gin craze' of the early eighteenth century had catastrophic results, not far removed from the anarchic mayhem depicted in Hogarth's famous satire *Gin Lane*. Roy Porter quotes a story from the *Gentleman's Magazine* of 1748, which reports how:

> *At a Christening at Beddington in Surrey the nurse was so intoxicated that after she had undressed the child, instead of laying it in the cradle she put it behind a large fire, which burnt it to death in a few minutes. She was examined before a magistrate, and said she was quite stupid and senseless, so that she took the child for a log of wood; on which she was discharged.*

A few years later an observer noted of the capital's nurses, 'These infernal monsters throw a spoonful of gin, spirits of wine or Hungary water down a child's throat, which instantly strangles the babe,' the nurse recording the cause of death as 'convulsions'. Even the clergy were not exempt from this madness. In 1743 John Wesley recorded that, during a sermon, 'a gentleman rode up very drunk, and after many unseemly and bitter words, laboured much to ride over some of the people. I was surprised to hear he was a neighbouring clergyman.'

By the middle of the century the problem was acute. A measure designed to limit excessive drinking by imposing a tax on spirits merely prompted the mob to riot, which in turn encouraged the authorities and vendors alike to largely ignore the Act's provisions. In 1751 the novelist and social reformer Henry Fielding observed that gin 'is the principal sustenance (if it may be so called) of more than a hundred thousand people in [London]. Many of these wretches there are who swallow pints of this poison within the twenty-four hours: the dreadful effects of which I have the misfortune every day to see, and to smell too.'

Gin or 'Geneva' shops were to be found liberally sprinkled about all of the poorer urban areas, selling a 'gin' made from such healthy ingredients as sulphuric acid and turpentine and promoting what Dorothy George has called 'an orgy of spirit-drinking'. Ultimately, it was Hogarth's popular exposé of the evils of spirits – his celebrated *Gin Lane* of 1751 – which

Joseph Highmore's paintings intended as the basis for the illustrations to Samuel Richardson's novel *Pamela* of 1740 provide rare glimpses of the more modest interiors of the period. This particular scene, 'Mr B finds Pamela writing', shows a very demure room, with simple, uncovered deal floorboards, wood-coloured walls, a basic Palladian chimneypiece and a hefty rim lock on the door. The only note of richness is in the red damask chair upholstery.

prompted the government to action. By an Act of 1751, the duty on spirits was vastly increased and most gin and brandy outlets were made illegal. Thus was pernicious Gin Lane demolished and rebuilt as healthy Beer Street.

Hogarth's influence was not only felt in the area of social reform. In 1715 the art establishment was dominated by old Godfrey Kneller, already a knight and about to be made a baronet by George I. Kneller's portraiture could on occasions reach inspiring depths; mostly, however, he confined himself to ensuring that his studio churned out stock depictions of the leading courtiers of the day, the great man himself turning up to paint the face, and possibly even the hands, while assistants and professional drapery painters filled in the rest. Potential sitters could simply choose a pose from a catalogue, and it was done. Into this tired and highly formulaic cosiness burst William Hogarth, a fierce and xenophobic patriot whose disdain of the 'Grand Style' and whose abiding interest in depicting the humble citizen and the everyday event transformed British art. Hogarth's fresh, naturalistic art of the 1730s and '40s in turn paved the way for Thomas Gainsborough's astonishingly refreshing early portraits of the later 1740s and early 1750s, depictions of unpretentious Suffolk gentry or his own charming daughters. Hogarth also injected a strong element of personal rancour into his works, much of this directed at no less a personage than the Earl of Burlington.

Two scenes from Jonathan Swift's *Tale of a Tub* of 1704, engraved for the edition of 1754. The scene shown on the left features a typical middle-class room of the mid-eighteenth century, with its characteristic stile-and-rail panelling; the room on the right is somewhat grander, with a rather fanciful Corinthian pilaster.

As the son-in-law of Wren's favoured historical painter Sir James Thornhill, Hogarth saw Thornhill ejected as Serjeant Painter to the King in favour of Burlington's ally William Kent; Kent also replaced Thornhill as the author of the new murals at Kensington Palace. Hogarth's revenge was his bitter satire *The Man of Taste* of 1731, which mercilessly pilloried Burlington and his Palladian followers; in return, Kent barred Hogarth from the Chapel Royal in 1734 when the latter sought to make engravings of the wedding of the Princess Royal.

In literature, too, the Palladian era was one of glittering achievements – of Swift and Steele, Pope and Gay, Defoe and Addison, of Richardson's *Pamela* and Fielding's *Tom Jones*. (At the same time, it must be remembered that the much-ridiculed Poet Laureate, Laurence Eusden, was succeeded by the even more notorious Colley Cibber, Pope's 'King Dunce' of the 1743 *Dunciad*.) In music, George Frederick Handel progressed from Italian operas to British oratorios, proving himself the worthy successor to Purcell and establishing himself as one of Europe's leading composers. And behind many of these artistic figures was the patronage of the most famous Palladian of all, the Third Earl of Burlington, an enormously influential individual to whom many of the architects, sculptors, painters and musicians of the day owed their livelihood. How Burlington came to occupy such a position of pre-eminence in the arts of early Georgian Britain is explained in the next chapter.

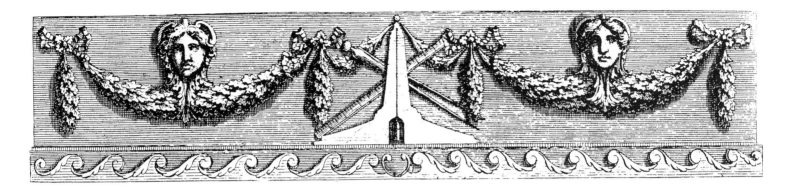

WE CAME AT LENGTH TO THE HOUSE, WHICH WAS INDEED A NOBLE STRUCTURE, BUILT ACCORDING TO THE BEST RULES OF ANCIENT ARCHITECTURE…I GAVE DUE PRAISES TO EVERY THING I SAW, WHEREOF HIS EXCELLENCY TOOK NOT THE LEAST NOTICE TILL AFTER SUPPER WHEN…HE TOLD ME WITH A VERY MELANCHOLY AIR, THAT HE DOUBTED HE MUST THROW DOWN ALL HIS HOUSES IN TOWN AND COUNTRY, TO REBUILD THEM AFTER THE PRESENT MODE. Jonathan Swift, *Gulliver's Travels*, 1726

Left **The frontispiece from the 1770 edition of Kent's** *Designs of Inigo Jones* **of 1727. Designs by Jones' pupil John Webb were actually included in this volume but, predictably, were assigned to Jones (who can be seen in the medallion on the left).**

The inspiration for the Palladian style of Burlington and his contemporaries was indirectly derived from the buildings of the classical world – in particular, from the architecture of the early years of the Roman Empire. In most cases, this message reached the English Palladians fourth-hand, via the successive reinterpretations – by Alberti, by Palladio, Barbaro and their sixteenth-century contemporaries, and latterly by Inigo Jones – of the architecture of Ancient Rome as described in the pages of Marcus Vitruvius Pollio's *De architectura* (translated as *Ten Books of Architecture*). Vitruvius was an architect and engineer of the first century BC who – appropriately for Augustan Britain – wrote at the time of the Emperor Augustus. The importance of Vitruvius' work to the European Renaissance cannot be

Above **A detail from the same edition of Kent's** *Designs of Inigo Jones*, **taken from the contents page.**

underestimated. Vitruvius was by no means the only, nor indeed the leading architect of early Imperial Rome; nor was he a particularly accomplished writer. However, his *Ten Books* constituted the only detailed guide to Ancient Roman building techniques and philosophies that survived in the modern world. From the fifteenth century onwards, Robert Tavernor has remarked, Vitruvius 'remained the only key to a true understanding of the ruins of Roman antiquity which were still to be marvelled at throughout Italy'.

Vitruvius and his fellow Romans laid great stress on the need for rules and regimentation, an emphasis which was enthusiastically taken up by the English Palladians 17 centuries later. 'Architecture depends on Order,' proclaimed Vitruvius, since 'Order gives due measure to the members of a work considered separately, and symmetrical agreement to the proportions of the whole.' In the *Ten Books* he laid out the rules devised for the three ancient classical orders on which all Roman architecture had been based. The inherent order of Roman architecture, he declared, drew its inspiration directly from Nature; from the perfection of Nature Vitruvius divined three principal prerequisites for all buildings: the fundamental criteria of Utility, Strength and Beauty which all structures should meet. As explained and clarified by Alberti and Palladio, it was these criteria which formed the basis for the designs of the eighteenth century Palladians.

Vitruvius' *Ten Books* not only contained rules and guidance for construction. They also dealt with decorative matters. Vitruvius described in great detail how white lead and verdigris were made, and how Imperial purple dye – which 'exceeds all the colours...both in costliness and in the superiority of its delightful effect' – was obtained from shellfish ('broken up with iron tools, the blows of which drive out the purple fluid like a flood of tears'), a mixture of chalk and madder root, or a less likely combination of bilberries and milk.

In the centuries following the demise of the Western Roman Empire, Græco-Roman architecture was allowed to decay and its lessons were forgotten. Dimly remembered Roman precepts found their way into Norman buildings of the eleventh and twelfth centuries, but the rational rock on which Vitruvius' architectural gospel had been founded was almost entirely buried. With the Italian Renaissance of the later Middle Ages, however, came a renewed interest not only in the surviving monuments of Ancient Rome but also in the theory and practice of their construction. Following the discovery of a reliable copy of Vitruvius in the monastic library of St Gallen in Switzerland in the fifteenth century, the manuscript was taken to Florence to lay the foundations of the classical revival.

The prime instigator of this revival was the cinquecento architect Leon Battista Alberti (1404–72), long revered as one of the most important figures

Right Staircase designs from Book I of Palladio's *Quattro libri*, taken from the second, 1721 edition of Leoni's *The Architecture of A. Palladio* of 1715. As Eileen Harris has observed, 'This lavish edition of Palladio's works... proved far too fanciful for the didactic perfection demanded by Burlington'. Campbell died after publishing only the first book of a new, more pedantically precise edition in 1728, and it was not until 1737 that an edition of Palladio appeared on which the Palladians could rely.

Left **Courtyard elevation of the Palazzo Thiene in Vicenza, begun in c.1545 and illustrated in Palladio's *Quattro libri* of 1570.**

Right **Bramante's Tempietto at S Pietro in Montorio, Rome, of 1502–14, has been acclaimed as one of the most important monuments of Renaissance architecture. Its influence on secular as well as ecclesiastical design of the next three centuries was immense.**

of the Renaissance. Alberti began as an expert on fine art — writing the first Renaissance treatise on painting — before turning to architecture in his forties. While Englishmen won and lost half of France and then indulged themselves in the medieval tragi-comedy of the Wars of the Roses, Alberti was reinterpreting classical theory and using the resultant synthesis to build some of the most enduring monuments of the early Renaissance. His *De re aedificatoria*, written in about 1450 but published posthumously in 1485, was the first work on architecture to be compiled since the fall of Rome. One of the most influential of all Renaissance tracts, it was arranged in the form of ten books — in homage to Vitruvius — but did attempt to make classical theory a little more accessible than had been the case with Vitruvius' often obscure prose. As a direct result of the interest in Roman architecture engendered by the publication of Alberti's work, a year later Vitruvius' own *Ten Books* were republished for the first time since the reign of Augustus.

Alberti's lead was enthusiastically and energetically taken up by Donato Bramante who, in Palladio's opinion, was 'the first who brought good and beautiful architecture to light'. Bramante's Tempietto of 1502–14, a small temple attached to the church of S Pietro in Montorio in Rome which commemorates the martyrdom of St Peter, is one of the few buildings to have been consistently venerated since its construction. As historian Mark Wilson Jones has commented, the Tempietto 'has been praised as a model of perfection and a landmark in the history of architecture'. Bramante also produced a rigidly symmetrical design for St Peter's in Rome in 1506, based on a literal interpretation of the precepts of Vitruvius and Alberti and relying almost entirely on the simplest of geometrical shapes — the circle and the square. This, Bramante's contemporaries and successors believed, was surely the way ahead for architecture.

After Bramante, the tradition of Vitruvius was kept alive through Daniele Barbaro's new edition of the Roman architect's *Ten Books*, published in 1556. Barbaro (1514–70) was truly a Renaissance man: editor of Vitruvius, gentleman farmer, mathematician and diplomat, he was even designated Patriarch of Aquilea by the Venetian Republic. His Vitruvius was a vital element in the propagation of the neoclassical gospel, not just in Renaissance Italy but also in eighteenth-century Britain and Colonial and Federal America.

One of the minor contributors to Barbaro's work was an architect named Andrea Palladio, born Andrea della Gondola in Padua in 1508. His earliest patron and instructor was Count Gian Giorgio Trissino (1478–1550), a renowned Humanist scholar born six years after Alberti's death and 30 years before Palladio's birth. Palladio worked for Trissino in Vicenza when young; it was Trissino who gave him his new name of Palladio when he was

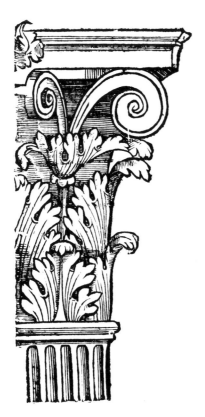

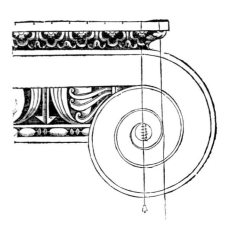

still a student at Trissino's academy in rural Cricoli, and took him to Rome in 1541. Palladio's father had been a stonecutter, so the young architect began with a sound knowledge of masonry and building practices. To this he was to add an expert acquaintance with the theory and practice of the architecture of the Ancients.

At the age of 32, Palladio, having learned much from Trissino and his contemporaries, returned to Vicenza and began to practise. Most of Palladio's early buildings were sited around the area of his home town of Padua and nearby Vicenza; indeed, most of his patrons were graduates of the internationally renowned University of Padua. However, Palladio's influences also came from further afield. One of the most important sources was the early-sixteenth-century oeuvre of Sebastiano Serlio (1475–1554), a Bolognese painter who, like Alberti, had turned to architecture late in life. Serlio's books were the first reinterpretations of classical theory and practice to rely not on prose but on newly commissioned engravings to convey the message. These illustrations were to have a profound effect on the young Palladio, and indeed on the architecture of the next two centuries.

Above and *right* Details of the classical orders from Books I and IV of Palladio's *Quattro libri*. Clear illustrations of the orders were an essential component not only of Palladio's guide but also of most of the British pattern-books of the eighteenth century.

Palladio believed, as had all his Renaissance predecessors (and as would his British and North American disciples), that perfection in architecture was to be achieved only by imitating Nature. Every element of every building should, he reasoned, be governed by one supreme set of proportions, all of which derived from the proportions of the human body – and thus, indirectly, from God himself. Like the Renaissance artists and sculptors, Italian architects of the fifteenth and sixteenth centuries made the study of the proportions of the human frame the centre of their system of building; the symmetry and proportions of the body were, surely, the key to God's architecture. In this respect, Alberti had improved upon Vitruvius' Roman precepts, shifting the proportional centre of the human body from navel to pelvis. Still, for Alberti as for Vitruvius, the human frame was the way to, quite literally, heavenly perfection. The Ancient Greeks and Romans, Alberti believed, having:

> considered man's body…decided to make columns after its image. Having taken the measurements of a man, they discovered that the width, from one side to the other, was a sixth of the height, while the depth, from navel to kidneys, was a tenth. The commentators of our sacred writings also noted this and judged that the Ark built for the Flood was based on the human figure.

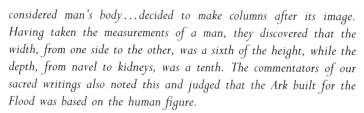

Having selected the human body as a divinely guided model, architects were keen to ensure that their buildings, in Palladio's own words, 'should appear an entire, and well finished body'. Thus basic services should be hidden, just as 'our blessed Lord has designed the parts of the body, so that the most beautiful should be in places which are exposed to sight and the less decent in hidden places' (a precept which held sway until temporarily rejected by the proponents of twentieth-century high-tech architecture). To translate these human proportions to the dimensions of a building, the Renaissance architects needed a standard module. This they found in the foot (of 12 or 14 inches), a standard which they proceeded to apply to every architectural element, from the height of a room to the length of a brick. This in turn provided the standard guide for construction throughout Western Europe.

Palladio's early works provided essential visual references for much of the Palladian architecture of the eighteenth century. His Villa Valmarana at Vigardolo, begun in 1541, displayed many of the traits that were to become hallmarks of English Palladianism two centuries later: prominent Venetian windows, circular openings and blank, unadorned wall space. His Villa Cornaro of 1551–3 and Villa Pisani of 1552–5 were devised around a simple architectural rhythm of bays, 1–3–1, which could be seen reproduced in

Left Rural Italian villas of the second half of the sixteenth century which had a significant impact on the British country house and town 'villa' of the early eighteenth century. *Clockwise from top left*, three villas by Palladio: Villa Cornaro at Piombino Dese of 1551–3, Villa Rotunda or Almerico, begun in c.1565, and Villa Emo at Fanzolo of the late 1550s. *Far left bottom*, Scamozzi's Villa Rocca Pisani at Lonigo of 1576.

Colen Campbell's Whitehall house for Lord Herbert (later Ninth Earl of Pembroke), built in 1724 and illustrated in the pages of the third volume of *Vitruvius Britannicus* the following year. Possibly influenced by Herbert himself, the design, in John Harris' words, 'brought the villa to town' for the first time. The first-floor loggia is a very Italian device, not altogether suitable for the English climate but also employed by Burlington at Chiswick a year or two later. The composition of the façade was clearly a major influence on that of Marble Hill House, the Twickenham villa of 1724–9 for which Herbert was an advisor. The house was demolished in the nineteenth century.

English villas of the 1720s, most notably Roger Morris' Marble Hill and Colen Campbell's Whitehall house for Lord Herbert, later the Earl of Pembroke. (The typical, 1–3–1 villa composition can even be glimpsed through the window in the first scene of Hogarth's vicious parody *Marriage à la Mode*.) The Villa Emo at Fanzolo was especially instructive for the British and North American Palladians, since its rich and sophisticated interiors were helpfully veiled by a plain and modest façade. It was this outward reticence which appealed most to the Georgians. As historian James Ackerman has written, often the entrance porch was 'the only antique reference in the design' of Palladio's villas – 'all the rest of the detail is simple geometry'.

More important than his executed works, however, was Palladio's *Quattro libri dell'architettura* of 1570. While few apart from Burlington and Kent had the resources or the luck to visit Palladio's buildings, many architects, patrons and builders were able to purchase Palladio's printed manual and thus learn the lessons of the Ancients for themselves. The *Quattro libri* together constituted a clear and concise reinterpretation of Vitruvius, Alberti and Barbaro; more unusually, though, the four sections were illustrated by a large number of Palladio's own works. Blessed with such topical references, it became the world's first popular architectural book.

Unfortunately, the year which saw the publication of the *Quattro libri* also represented the high-water mark of Palladio's career. Although in 1570 he succeeded Sansovino as the principal architect in Venice, the death of his two eldest sons the following year turned Palladio into a morose recluse. It was instead a pupil of Palladio's, Vincenzo Scamozzi (1552–1616), who carried the Palladian tradition into the seventeenth century. Most significantly, it was Scamozzi who in 1614 met the man who was to introduce the forms of the Ancient World into a Britain still largely oblivious of classical architecture: Inigo Jones. Having made a pilgrimage to see Scamozzi in Vicenza, Jones was not at all impressed with the Italian's surly and secretive nature. The brief and stilted conversation the two held was hardly an occasion which could be described as the passing on of the torch of Neo-classicism; however, it did help to convince Jones that the pure-bred classicism of the Roman Empire and of Renaissance Italy was the only worthwhile architectural style for a country with real political ambitions and true artistic pretensions.

Inigo Jones was born in Smithfield in the City of London in 1573, the son of a humble clothworker. He was born only nine years after Shakespeare, yet whereas the latter is always popularly associated with the age of Elizabeth I, Jones was very much a man of the early Stuart Court. Indeed, Jones' first major patron was James I's early first minister, Robert Cecil, Earl of Salisbury, for whom Jones designed the New Exchange in the Strand and who gave Jones ready access to the Jacobean Court. It was Cecil who helped Jones attain the coveted post of Surveyor-General of the King's Works in 1615 – before which, as Timothy Mowl dismissively but perceptively observes, Jones had only been used to 'ingratiating his way into royal favour by churning out ephemeral Mannerist candy floss' in the shape of sets and costume designs for the Court masques. Meanwhile Jones visited Italy in the train of another renowned patron, Thomas Howard, the Second Earl of Arundel; it was this trip which, in the words of John Newman, 'provided a vital formative influence on his subsequent achievement as an architect'.

By 1620 Jones was firmly established as the principal architect of the Jacobean and, after 1625, the Caroline Court. Jones was, however, ultimately handicapped by the fact that his architectural practice was intimately associated with what Parliament and the public saw as the quasi-Catholic and despotically-inclined Court of Charles I. This is not to say that the whole of the Court was Catholic, nor that in reality King Charles himself deviated in any way from a staunch, deeply-held Anglicanism. However, what mattered was that the Court – and Jones himself – was perceived as at best tacitly accepting, and at worst actively encouraging, the Papist evangelicism of Charles I's much-despised Queen, Henrietta Maria. The Queen's zealous promotion of her native religion tarred the rest of the Court, and indeed the

Right Van Dyck's splendid equestrian portrait of Charles I consciously recalled Titian's famous portrait of the Emperor Charles V a century earlier. However, while the expressions of martial ardour and regal power were wholly appropriate for the absolute ruler of half of Europe, they were rather absurd when applied to a British monarch whose revenue depended on the goodwill of his Parliament and who had, until 1638, never commanded troops in the field.

Thornton's engraving after Kneller of Charles I's execution on 30 January 1649. Jones' Banqueting House provides the backdrop – a touch of symbolism that was not lost on the crowd or the nation. This engraving shows the building with cross-frame windows which would have been filled with leaded lights. The introduction of sash windows later in the seventeenth century significantly altered the balance of Jones' façade.

whole of the Caroline government, with the Catholic brush. Ambitious courtiers rushed to confess their Papist enthusiasms in a bid to impress the highly influential royal consort: Richard Weston, Earl of Portland and Lord Treasurer, admitted his conversion to Catholicism on his deathbed in 1635; less fortunate was his rival Lord Cottington, who confessed to his Catholic leanings while seriously ill the following year – but subsequently recovered his health. And, whilst other key figures of the 1620s and '30s such as Archbishop Laud and the Earl of Strafford – and indeed Jones himself – do not appear to have espoused the Church of Rome, the popular impression at the time was most certainly that they had. Indeed, so widespread was the belief in Laud's Catholicism that the Papacy actually offered the Archbishop a cardinal's hat in 1633.

Long ago the historian Rudolf Wittkower took issue with the much-repeated allegation that Jones was a Catholic convert; however, the general belief was that the King's architect, like the King's Archbishop, was a closet Papist. (He was also, if John Harris is correct, a closet homosexual.) Certainly the Papal Agent Gregorio Panzani – the first Papal emissary to visit Britain since Henry VIII's Reformation a century earlier – had his suspicions. Observing Jones' embarrassingly sycophantic reaction to a gift of some mediocre pictures, Panzani noted that Jones ordered 'that these are pictures to be kept in a special room with gilded and jewelled frames, and in spite of being a very fierce Puritan he said this publicly in the ante-chamber of the

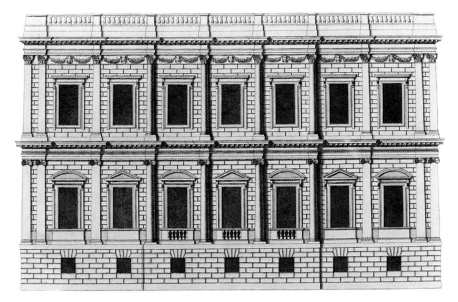

Inigo Jones' Banqueting
House at Whitehall Palace,
as engraved for *Vitruvius
Britannicus*. When Sir David
Conyngham's Jacobean
Banqueting House burnt
down in 1619, Jones rapidly
produced a scheme for
what was to become the first
public building in the
Palladian manner. These
early designs included a
central pediment, clearly
dropped from the final
version, and rustication only
for the basement rather than
on every floor, as was the
case with the executed
building.

Queen'. Panzani must have wondered what a 'very fierce Puritan' was doing
designing chapels for a Catholic Queen in which to convert her husband's more
pliable subjects.

Suspicion of the Caroline Court's innate Catholicism, rather than
Charles I's refusal to call a Parliament for 11 years after 1629, appears to
have been the primary reason why many took arms against the King in 1642.
Unsurprisingly, in the ensuing parliamentary and popular reaction both
Strafford and Laud, as well as the King himself, perished on the scaffold.
Inigo Jones was lucky that he did not share their fate. Being bundled naked
in a blanket out of the besieged Basing House in 1645 was certainly igno-
minious, but not fatal. However, the parliamentarian propagandists made
much of Jones' fall, crowing over the capture of 'the famous surveyor' who
had begun his career as the 'contriver of scenes for the Queen's Dancing
Barn'. The prose of such announcements illustrated the degree to which the
King's architect was associated with the pseudo-Catholic Court, and in
particular with the machinations of the Catholic Queen. The place of his
capture gave added resonance to Jones' downfall, since Basing House had
been notorious as an unofficial centre for the Queen's intrigues.

The first major work which Jones completed for the King was
effectively a representation in stone and wood of Charles I's regal and artistic
ambitions. 'Arguably the most unexpected creation in English architectural
history', as Timothy Mowl has described it, Jones' Banqueting House at
Whitehall Palace, begun in 1622 and finished in 1629, represents the apogee

of his work as architectural apologist and hagiographer of the Early Stuarts, as well as an excellent illustration of his devotion to the memory of Palladio and Vitruvius. The Great Hall – an exact, Neo-Palladian double cube, as the hall of the Queen's House had been a single cube – was initially the setting for Jones' and Jonson's royal masques, events in which the royal family sometimes took part. The installation of the Rubens ceiling in 1638 brought an end to these entertainments, since the smoke from the torches which previously lit the chamber and illuminated the masques would have blackened Rubens' precious scenes. However, Rubens' commissioned subject – the faintly ludicrous theme of the Apotheosis of James I ('who slobbered at the mouth and had favourites', as *1066 And All That* memorably puts it) – was the clearest encapsulation in art of the concept of the Divine Right of Kings yet executed. The space was thereby converted into what John Harris and Gordon Higgott have called the 'throne room or hall of state'. As Charles I had disrupted the fragile consensus of Early Stuart government, so the Banqueting House, in Timothy Mowl's words, represented in the clearest possible form the 'artificial intrusion of outdated Venetian classicism into the context of Jacobean design'. The crowning – and presumably intended – irony was that in 1649 Charles I was executed on a scaffold attached to the Banqueting House, a building which was such a theatrically evocative symbol of his artistic and political aspirations and which had provided such a colourful backdrop to his personal rule. To reach the block, the King had to emerge from one of the Jones windows whose Italianate formality and grandeur he had admired so much.

Not only was most of Inigo Jones' work undertaken for the Caroline Court; his principal client was Charles I's pernicious Catholic Queen. Jones' Queen's Chapel at St James's Palace of 1623 was a simple, chastely Neo-Palladian work which featured Jones' first Venetian window – dominating the east end – and a coffered, barrel-vaulted ceiling taken directly from Palladio. Begun for the Spanish Infanta whom Prince Charles had gone to collect as his bride in 1623 (but who refused to leave Spain), the chapel was completed for the Catholic French princess who was eventually prevailed upon to accept his hand, Henrietta Maria. Sixty years later the Chapel was, rather appropriately, refitted for another Catholic Queen: Mary of Modena, consort of the despised James II.

Jones' first major classical work was also finished to the requirements of Henrietta Maria. The Queen's House at Greenwich had been begun in 1616 to Jones' designs for James I's wife, Anne of Denmark, but work was halted on the latter's death in 1619 and was only recommenced 11 years later for Charles I's Queen. Jones' other commissions for the Queen included

The Queen's Chapel at
St James's Palace, London,
of 1623–5. This is one of the
best preserved of all Jones'
works, although the internal
woodwork dates from 1682.
The double-cube nave and
coffered ceiling (the latter
having been directly
adapted from a Palladio
design) are dominated by
the vast Venetian window
at the east end.

additions to Somerset House in 1626, the remodelling of Basing House in
c.1633, the erection of Oatlands in Surrey in 1636–8, and major works to
Wimbledon Palace in 1639–40. Most revealingly, in addition to his
Surveyorship of the Royal Works, Jones was also paid £20 a year for acting
as 'Surveyor of Her Majesty's Works' – a wholly unofficial post, presumably
invented by Henrietta Maria herself, which was quite outside the administration of the Office of Works. Few royal servants were as closely linked
with the Queen as Inigo Jones, her private architect.

Even those commissions which were not directly intended for the
monarch or his wife were tainted with this Court connection. The centrepiece of Jones' heavy-handed restoration of St Paul's Cathedral, for example,
was a new, classical West End strewn with statues of James I and Charles I,

Samuel Scott's view of Covent Garden in c.1750. The west end of the church of St Paul's, Covent Garden, built in 1631–3, is notable for its overhanging eaves and its robust Tuscan order, features employed by Jones in an attempt to create a simple, rustic yet distinctly Italian composition.

as well as some of England's genuinely illustrious rulers. This grandiose but blatantly inappropriate statement was completed just in time for the outbreak of civil war in 1642; 24 years later it burned down with the rest of the medieval cathedral in the Great Fire of London.

The one major commission that brought Jones out of this claustrophobic and increasingly isolated Court circle was his creation of a new church and accompanying townscape at Covent Garden in the West End of London. The patron of this development – Francis Russell, the Fourth Earl of Bedford – was at best a semi-detached member of Charles I's Court; indeed, in the months before his untimely death in 1641, Bedford led the moderate parliamentary opposition to the Court. The church of St Paul's that he founded was not only the first church built in London since the Reformation, a century earlier; it was also the first classical church of any kind built in Britain, and shockingly different to anything that had gone before. The presumably apocryphal story (according to that inveterate storyteller, Horace Walpole) was that Jones, having been asked by the Earl to provide a simple, barn-like structure, replied that, in that case, 'You shall have the handsomest barn in Europe.' A century later the church was still much admired. St Paul's was, decreed the architectural critic James Ralph in 1734, 'without a rival'; indeed he deemed it to be 'one of the most perfect pieces of architecture that the art of man can produce'.

The piazza which Jones created to surround the church was even more impressive. And as a model for the Georgian terrace a century later, it was highly influential. As John Summerson wrote in 1945: 'The Piazza must have presented a fine picture. The big Italian scale, the total absence of ornament

Right **Plan of the Covent Garden Piazza, erected during the 1630s for the Fourth Earl of Bedford to Inigo Jones' innovative design.**

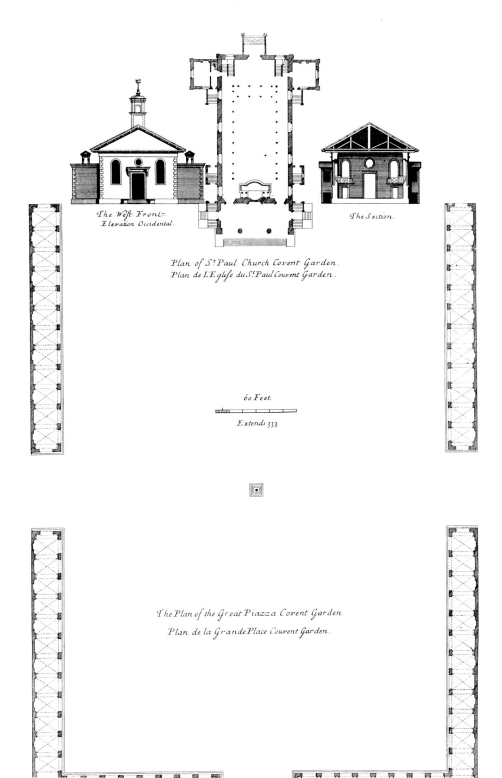

The West Front.
Elevation Occidental.

The Section.

Plan of St Paul Church Covent Garden.
Plan de L'Eglise du St Paul Couvent Garden.

60 Feet.

Extends 333

The Plan of the Great Piazza Covent Garden
Plan de la Grande Place Couvent Garden.

that was not of perfect academic propriety, the use of external stucco to give the effect of stone – all these things were new, and suggested new standards for London street architecture.'

Jones' academically impeccable and markedly Italianate classical detailing, his flat roofs and cubic rooms, were astoundingly new in a country which had rarely been in the vanguard of architectural innovation. And his approach to building was as novel as the vocabulary which he employed. As John Bold has written, Jones was 'the first to apply the classical principles of architecture as a thoroughgoing system of design which permeated all aspects of a building'. Not only were his elevations unlike anything produced by his English contemporaries; even his roof structures were wholly innovatory, Jones using not the traditional tie beam method but the new, Italian trussed roofs to construct the large, unsupported ceilings of the Banqueting House and St Paul's, Covent Garden. He thought as long and hard about the provision of elements such as the staircase – 'a hard Thinge to find place fitt for…and not offend the Rest of the Buildinge' – as he did about Palladio's ideal system of proportion. Yet Jones' architecture was not always recognizably Italian or Neo-Palladian. His elevations – particularly those of the Banqueting House and of the Covent Garden piazza – bore none of the calm, astylar reticence which had so marked Palladio's villas, nor were they especially three-dimensional. It was not until the 1720s that such elements as astylar façades, heavily emphasized single features and large expanses of bare masonry found expression in British architecture.

While not always truly Italianate in conception, neither were Jones' stark innovations necessarily superior to what was being built by his British contemporaries. Harris and Higgott have observed that in 1623 – the year in which Jones' simple Chapel at St James's Palace was being constructed – Jones' second-in-command at the King's Works, Thomas Baldwin, 'built Bray Hospital as if Palladio or Serlio had never existed'. And as late as 1638 the accomplished sculptor, mason and architect Nicholas Stone was building the north front of Kirby Hall in Northamptonshire 'in a northern Mannerist style boasting no less than ten different window openings'. However, this is not to say that such works were intrinsically inferior to those of Inigo Jones. Timothy Mowl in particular has taken Jones to task for stifling the energetic, native Jacobean style of the early seventeenth century, convincingly arguing that what was astonishingly new to the British was actually rather old-fashioned to the Italians. Judging the effects of Jones' Banqueting House, Dr Mowl has argued that 'a great and vital artistic episode had been decisively ended by the craven desire of a few strategically placed courtiers to conform to what they believed was a superior continental norm'.

Whatever the merits of Jones' architecture, the Revolution which erupted in 1642 brought an abrupt end to his career. The royal architect recognized that his intimate association with Charles I's Court, and in particular with Henrietta Maria, precluded the establishment of any successful private practice. (Harris and Higgott have recently noted how Jones' close connections with the Queen meant that 'few courtiers...sought his services, and no-one from the trading or banking classes'.) Accordingly, in 1642 he followed his royal master to the Siege of Beverley. Two years later Parliament – having disposed of Charles I's former lieutenant Strafford, imprisoned Archbishop Laud and come within sight of winning the war – finally struck at Jones himself. Parliamentary order dismissed Jones from his post as Surveyor-General and installed in his place Edward Carter. (Carter was by no means incompetent or inexperienced, having been Jones' Deputy at St Paul's Cathedral.) Following his capture at Basing House in 1645, Jones saw his estate temporarily sequestrated, but a forgiving Parliament pardoned him in 1646. With the execution of Charles I at the Banqueting House in 1649, any hope of future royal commissions died too. As John Summerson has graphically commented, with the death of Charles I, 'Court architecture was dead – as dead as the King who walked to his execution through an Italian casement.'

Jones lingered on for three years until his death in June 1652. For the remainder of the Republic and Protectorate, it was his pupil John Webb who almost single-handedly kept the Palladian ideal alive. Webb had been intimately associated with Jones; not only had he worked with the great master at Wilton House and other sites, he married Jones' cousin and heir Anne. Webb was vehement in his defence of Jones' legacy, declaring that his teacher had been 'the Vitruvius of his age' and alleging that he had been more 'famous in remote parts...than at home'. Yet, while his intended treatise on Jones' life and works never got beyond the planning stage, his own career prospered. Despite the image which has been popularly projected since 1660, architecture did not come to a halt under Cromwell's Protectorate. Webb – a figure who, as John Harris has lamented, 'has been sadly demoted in the roll call of great British architects' – in fact built up a healthy practice during the 1650s. It was not the Commonwealth but the restored Stuart monarch, Charles II, who did most to stifle the legacy of Palladio and Jones, passing over Webb, the obvious candidate for the royal Surveyorship, in favour of a Cavalier nonentity in 1660 and an unknown academic nine years later. Far from Cromwell having extinguished the lamp of Palladian Neoclassicism, it was rather Charles II – whose parents had been Jones' greatest patrons – who did most to defer the style's acceptance in Britain.

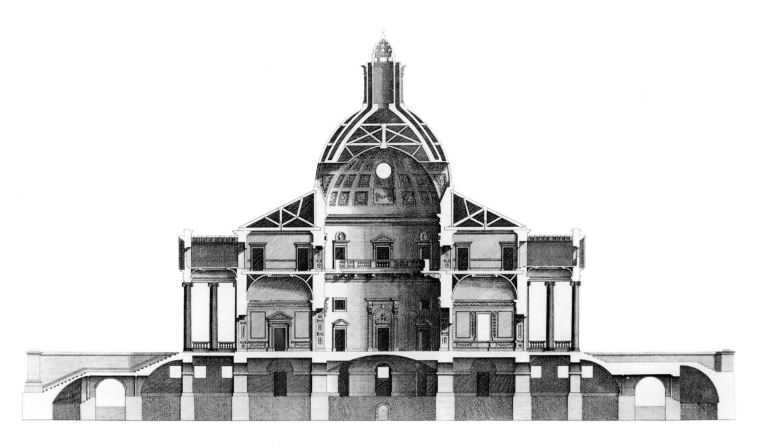

YOU SHOW US, ROME WAS GLORIOUS, NOT PROFUSE,
AND POMPOUS BUILDINGS ONCE WERE THINGS OF USE.
YET SHALL (MY LORD) YOUR JUST, YOUR NOBLE RULES
FILL HALF THE LAND WITH IMITATING-FOOLS.

Alexander Pope, *Epistle to Richard Boyle, Earl of Burlington*, 1732

Left **Joseph van Aken's**
***The Music Party* of 1725.**
The classical urn, statue and
temple were all key elements
of the typical Palladian
country house garden.

The 60 years which followed the death of Inigo Jones in 1652 were dominated by one architect: the master mathematician and superlative pragmatist, Sir Christopher Wren. By the turn of the century, however, leading commentators were publicly questioning both the Baroque style favoured by Wren – which in the hands of his pupils Hawksmoor and Vanbrugh was becoming increasingly eccentric – and the stranglehold which the wily old Tory (who had already managed to survive four major changes of monarch and government) continued to exercise on the hub of national architectural patronage: the royal Office of Works, over which Wren had presided as Surveyor-General since 1669. In Late Stuart Britain, success as an architect depended as much on having the right contacts as on sheer talent; and in

Above **Cross-section of**
Mereworth Castle of 1722
from *Vitruvius Britannicus*,
showing the contrast in
decorative treatment
between the ground-floor
reception rooms and the
simpler first-floor bedrooms.

Sir Christopher Wren, Surveyor-General of the King's Works during five reigns and for almost 50 years, from 1669 until 1718. In this engraving by Wenceslaus Hollar, Wren's greatest achievement, St Paul's Cathedral, is clearly visible in the background.

Right Title page from the first volume of *Vitruvius Britannicus* of 1715. The work was largely financed by subscribers who, according to the original proposal of 1714, constituted 'Persons of Quality and gentry'. The Scots architect Colen Campbell appears only to have been brought in at the eleventh hour as an experienced draughtsman who, fortuitously, could supply engravings in the latest Palladian mode.

1714 Wren, who for 45 years had disposed every scheme commissioned by the royal household, still held the key to all the requisite political and artistic contacts. Such a monopoly inevitably aroused widespread resentment. At the same time, Wren's English Baroque style was denounced – in a xenophobic manner so typical of Britain's attitude to the arts – for its foreign and, even worse, for its Catholic antecedents. As Dan Cruickshank has observed, 'it was because Wren's architecture was comparable with European building –

VITRUVIUS BRITANNICUS,

or

The British Architect,

Containing

The Plans, ELEVATIONS, and Sections

of the Regular Buildings, *both*

PUBLICK and PRIVATE,

IN

GREAT BRITAIN,

With Variety of New Defigns; *in* 200 *large* Folio Plates, *Engraven by the* beft Hands; *and Drawn either from the* Buildings *themfelves, or the* Original Defigns *of the* Architects;

In II VOLUMES

__VOL. I.__ *by* Colen Campbell Efq.r

VITRUVIUS BRITANNICUS,

ou

Contenant

Les Plans, ELEVATIONS, & Sections

des Bâtimens Reguliers, *tant*

PARTICULIERS que PUBLICS

de la Grande Bretagne,

Compris en 200 *grandes* Planches *gravez en* taille douce *par les* Meilleurs Maitres, *et tous ou deffinez des* Bâtimens *memes, ou copiez des* Deffeins Originaux *des* Architectes:

EN DEUX TOMES.

__TOME I.__ *Par le* Sieur Campbell.

CUM PRIVILEGIO REGIS.

Sold by the Author over againft Douglas Coffee-houfe *in* St. Martins-lane. John Nicholfon *in* Little Britain, Andrew Bell *at the* Crofs-Keys *in* Cornhil, W. Taylor *in* Pater-Nofter-Row; Henry Clements *in* St. Pauls Church-yard, And Jof. Smith *in* Exeter-Change. LONDON MDCCXVII

J. Shut fculp.

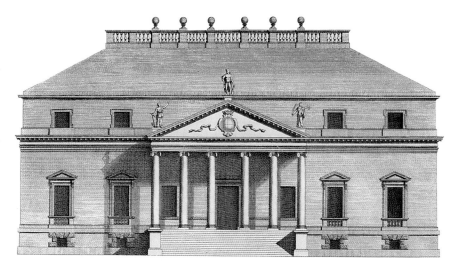

A design for the west elevation of Goodwood House in Sussex, as engraved for volume III of *Vitruvius Britannicus*. The design formed part of a grand plan, drawn up by Colen Campbell in 1724, for rebuilding the Second Duke of Richmond's country house. In the event little of the scheme seems to have been executed; indeed, by the mid-1720s, Campbell appears to have developed a knack of falling out with his most important patrons.

empiricist in character and influenced by French and Italian architects – that it was open to criticism by those who felt that the playful varieties and extravagance of Baroque Counter-Reformation architecture of Catholic Europe was not for England.' Such attacks were somewhat ironic given that the architectural style that was introduced to replace Wren's Baroque synthesis, Palladianism, was even more dependent on Italian influences.

The first British experiments in an Italianate, Palladian style were carried out by a Scot, James Smith. Smith visited Italy in the 1670s, and subsequently made a number of Italian-inspired designs. Few of Smith's executed buildings, however, betrayed any particularly Palladian traits: his importance lies in his unexecuted drawings, which passed to the architect Colen Campbell on his death. By 1715 Campbell had built a number of miniature Palladian villas and was beginning to turn his attention to grander projects. Yet the first truly 'Palladian' building in Britain had actually been executed some years before Campbell's early villas. In 1707 work began on the new Peckwater Quad at Christ Church College, Oxford. Designed by an amateur architect, the talented Oxford don Dr Henry Aldrich, it was a composition of surprising sophistication. In particular, its regular, rusticated base, its central, hexastyle portico and its Ionic pilasters on the first floor were very much in the tradition of Palladio and his Italian contemporaries rather than that of Wren and Hawksmoor.

When the Peckwater Quad was completed in 1714, Wren and his pupils continued to dominate the architectural mainstream. With the succession of George I, however, that situation was about to be radically transformed.

The first dissenting voice to be heard attacking the established architectural order did not belong to an architect or a politician but to a philosopher:

Dean Henry Aldrich's Peckwater Quad at Christ Church College, Oxford. Begun as early as 1707, this seminal building, perhaps the most influential of all proto-Palladian schemes of early eighteenth century Britain, was designed not by an experienced architect but by an amateur university don.

Anthony Ashley Cooper, Third Earl of Shaftesbury. He was an aristocrat, but one with impeccable Whig credentials, his grandfather having died in exile following his involvement in a plot against the Catholic Duke of York, subsequently King James II. In 1712 Shaftesbury published a public letter denouncing Baroque architecture, directing especial venom at 'false and counterfeit pieces of Magnificence' such as Vanbrugh and Hawksmoor's pompous pile of Blenheim Palace, then under construction. He also attacked Wren's personal control of the Office of Works:

> thro' several reigns we have patiently seen the noblest publick building perish (if I may say so) under the hand of one single court architect; who, if he had been able to profit by experience, wou'd long since, at our expence, have prov'd the greatest master in the World. But I question whether our patience is like to hold much longer.

To replace Wren's hegemony at the Works, Shaftesbury proposed the promulgation of a 'National Style' – a style free from any taint of foreign Catholicism (Shaftesbury never once mentioned the name of Palladio) and under the direction of hands other than those of the present Surveyor-General and his cronies.

Shaftesbury's radical viewpoint was rather undermined by the fact that he had a well-known grudge against Wren: at the time when his grandfather, the First Earl, was being hounded to his death for championing Whig

Sir Godfrey Kneller's
portrait of Lord Burlington
of c.1720 shows a successful
and confident landowner
and courtier who appears
remarkably assured for his
relatively few years.

Right Burlington House,
Piccadilly: Burlington's West
End residence, abandoned
for Chiswick in 1733, as
engraved for *Vitruvius
Britannicus*. Rebuilt by Colen
Campbell in 1718–19, it was
substantially remodelled by
E M Barry in 1868 and now
houses the Royal Academy.

Protestantism in the face of what was perceived to be a royal Catholic conspiracy, the Tory Wren was contentedly serving as the loyal MP for Plympton in Devon. (Not only was Wren part of the parliamentary majority which had condemned the First Earl and his Protestant allies; he was also happy to remain an MP during the subsequent reign of James II, who attempted to dismantle the Anglican Church and State in order to liberate his fellow Catholics.) More importantly for the prospects of Palladianism, Shaftesbury was no politician. Thus, whilst Shaftesbury did help to weaken Wren's position, the overthrow of the Surveyor-General, the capture of architectural officialdom and the establishment of a wholly new architectural

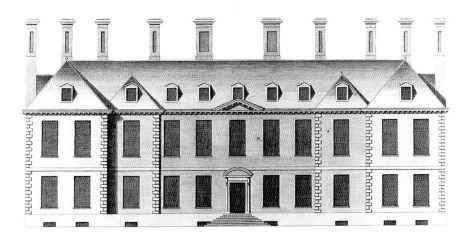

style was left to a far more determined figure, who was able to combine an obsession with architecture with high political rank.

Richard Boyle, Third Earl of Burlington and Fourth Earl of Cork, was only ten years old when he inherited his titles and the vast tracts of land in Middlesex, Yorkshire and Ireland which went with them. Like Shaftesbury from an impeccably Whig family, he became one of the first Whig peers to profit from the arrival of the Hanoverians in 1714. In that year, while still only 20, he was appointed to George I's Privy Council and the following year, 1715, was awarded the sinecure of Lord Treasurer of Ireland. Buoyed by this sudden success, in 1714 Burlington embarked on his own Grand Tour, taking with him the accustomed entourage of artists and self-appointed experts.

This first visit to Italy was to have momentous consequences for the development of architecture in Britain and North America. Burlington returned – with 878 trunks and two harpsichords – a confirmed Italophile, and immediately set about establishing Italian culture in his own, far chillier northern climes. The composers Giovanni Maria Bononcini and George Frideric Handel (then at the start of his illustrious career) were invited to Burlington House and commissioned to write a series of Italian operas for the new but short-lived Royal Academy of Music, which Burlington founded in 1719 with Handel as its first Director. Also established at Burlington House was the Italian sculptor Giovanni Battista Guelfi, whom Burlington rather optimistically lauded as the greatest sculptor of the age. At the same time, Burlington commissioned the Scots architect Colen Campbell to remodel his own London home in the style of Andrea Palladio and Inigo Jones. As James Lees-Milne has written, during 1719 'The inhabitants of London were amazed to see rising in their midst a palace taken from a north Italian city'.

However, not all of Burlington's Italian ventures prospered. His two pet composers – and their respective fans – quarrelled constantly, as the poet John Byrom gleefully testified:

Some say, compared to 'Bononcini'
That Mynheer Handel's but a ninny,
Others aver that he to Handel
Is scarcely fit to hold a candle.
Strange that all this difference should be
'Twixt Tweedle-dum and Tweedle-dee.

In the event, Burlington's ambitious Royal Academy of Music was a notorious flop. The inveterate gossip Lord Hervey described the King and Queen sitting 'freezing at his empty Haymarket opera, while the Prince with all the chief of the nobility went as constantly to that of Lincoln's Inn Fields'. In the same year (1728) that John Gay's notorious anti-government play *The Beggar's Opera* was premièred at Lincoln's Inn, the Royal Academy finally closed its doors. And soon both the taciturn and argumentative Guelfi and Burlington's newest protégé, the historical painter William Kent (already being compared by Gay and others to Raphael and Titian), proved substantial disappointments. Guelfi returned to Italy in 1734, by which time Kent had been successfully recast as an architect and landscape gardener.

Burlington's architectural forays were, thankfully, far more successful and long-lasting. Campbell's new-look Burlington House won widespread praise: John Gay wrote of it that whilst there was 'Beauty within, without proportion reigns', whilst to Horace Walpole, invited to a ball at the Piccadilly mansion, 'It seemed one of those edifices in fairy-tales that are raised by genii in a night's time.' Within a few years, largely thanks to Burlington, a far wider public was able to admire the design of Burlington House and other new Palladian structures at their leisure. Between 1715 and 1725 appeared the three volumes of the first new British work on architecture since John Shute's *The First and Chief Groundes of Architecture* had been published in 1563. *Vitruvius Britannicus*, edited by Burlington's architect Colen Campbell, was a collection of plates of contemporary houses which, whilst it attempted primarily to be a celebration of things British ('so many of the British Quality have so mean an opinion of what is performed in our own Country', moaned Campbell in the Preface) also served as a handy piece of propaganda for Burlington and his new Palladian taste. The original idea for the project was not Campbell's, nor indeed Burlington's; however, on his arrival in London from Scotland in 1713, Campbell was enlisted by the work's originators (an alliance of printers led by David Mortier and Joseph Smith)

Right View by Peter Rysbrack of the gardens at Chiswick in c.1728, showing the Bollo Brook to the left, the newly created pond and, on the right, Burlington's Tuscan pavilion, with a portico based on that of Inigo Jones' St Paul's, Covent Garden.

as a useful 'front man', while Burlington was kept apprised of the work's contents. Campbell proved his worth when, in order to rush out the first volume of *Vitruvius Britannicus* so as to beat Giacomo Leoni's rival publication, an edition of Book I of Palladio's *Quattro libri*, he contributed several unexecuted designs at the last minute to fill the required number of pages.

Leoni was one Italian whom Burlington shunned. Born in Venice in 1686, Leoni came to England around 1713 – the year in which Campbell travelled down to London in search of richer pickings than Scotland could offer. Yet he was forever in Campbell's shadow. Although his translator Dubois referred to Leoni as a 'generous foreigner…who makes a very considerable present to the public', and Leoni's 1716 English edition of Palladio's first book spoke of reviving old English traditions while promising 'general Notes and Observations of Inigo Jones never printed before' (which actually only appeared in the 1742 edition), Leoni lost the chance to lead the emerging Palladian movement when his work was beaten to the libraries of the cognoscenti by the first volume of Campbell's *Vitruvius Britannicus*. Despite

This delightful illustration by William Kent for John Gay's *Fables* shows the Casina (visible in the middle distance) in the grounds of Chiswick House. Built by Burlington to his own design in 1717, this small temple (demolished in 1778 by the Fifth Duke of Devonshire) terminated the north-western walk of the Earl's newly created 'natural' garden. The snail included in the foreground is typical of Kent's irreverent drawing manner.

the praise which Leoni lavished on Burlington, the fact that Leoni altered many of the great Palladio's designs in his edition of Book I in order to accommodate them to modern tastes did not endear him to the hagiographic Earl. And for the world outside Burlington House, Leoni – like that other architectural outsider of the period, the Scot James Gibbs – remained that most detested of creatures; a Catholic.

Whilst Campbell was busy promoting himself and his work through the new medium of *Vitruvius Britannicus*, Burlington was furthering his own architectural education. Emboldened by the success of Campbell's Burlington House and of *Vitruvius Britannicus*, in 1717 he designed and built a small Jonesian 'Casina' in the grounds of his Middlesex country retreat at Chiswick. And in 1719 he returned to Italy. The long-term effect of this second Italian journey was considerable, since it enabled him to visit Palladio's Veneto villas, to buy a copy of Palladio's *Quattro libri* in Vicenza and, whilst at the Villa Maser, to purchase a pile of Palladio's own drawings – to which he subsequently added the 'Parcell of Architectonicall Designes and Drawings by Palladio' which he bought from the connoisseur and collector John Talman. In Italy, Burlington also met the man who was to be his lifelong companion: William Kent.

Fortified by their political and architectural triumphs, Burlington and his allies felt confident enough to strike at the architectural establishment itself. In 1715 Wren had stood powerless while the Surveyor-Generalship was converted into a commission, with Wren himself included only as one member of the new Board of Comissioners. Four years later, despite the fact that the 86-year-old Wren had missed only 43 of the over 200 board meetings held since 1715, Burlington engineered the brusque dismissal of the aged architect.

In Wren's place, Burlington encouraged the government to install a figure who was soon to become the most notorious of all architectural nonentities: William Benson. His appointment was, admittedly, in the best Works tradition. In 1660 established, experienced architects such as Hugh May and John Webb had been passed over for the post of Surveyor-General in favour of an obscure Cavalier poet, Sir John Denham, who had no architectural ability (or interest) and who was soon exhibiting periodic symptoms of insanity. In 1669 May and Webb were once again ignored in favour of Wren himself – then known more for his scientific achievements and for his family's excellent royalist connections than for any architectural genius.

William Benson had, it is true, been partly responsible for what can be called the first Palladian villa in Britain. However, Wilbury House in Wiltshire, begun in 1708, was not a product of innovative inspiration. Campbell probably had a hand in the design, which was taken directly from a drawing by Inigo Jones and which, as the very name of the house acknowledged, borrowed heavily from two Neo-Palladian icons: Wilton House and Amesbury House, two Wiltshire houses which were at the time believed to have been designed by Jones. (In fact, Webb was the author of Amesbury and Jones, it seems, had only designed the interiors at Wilton.) Yet, when completed, Wilbury was found to be excessively cramped and undersized, and had to be substantially enlarged over the next two centuries. Apart from Wilbury, Benson's architectural experience was virtually non-existent. His only achievement in this field prior to 1718 had been to ingratiate himself with the new King by advising him on projected waterworks at the Hanover palace of Herrenhausen. 'It is very well known', commented his contemporary John Ker, 'that Mr Benson was a favourite of the Germans.'

Benson's unsuitability for office was quickly demonstrated. He had already admitted to his friends that he aimed to hold the Surveyorship only long enough to 'be in possession of one of the two offices of Auditor of the Imprests and Foreign Accounts or...some other office or place'. And one of his first acts was to replace the highly talented Baroque architect (and pupil of Wren), Nicholas Hawksmoor, as Secretary to the Board of Works at

Design by Burlington for the kitchen pavilion at Tottenham Park, Wiltshire. The Earl uses blank wall space in what was (for Britain, at least) a radical new manner to create a restrained, tastefully proportioned façade. The geometric perfection of this drawing was mirrored in the executed elevations of the main house, a four-towered composition begun in 1721.

Right Joseph Goupy's painting of 1740–41 showing Sir Robert Walpole addressing his cabinet includes a modest Palladian fire-surround, a brown-painted door with rim lock and grained or brown-painted (or possibly even real oak) sash windows.

Whitehall with his own brother Benjamin, whose only recommendation was that he had 'lately come from a merchant in Holland'. At the same time, he foolishly angered the Treasury by his 'unusual piece of presumption in an inferior officer' in personally relaying the King's wishes to the government in an ill-advised and high-handed manner. Unsurprisingly, his downfall soon followed. In January 1719 Benson, his brother and his 'agent' Colen Campbell (the only experienced architect in the new administration) told the House of Lords that their ancient chamber was in imminent danger of collapse. Yet, as Benson's workmen shored up the building and the peers were moved to temporary accommodation in Westminster Hall, the Master Mason, Benjamin Jackson, refuted Benson's claims. His assertion that he 'did not perceive that there has been any considerable sinking or settling of the Rafters' was supported by many of the leading architects of the day – Campbell's bitter enemy, James Gibbs, among them. Accordingly, retribution was swift. On 16 April 1719 the Lord Chamberlain announced not only that His Majesty 'had given Order for suspending the said William Benson from the Execution of his Office' but that he 'would give further Order for his effectual prosecution'. In the event, Benson escaped scot-free, having, in Hawksmoor's words, 'got more in one year (for confusing the King's Works) than Sr Chris Wren did in 40 years for his honest endeavours'. Doubly galling for Hawksmoor, just before he died, must have been the news that in 1735 Benson actually attained his stated desire: the sinecure of Auditor of Imprests. The admirers of Wren and Hawksmoor must surely, though, have derived some satisfaction from the newspaper report of 1741 that stated that Benson had been 'seized with a violent disorder of the mind'.

Campbell's reputation was severely dented by the débâcle of 1719. Burlington himself, having begun the rot, now found himself powerless to stop the further deterioration of the Office of Works. For Benson's successors were little better. While the former Works stalwarts Vanbrugh and Hawksmoor were again passed over ('I have…had a very hard Disappointment', wrote Vanbrugh to his friend Jacob Tonson, 'of not being made Surveyor of the Works; which I believe you remember, I might have had formerly, but refus'd it, out of Tenderness to Sr Chr Wren'), the Earl of Sunderland engineered the appointment as Surveyor-General of Thomas Hewett, an amateur architect and, more importantly, a staunch political ally. Hawksmoor, admittedly a far from impartial observer, derided Hewett's stables at Thoresby in Nottinghamshire as 'the only piece of Building that Sr Tho Hewett was Guilty of, dureing his being Architect Royall…and the most infamous that ever was made'. He also noted, with typical bitterness, that Hewett had given the post of Clerk of Works 'to a person who was Lately a country Joyner'.

Three years later, on Hewett's death, Burlington again failed to secure the important post of Comptroller of Works for William Kent, as Prime Minister Robert Walpole had reserved it for Thomas Ripley – another architectural mediocrity, who just happened to have married one of Walpole's servants. As historian Howard Colvin has noted with masterly understatement, Ripley (who, despite his limitations, was showered with posts and sinecures by Walpole) 'has not been much esteemed either by his contemporaries or by posterity', his one major work, the Admiralty portico, being 'a notorious failure'. Ripley was considered fair game by the satirists of the day: 'See under Ripley rise a new White-hall,/While Jones' and Boyle's united labours fall' wrote Pope in his *Dunciad*. However, in truth, both Hewett and Ripley never really had much of a chance: neither George I nor George II bothered themselves with building projects nor, indeed, in the best traditions of the British monarchy, with artistic patronage of any kind.

After the embarrassment of Benson's Surveyorship, Campbell attempted to salvage his career by an adroit piece of political gamesmanship. First, he attached himself to the Leicester House circle, the group of politicians and courtiers centred around the unofficial Court of George I's fractious and troublesome son, Prince George Augustus. In 1716 the Prince – always at loggerheads with the King in what was to become a fine Hanoverian tradition – had broken publicly with his father and with his father's Court, and had set up his own rival establishment, which by 1718 was permanently based at Leicester House. Although the Prince was formally reconciled with his father through the agency of Sir Robert Walpole in 1720, relations between the

Colen Campbell's Houghton Hall, Norfolk, built for Prime Minister Walpole between 1722 and 1732. *Above*, the Stone Hall (a perfect, 40-foot cube) and *above left*, the White Drawing Room, hung in the modern manner. *Right*, the Saloon at Houghton. The massive doorcase is in the heaviest of Palladian manners; the similarly weighty and almost oppressive ceiling was inevitably painted by William Kent, who was also responsible for the design of the sturdy, gilt mahogany furniture.

King and his heir were far from cordial, and for the next seven years the Prince maintained both his residence at Leicester House and the connections he had secured during these years – the majority of these adherents being rewarded with Court offices when the Prince came to the throne in 1727.

Campbell quickly ensured that he was well connected to the luminaries of the Prince's set. He was working on the fabric of Leicester House itself during the early 1720s, and between 1726 and 1727 built Compton Place in Sussex for Spencer Compton, a Leicester House crony who was used by the new King in 1727 in an ultimately unsuccessful attempt to supplant Walpole as First Minister. At the same time, however, Campbell provided himself with what he hoped would be invaluable political insurance. For in 1722 work was begun on a house designed by Campbell for Robert Walpole himself: Houghton Hall in Norfolk. Such was Campbell's self-confidence that by 1725 he was ambitiously styling himself 'Architect to His Royal Highness, the Prince of Wales' on the title page of the third volume of *Vitruvius Britannicus*, and clearly hoping for great things once the Prince succeeded to the throne.

However, all Campbell's carefully laid plans came to nought. He did succeed Vanbrugh as Surveyor at Greenwich Hospital in 1726, but George II's accession brought little more likelihood of royal architectural patronage than had George I's. To add insult to injury, Campbell was dropped by his patron the Earl of Pembroke in favour of the relatively unknown architect Roger Morris, and before his early death in 1729 had been replaced in Burlington's affections by the more versatile and personable figure of William Kent.

Meanwhile, Burlington himself was busy with Chiswick House (the development of which is outlined in the next chapter), with securing architectural commissions for friends and acquaintances, and with his own academic pursuits. Many of the original Palladio drawings which Burlington had bought in 1719 were expensively published as *Fabbriche Antiche* in 1730. The following year work was begun on Burlington's radical new Assembly Rooms in York. This undemonstrative and chaste evocation of an ancient hall was kept deliberately simple and austere, resulting in what Rudolf Wittkower has called 'probably the most severely classical building of the early eighteenth century'. Its interior was, as the researches of Ian Bristow have revealed, originally decorated from floor to ceiling in a pale stone colour. (Burlington's Palladian vision stands in marked contrast to the lurid 1950s greens and 'school hall' floorboards which currently disfigure this seminal building.) However, Burlington's coolly neoclassical effect was achieved at the expense of the hall's function. It was soon apparent that the colonnade had been squashed far too closely together to allow the latest fashions to emerge unscathed. As the Duchess of Marlborough remarked, the columns stood 'as

York Assembly Rooms, Burlington's essay in classical austerity of 1731–2 and, according to John Harris, 'conceivably the most novel and significant building in Europe' of the period. In 1751 the seating, formerly placed against the wall, was brought forward to be re-sited between the columns, ruining Burlington's Vitruvian proportions but preventing any more socialites from getting their ballgowns stuck between the densely packed pillars. This engraving of 1759 shows the new arrangement.

close as a row of nine pins. Nobody with a hoop petticoat can pass through them.' More recently, even Wittkower has admitted that even those resting on the seats behind 'must have felt squeezed in and uncomfortable'.

Despite these practical problems, by the mid-1730s Burlington was widely acknowledged as the supreme arbiter of architectural taste. Even Horace Walpole (who had, characteristically, become disenchanted with the Earl some time after his rapturous visit to Burlington House in 1715) was prepared to bestow on him the backhanded compliment of 'knowing the minute and mechanical parts of architecture too well'. And in 1734 James Ralph – an architectural writer who had spent his early years in America and who had returned to England in 1725 in company with Benjamin Franklin – dedicated his highly influential *Critical Review of the Publick Buildings…in and about London* to the Earl alone.

During this time, Burlington worked increasingly closely with his companion and protégé William Kent. Kent was born in 1685 – the same year as Handel and Bach. He had settled in Rome in 1710, and did not return to England until that most auspicious of Palladian years, 1715. Shortly before he left he met Burlington, then on his first Grand Tour; it was during Burlington's second visit of 1719, however, that their friendship ripened. Having met the Earl at Genoa, Kent was soon gleefully confiding that 'His Lordship lik'd my designs so well, both painting and architecture, that he

Above and *above right* The
Landscape Room and Green
Room from William Kent's
Holkham Hall, begun in 1734
but not finished until 1765.
Most of the ceilings and
chimneypieces in the house
were taken from designs
by Inigo Jones. The result,
in the opinion of Admiral
Boscawen who visited
Holkham in 1757, was a
building 'so elegant that it
is far beyond conception or
description'.

would make me promise at least to begin with to paint for him the first when I come over, which if he comes soon may be with his Lordship'. By 1720 he was firmly established at Burlington House as the Earl's pet history painter, his hagiographical but also faintly absurd *Apotheosis of Inigo Jones* being accorded pride of place in Burlington's London home. Two years later, Burlington engineered Kent's capture of the commission for painting George I's new state rooms at Kensington Palace – a job won over the head of the enraged Serjeant Painter, Sir James Thornhill. Thornhill was linked with the discredited Wren and the ousted Tories; Kent's patron, on the other hand, was one of the leading lights of the youthful new Whig administration. Kent's work at Kensington – the additions to which represent virtually the only major royal commission of George I's colourless reign – includes some of his finest painting. In particular, the 'grotesque' ceiling of the Presence Chamber was not only remarkably evocative of the domestic ceilings of Ancient Rome but also suitably respectful towards Jones' Queen's House; indeed, so innovative was the design that 50 years later it was to prove a major influence on Robert Adam's virtuoso ceiling compositions. However, few of Kent's other paintings were so successful. His altar-piece for the Wren church of St Clement Danes, for example, was so bad that it was removed and put into storage soon after its installation in 1725, a development that Thornhill's son-in-law Hogarth was quick to exploit in a satirical print. Hogarth's malicious captions ('F/The inside of his leg but whether right or left is yet undiscover'd', and 'H/The other leg judiciously omitted to make room for the harp') poked fun at Kent's approximate drawing style.

For Burlington, though, the question of Kent's innate talent was never in doubt. In 1726 he secured for his protégé the commission to design and dispose the interiors at Robert Walpole's Norfolk palace of Houghton Hall, the shell of which had been begun under the direction of Colen Campbell (by now dropped in favour of Kent) in 1722. Here money was clearly no object. Kent used highly expensive mahogany not just for select items of furniture but throughout the house; as Michael Wilson has noted, 'the doorway of the Saloon alone is said to have cost £1,000'. The vast State Bed, with its pronounced Palladian cornice, fabulously expensive green velvet hangings and typically Kentian shell motif, cost an enormous £1,219 to make.

Yet Kent's attitude was growing increasingly complacent. Already notorious for his rather un-English love of good food, he was frequently drunk on site at Houghton. 'The Signior, as he was called,' wrote Burlington's friend, the amateur architect Sir Thomas Robinson, 'often gave his orders when he was full of claret'; in addition, 'he did not perhaps see the works for several months after'. His interiors at nearby Raynham, designed at the

The exterior of Holkham. In planning this ambitious house Kent was apparently assisted not only by Burlington but also by the owner himself – Thomas Coke, Earl of Leicester. Holkham Hall, however, took over 30 years to complete, by which time Kent, Burlington and Leicester were all dead. The architect who actually supervised the erection of most of the house, Matthew Brettingham, took advantage of this to pass off the Hall's design as his own; it was only in 1773 that Brettingham's son admitted that the house was largely Kent's invention.

same time as the work at Houghton, were soon the target of much criticism. 'The rooms are fitted up by Mr Kent,' wrote the Earl of Oxford after a visit of 1732, 'and consequently there is a great deal of gilding', as well as 'very clumsy over-charged chimney-pieces to the great waste of fine marble'. Sir Thomas Robinson could only report that the rooms at Raynham were 'prettily ornamented in the inside by Mr Kent', but 30 years later the architect James Adam was perhaps being more frank when he noted: 'The apartments have been fitted by Mr Kent but are by no means elegant or pleasant.'

Even Burlington now could no longer ignore the fact that Kent had proved an embarrassing failure as an artist. Observers such as the antiquary George Vertue testified that 'Courtiers declared him the best History painter', while John Gay famously – and ludicrously – compared him to the greatest of all Renaissance painters ('Why didst thou, Kent, forego thy native land,/ To emulate in picture Raphael's hand?'). But his undistinguished work at Burlington House and later at Chiswick must have revealed even to the adulatory Earl that there was an element of 'the Emperor's new clothes' in the public reception of Kent's art. As Horace Walpole testified some years later, while 'a restorer of the science of architecture and the father of modern gardening', as a painter Kent remained 'below mediocrity'.

Undaunted, Burlington set about making his friend into an architect instead. It was to this end that in 1727 he financed the publication of Kent's *Designs of Inigo Jones*, which actually featured more drawings by Burlington, Kent and Webb than by the great master himself. By the mid-1730s Kent was well established as an architect fluent in both Gothick and Palladian styles. In 1734 work was begun on Holkham Hall, a vast Palladian pile built for Thomas Coke, Earl of Leicester, which was even grander than its Norfolk neighbour, Houghton. Holkham's elevations were built not in stone, as at

Houghton, but in local yellow brick, following Vitruvius' precept that brick was the most suitable material for the walls of villas. By the time Kent died in 1748, however, work on Holkham was barely half finished, and by the mid-1750s even the Earl of Leicester himself had lost interest in this most costly and ambitious of projects. ('I look around,' wailed the Earl, 'not a house to be seen but my own. I am Giant, of Giant Castle, and have ate up all my neighbours.')

   Kent, it is clear, was far more than Burlington's architect and companion. (In this, the Earl may have been unconsciously imitating Jones yet again: Jones, John Harris has suggested, 'was probably a homosexual'.) Their correspondence is overtly affectionate, and when Kent was away on site Burlington obsessively re-read all of Kent's letters. 'The person I mention to you for a servant in your house', Kent once wrote to Burlington in his usual, tortuous prose, 'is such a one, that I don't know but by people loving and living with them may in time think the same way, as I flatter myself I do with you.' James Lees-Milne remarked that Burlington's marriage in 1721 'made not the slightest difference to their relationship'. Indeed, this does seem to have been the case. Michael Wilson has pointed out the significance of Kent's use of

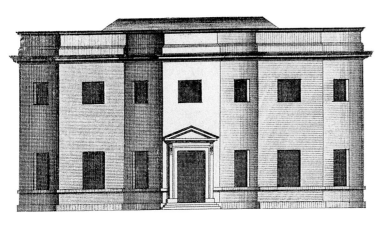

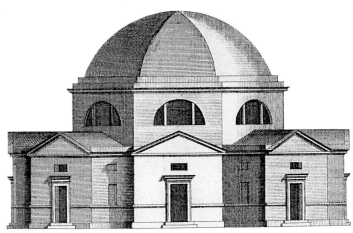

Left **Canaletto's splendid view of the pre-Kentian Horse Guards, as seen from St James's Park in 1749. The terrace on the right is particularly interesting, with its white-painted sashes and pre-Georgian dormers. In front of the terrace two servants are dusting down an expensive oriental carpet.**

Plates 30 and 47 from Robert Morris' influential pattern-book *The Architectural Remembrancer* of 1751. The use of large, protruding octagonal rooms was a particularly new concept, one which taken up with enthusiasm by Robert Taylor, John Carr and James Paine in Britain and, later in the century, by Thomas Jefferson in America.

the word 'our' in his strained comment on the union: 'I hope the *vertu* will grow stronger in our house and architecture will flourish more.' Kent was clearly allowed to have a mistress – but then such an accoutrement was an essential accessory for any fashionable man about town. More significantly, Burlington's new wife, Lady Dorothy Savile (soon reputed for her notoriously short temper and highly abusive vocabulary), was freely permitted to indulge her notorious passion for the Duke of Grafton. The Burlingtons did, though, find time to perform their dynastic duties and beget three daughters.

The 1740s saw some of Kent's finest architectural works, among them the stunning interior of 44 Berkeley Square, begun in 1742, and Kent's grand design for Horse Guards, erected posthumously in 1750. In 1744 Kent was accorded the unparalleled honour of being linked with the very inspiration of English Palladianism in John Vardy's flattering sourcebook *Some Designs of Mr Inigo Jones and Mr William Kent*. For his patron, however, the 1740s had an entirely different aspect. Burlington's achievements had begun to pall; deeply in debt, he saw his gods being derided and his enemies lauded. (In Abraham Swan's highly successful pattern-book, *British Architecture*, of 1745, the author, as Eileen Harris has noted, 'took every opportunity to tarnish the reputations of the celebrated Italian authorities – Scamozzi, Vignola and especially Palladio – in order to add to the lustre of Wren'.) Bowed down by an acute sense of failure, the Earl built little during the ensuing decade, and appears to have become a semi-recluse. Shortly before his death in 1748, he even fell out with his dear 'Kentino' – a breach which was possibly instigated by the quarrelsome but understandably jealous Countess.

But what exactly was the English Palladianism being propounded by Burlington and his followers? When Robert Morris, a kinsman of Roger Morris

Right The rusticated doorway from Kent's Palladian garden at Rousham, Oxfordshire of c.1740. *Far right*, a more complex rusticated doorway design by Inigo Jones.

and the only real architectural theorist of the period, referred in 1751 to 'the *Paladian* [*sic*] manner', he clearly believed that his readership already understood what this term meant. Yet even today there is often much confusion over exactly what 'Palladianism' is, and how it relates to Georgian architecture as a whole. Strictly speaking, the term should be 'Neo-Palladian' – architecture after the manner of Palladio. However, 'Palladianism' is the shorthand generally used here as elsewhere. This is the style which, whether expressed in the form of a great house, a country villa or an urban terrace, created what we understand today as 'Georgian' architecture.

In 1945 Rudolf Wittkower pointed out that not all of the influences on English Palladian architecture were actually Neo-Palladian, and that English Palladianism was to a large extent derived from English traditions and English adaptations. The Early Palladians, he declared, were 'a good deal more English than is generally realized' in their buildings:

> These men could neither ignore the development of the previous hundred years in English architecture nor their own national tradition, and it can be shown that they gave a new meaning to almost all the elements which they derived from Palladio... Moreover, certain recurrent motifs of importance in English academic architecture between 1720 and 1760 are not Palladian at all.

Especially English was the tendency for the flagbearers of Palladianism to understate the influence and importance of Andrea Palladio himself. Instead,

English commentators and designers preferred to elevate the figure of the native 'master' of the seventeenth century, Inigo Jones. As an Englishman, Jones was far more compatible with the image of an architectural style grounded on national sentiment and characteristics than Palladio or his fellow countrymen, and the style's recurrent use of Jonesian rather than pure 'Neo-Palladian' (ie sixteenth-century Italian) motifs reflects a conscious desire to emphasize a peculiarly English heritage and style. Jones was the object of continual praise by the Early Palladian architects, who frequently lauded the Englishman at the expense of Palladio (who, while still venerated as a genius of design, nonetheless remained an Italian). To Colen Campbell, Jones was a genius more than equal to Andrea Palladio: 'It is then with the Renowned Palladio we enter the Lists, to whom we oppose the Famous Inigo Jones'. Indeed, in the first volume of *Vitruvius Britannicus* of 1715, Campbell stressed with monotonous regularity the undeniable superiority of the 'great Master' of British architecture: he was the author not only of 'those excellent pieces at Greenwich' but also of that 'incomparable piece', the Banqueting House in Whitehall ('designed by the immortal Jones'), while it was confidently declared of Jones' designs for the palace at Whitehall that 'There is no Palace in the World to rival it'. It is evident that Campbell intended *Vitruvius Britannicus* not so much as a monument to Palladio as a celebration of Jones. Campbell actually went out of his way to be rude about the Italian Baroque masters:

> *How affected and licentious are the works of Bernini and Fontana. How wildly extravagant are the Designs of Borromini, who has endeavoured to debauch mankind with his odd and chimerical beauties, where the parts are without Proportion, solids without their true Bearing, Heaps of Materials without strength, Excessive Ornaments without Grace, and the Whole without Symmetry.*

Over 30 years after the appearance of the first volume of *Vitruvius Britannicus*, Robert Morris was saying much the same thing: 'An Age scarce produceth a *Corelli* or a *Handel*; An *Angelo* or a *Raphael*, a *Palladio* or a *JONES*.'

Jones' buildings were accordingly pillaged by the Palladians for any knowing references that could impress Burlington and his fellow arbiters of taste. Jones' works – having, as Robert Morris put it, 'so sensible and strong Ideas of the Beauties of the Ancients' – provided an artistic touchstone that was eagerly quoted by Early Palladian designers such as Burlington, Campbell and Roger Morris. Virtually all Palladian architects of the first half of the eighteenth century, for example, made some reference in their works to the towers with pyramidal roofs which had been placed at either end of the south front of Wilton House. Indeed the Wilton towers (which Jones himself had

borrowed from Vicenzo Scamozzi's *L'idea della architettura universale* of 1615) represent perhaps the most characteristic motif of Early Palladianism – a rather ironic development, given that it is doubtful whether Jones was actually the real author of the south front of Wilton. Wiltonesque towers, inset with single Venetian windows, first appeared at Burlington's Tottenham Park of 1721; they subsequently featured in Campbell's Houghton Hall of 1722, and became a recurrent motif in the country houses of Roger Morris – hardly surprisingly, since the owner of Wilton, the eccentric 'Architect Earl' of Pembroke, was one of Morris' principal patrons.

Jones was chosen as the godfather of English Palladianism not necessarily for his architectural achievements but primarily because of his symbolic value to a national architectural style designed to match the grandiose political aspirations of Georgian England. The inaccuracy with which Palladians attributed works to Jones suggests that here it was not the content of the Jonesian-Palladian style that mattered so crucially as its essential Englishness, a nationalistic image which could be based on the myth of an incomparable English Master. The fact that Jones is now believed *not* to have designed the south front at Wilton – debate still rages over the respective claims of Isaac de Caus, John Webb and Jones – is academic. What matters is that the Palladians *believed* that this building was wholly by Jones, as they thought that Cobham Hall (where neither Jones nor Webb had ever set foot), Amesbury House (by Webb), Coleshill (by Roger Pratt) and the York House Water Gate (actually by the amateur Restoration architect Sir Balthasar Gerbier) were also by the great master. Thus these works remain vitally important as Jonesian icons for the eighteenth century.

Genuine Jonesian motifs were, of course, also in plentiful supply. Jones' sumptuous Single Cube and Double Cube Rooms from Wilton, for example, were copied – in dimension if not in decoration – throughout the Palladian era. At Roger Morris' Marble Hill House of 1724–9, for example, the borrowings from Jones (or Jones' pupils) were numerous: the alcoves recall the Jones/Webb alcove room at Greenwich; the Breakfast Parlour frieze is taken directly from Jones' designs for St Paul's Cathedral; the ceilings to the principal floor derive from Jones and Webb designs used by Campbell at Compton Place; while the mahogany stairs recall the double stair at Coleshill (in 1724 still attributed to Jones, though actually by the enigmatic Roger Pratt). Books of Jones' designs, most notably Kent's *Designs of Inigo Jones, with some Additional Designs* of 1727, helped popularize Jonesian Palladianism further. References to Jones thus filled the interiors of the period.

This is not to underestimate, however, the importance of Palladio's own works to the evolution of English Palladianism. Many of Burlington's

Roger Morris' Marble Hill House, Twickenham, Middlesex, built in 1724–9. *Above*, detail of Morris' bold egg-and-dart moulding and of the shutters in the second-floor windows, which are operated with cords, pulleys and weights. *Above left*, detail of the Breakfast Room. This alcove, with its curious paired brackets, may well have been designed by a more amateur hand than that of Morris – perhaps by Lord Herbert, or James Richards. *Right*, detail of the ground floor hall, with its rustic 'beams' (taken from Vitruvius) and utilitarian, tessellated stone floor.

designs, in particular, relied heavily on the Earl's collection of original Italian drawings, the bulk of which were by Palladio himself. His house for General Wade, for example, was virtually an exact copy of a project by Palladio for a waterside palace. (Although the house was eulogized by the architectural critic James Ralph as 'one of the best things among the new buildings… intirely chaste and simple', Horace Walpole revealed that its interior was very poorly proportioned, 'all to humour the beauty of the front'.) Yet within a few years the style of the English Palladians had evolved beyond the mere mimicry of Italian precedents; Burlington's Italianate house for Wade, of 1723, contrasts strongly with the stark, unhurried Palladianism of Roger Morris' Combe Bank, begun only two years after Burlington's house.

Already elements which owed little to Palladio himself were beginning to dominate the style of the English designers, as English architects went to enormous pains to incorporate recognizably native elements into what was in origin a wholly Italian style. Jones' surviving works were treated with almost hagiographical reverence. During the 1730s, for example, Burlington not only repaired the famous Jones icon of St Paul's Church in London's Covent Garden, but had Jones' gateway for Beaufort House in Chelsea re-erected in the grounds of his own rural retreat at Chiswick. And, while Campbell was reproducing Palladio's Villa Rotonda at Mereworth in Kent during the early 1720s, he was also competing with Thomas Hewett's architectural 'junta' to rebuild Whitehall Palace to Jones' monumental and repetitive designs.

In this context, Burlington's not entirely welcomed devotion to Italian culture in the early years of the Palladian movement – so evident during the 1720s with his sponsorship of Italian opera and sculpture – served to muddy the prospects for a distinct 'National Style' already based on dubious attributions and borrowings. However, by 1730 writers such as Robert Morris were strongly emphasizing the Englishness of the new Palladian style and preferring to draw a veil over Burlington's Italophile tendencies. Morris, while daring to censure Palladio in his *Lectures* of the early 1730s for the heinous sin of superimposing the five classical orders (a practice condemned as 'contrary to all the stated rules of *Architecture*' and 'disagreeable to the eye'), lavished praise on Jones for his 'sensible and strong Ideas of the Beauties of the Ancients'. Even Horace Walpole, who was not slow to castigate the Palladians when it suited him, was ready to acclaim Jones as an architect who 'soon stepped into the true and perfect Grecian'.

Having established the essential Englishness of their style, the Palladians were keen to give the new manner a rational and watertight philosophical pedigree. English Palladianism was thus quickly bound to a rigid set of building rules, all of which were designed to achieve that most tantalizing of

Right Elevation of General Wade's house in Old Burlington Street (now demolished). Designed by Burlington, and sited in the midst of his London estate to the north of Piccadilly, the elevation was taken directly from a Palladio scheme for a town house, and constituted the most purely Palladian composition in the capital. Wade – later to become famous as the subjugator of Jacobite Scotland – was a friend of Burlington's; Sir John Clerk, observing the house in 1727, acknowledged that the Doric order was eminently suitable for a general, since in the ancient world 'monuments … to Heroes were of this order'.

goals – aesthetic and functional perfection. 'Perfect' architecture was not a mere theoretical ideal for the Palladians; they believed that, by modelling their works on the buildings of the Antique world (or on the Renaissance's various reinterpretations of these classical ideals), they would attain the perfection readily found in Man and Nature.

Robert Morris was the first to emphasize that perfection lay within the compass of most designers – or at least those of talent and application. By following the 'Universal rule' of proportion (that could 'serve for all Manner of Rooms whatever') devised by Morris during the early 1730s, an architect could soon find the perfection of Nature within his grasp. Beauty and perfection, Morris asserted, derived from a consummate harmony of parts; 'the nearer we approach to Nature', he concluded, 'the more agreeable will that *Harmony* be.' The uniformity and simplicity of Nature should, he declared, provide all designers with the very model of perfection. This blissful state of perfection was also one which encapsulated ideals in *all* spheres of human experience – not just architecture. As there existed for Morris 'only seven distinct Proportions which produce all the different Buildings in the Universe', there also existed similarly immutable forms in music and other artistic disciplines.

This reliance on Nature – and implicitly in God, who created it – was based on a firm philosophical bedrock. The Third Earl of Shaftesbury, following Plato, declared that the eye and the ear operated solely through the agency of the mind, and that beauty was to be perceived merely as an expression of this rational process and not the result of latent, instinctive emotions. Sensuous, Baroque passions were firmly under control in Shaftesbury's rationalist vision of beauty. Colour, for example, was deemed 'plainly foreign and separate' to the ideal of corporeal beauty, 'having no concern or share in the proper delight or entertainment'. Nature was to be judged 'beautiful' not merely because it functioned according to predetermined scientific laws – the beauty of Nature, he stated, was far more profound than 'mere mechanic beauties' – but because it could be appreciated on a strictly rational basis.

Since Nature itself had been founded and propagated in the principles of rationality, the Palladian theorists held that, in espousing a rationalist approach to their discipline, architects would be able to achieve the ideal goal of imitating the natural environment in their works. Philosophers were indeed already exhorting designers to follow Nature's lead. Francis Hutcheson celebrated the '*Beauty* in Animals, arising from a certain proportion of the various Parts to each other, which still pleases the sense of spectators', and was echoed, in a rather more lyrical vein, by George Berkeley ('Oh Nature! thou art the fountain, original and pattern of all that is good and wise…You

Right Venetian windows, plain and rustic, from Edward Hoppus and Benjamin Cole's *The Gentleman and Builder's Repository* of 1737. As Eileen Harris notes, 'Hoppus and Cole were unscrupulous pirates but they were well-meaning, their whole purpose being to provide the lower ranks of builders with architectural information that otherwise would have been beyond their means.'

wou'd like then to follow Nature, and propose her as a guide and pattern for your imitation') and by Pope:

> *To* build, *to plant, whatever you intend,*
> *To Raise the* Column, *or the* Arch *to bend,*
> *To swell the* Terras *or to sink the* Grot,
> *In all let* Nature *never be forgot.*

Nature presented Robert Morris with the basic guidelines for his architectural rules. His magical proportions were, he averred, the logical result of simply observing Nature, 'constant and invariable in her Production'. Morris, like the Abbé Laugier later in the century, advocated the mimicry of elemental natural forms as the surest way to attain artistic perfection. The use of such forms was evident both in the delineation of his general theory and in the evolution of his particular system of proportions. 'The nearer we approach to Nature in Form, Colour or Number,' he wrote in 1739, 'or from the Nature and Occurrence of Things, the more agreeable will that *Harmony* be.' And, as 'The Harmony of *Nature* consists in Proportion', then for the Palladians it followed that proportion was the key to architectural success.

To reach their goal of perfect proportionality, the Palladians devised a wide variety of instant mathematical solutions to all manner of design problems. Robert Morris' scheme of seven proportions, ranging from a square and a circle to the complexity of a cube magnified by 72, was intended to be as relevant to the construction of a country villa as to the design of a London terrace. Such systems of proportion were taken from the works of Palladio, who in turn had derived his inspiration from none other than Plato.

Plato had made extensive use of the cosmic number seven: both the zodiacal band around the planets and the universal 'World-Soul' were, he believed, divided into seven harmonic intervals, derived mathematically from the progression of two-dimensional square forms and three-dimensional cubic forms. From these, Plato had produced his system of seven proportions – 1, 2, 3, 4, 8, 9, 27 – which could be infinitely prolonged in either direction. Palladio's and Morris' proportions were merely simpler variants of the Platonic scale, based on progressive addition rather than multiplication.

Morris also followed Plato in providing copious musical analogies for his proportional scheme. Plato's proportions corresponded to the relative lengths of string required, in Greek musical practice, to produce the seven notes of the scale. Morris, too, cited the example of the musical scale in providing a valuable analogy for his 'Harmonick Proportions of Rooms'. In *Music* are only seven distinct Notes,' he declared, 'in Architecture likewise are only seven distinct Proportions.' To him the natural 'affinity of Numbers and Sounds' extended both to solid forms and musical compositions: 'A Jarring and Discord in Music immediately offends the Ear', as 'a disproportionate Building displeases the Eye.'

In addition to building on Platonic theories to construct a firm philosophical basis for English Palladianism, the Palladian pioneers were also keen to establish the style's political correctness. In emphasizing the Grecian, rather than the Roman or Italian, origin of eighteenth-century English Palladianism, Morris neatly avoided any undue enunciation of the connection between the new English 'National Style' and either the notorious excesses of the Roman Empire (in particular its anti-Christian campaigns) or the Catholic absolutism of contemporary Rome, cradle of the Jesuits and the Counter-Reformation. Furthermore, it diverted attention from the inordinate reliance of many of the early English Palladians on the designs of Palladio and the other Italian masters of the previous two centuries. Morris' appeal to a semi-mythical, politically neutral Greek past also helped to emphasize the ties between his vision of rationalist architecture and the Platonic realism on which much of contemporary British philosophy was based. Morris deliberately blurred the distinction between Greek and Roman in the Preface to *Rural Architecture*, where he recalled 'the *Grecian Architecture*, which *Vitruvius* and other great Genius's practised in *Rome*'. By associating the legacy of Vitruvius with Greece, he attempted to avoid the identification of English Palladianism with Ancient Rome or the contemporary Papacy.

Since Palladianism was almost exclusively employed for domestic building in Britain, the objection that Ancient Greece was a heathen culture alien to a Christian society was rarely made. Accordingly, Morris was able

Right The garden front of Peckover House in Wisbech, Cambridgeshire of 1722, showing two of the most commonly used Palladian elements: the Diocletian window (top) and the Venetian window (middle). Swept-head windows such as these were a frequent feature of the homes of the 1720s; by 1740, however, the more regular (and cheaper) rectangular window had become the rule in most metropolitan areas.

The Saloon doorway at Rokeby Park, Yorkshire, rebuilt by Sir Thomas Robinson to his own designs between 1725 and 1730.

to recall an idealized, idyllic, pre-Roman past: 'the three *Greek* orders are of themselves sufficient to raise the greatest, noblest and most magnificent Structure that mankind can possibly invent, without the least Assistance of the *Latin* or *Roman*.' Indeed, he frequently stressed how these pure Greek forms had been debased by Roman practice: 'I do not find a single Beauty has been, or could be, added to the three *Greek* Orders…The Romans, indeed added two other, which I wish were nameless Orders: the *Tuscan*, sunk into Dullness and Heaviness in Composition…[and the] *Composite Order*, consisting of a Redundancy of Mouldings.'

And things had got far worse since the Romans. Gothic was, to Morris, 'irregular, disproportion'd, or deformed', and masterpieces of the style such as Westminster Abbey 'only a heavy, lumpish, unrein'd Mass of Materials jumbled together without Design, Regularity, or Order'. Eighteenth-century architects (presumably even including his cousin Roger Morris, who had already experimented with a consciously neo-medieval Gothic style) had no business employing such barbaric forms: 'K–T has no Excuse, to copy these,/ Unless he has NO other Way to please'. And Baroque classicism was castigated in similarly dismissive terms. Baroque architects may have taken the architecture of the Ancients as their original inspiration, but they had 'rejected its sublime Principles, and treated it with so much malicious Barbarity, that the original Beauties of Architecture were almost extinct and lost'. Even today there was, thundered Morris, 'a daily Application of combined Force to destroy that Beauty, Sweetness and Harmony united in the Composition of ancient Architecture'. Naïve, Burlingtonian Neo-Palladianism was no answer. Palladio, Morris insisted, was only mortal. 'He sometimes follows the Caprice or Humour of the Person for whom he built' and 'sometimes deviates from that Nobleness and Grandeur,' appearing 'inconsistent with himself'.

Curiously, the wholly out-of-favour Catholic architect James Gibbs – whose style was neither Palladian nor Baroque – escaped Morris' censure. Gibbs won approval for 'that beautiful and noble building of St *Martin's* Church', and was even accorded the accolade 'immortable' and provided with a niche in Morris' Palladian pantheon:

> Learn of PALLADIO, how to Deck a Space,
> Of JONES you'll learn Magnificence and Grace:
> CAMPBELL will teach, the Beauty they impart;
> And GIBBS, the Rules and Modus of the Art.

This politically incorrect commendation of Gibbs (who appears to have been deliberately omitted from all three volumes of Campbell's *Vitruvius Britannicus*) is quite out of character for the normally acerbic Morris. There

The magnificent top-lit staircase at 44 Berkeley Square, London. Begun in 1742, the interior of number 44 is one of Kent's finest and most mature works. The dividing staircase, with its revolutionary, serpentine iron balusters, won unqualified praise even from Horace Walpole, who called it 'as beautiful a piece of scenery and, considering the space, of art, as can be imagined'.

were many eminent Palladians Morris could have cited, most notably William Kent. However, it seems that for a time the two men had been neighbours. Gibbs designed a number of buildings in the Middlesex parish of Twickenham in which Robert Morris lived; it therefore seems likely that the two met here and became friends. It was at Twickenham that Gibbs wrote what was to become perhaps the most influential pattern-book of the eighteenth century, his *Book of Architecture* of 1728.

The English Palladian style being propagated by Burlington, Kent and Robert Morris can be identified in a number of ways. The first distinctive trait was the Palladians' interest in the honesty of design. This radical and striking theme – which anticipates the Arts and Crafts Movement of the mid-Victorian era as well as twentieth-century Modernism – was best expressed in the writings of Robert Morris. In the Preface to his *Rural Architecture* of 1751, Morris made frequent and explicit reference to the subject of utility and the expression of function, in a manner oddly similar to that of the

The principal façade of Roger Morris' Council House at Chichester, Sussex. This small, modest building is in fact one of Morris' most Italian-inspired compositions. Features such as the double temple front and the prominent Venetian window strongly recall Palladio's Venetian churches of San Giorgio Maggiore and Il Redentore.

Bauhaus designers two centuries later. 'Your structure must answer the End for which it was erected', stipulated Morris, since 'Every *Cave* and *Hut* was made to answer some End'. Each structural and decorative item was deemed unworthy unless it served a particular constructional or aesthetic purpose. 'All Breaks arise or spring from some proper Bearings,' he declared, and must be 'useful for the End they are introduc'd'.

Palladianism in Britain and North America is easily recognized by its vocabulary of stock architectural features. The most famous of these motifs was the Venetian window, known in North America as the 'Palladian window'. This was an old Italian window form which Palladio had taken from Serlio, and which was introduced into British practice by Jones (who used not Palladio but Scamozzi as his direct inspiration). Centrally placed Venetian windows, remarkably similar in context and form to those used by Scamozzi in schemes for palazzi in his *L'idea della architettura universale* of 1615, appear in Jones' projects for Somerset House, Worcester College and Whitehall Palace. From Jones the motif passed into the repertoire of the eighteenth-century Palladian designers.

The manner in which the Venetian window was used in Britain and North America, however, differed sharply from Italian custom. In the English-speaking countries it was employed generally as a single, enlarged and isolated feature. Palladio himself rarely used Venetian windows in this

The north front of Lord Burlington's Chiswick House, with a Diocletian window visible in the octagonal dome. The wall below is punctuated by three isolated Venetian windows.

manner: the only isolated window in Palladio's oeuvre occurs at the Villa Angarano, which was not only one of Palladio's earliest works (being begun around 1548) but was also never finished. Far more typical of Palladio's use of Venetian windows was the design of the celebrated Basilica in Vicenza, where large, continuously repeated openings of this kind occupied most of the wall space on both storeys. Rhythmic sequences of more than three windows did not appear in the buildings of the English Palladians until the great houses designed by Robert Adam in the 1760s and '70s. Early Palladian usage of the Venetian window remained directly opposed to the Italian tradition, in which every structural element possessed its own functional energy and linear movement. In Palladian Britain and Colonial America, Venetian or Palladian windows provided the primary punctuation for façades that were otherwise comparatively undecorated. In this, as in so many other aspects of Palladian design, architects took their cue from Burlington – in this case, from the

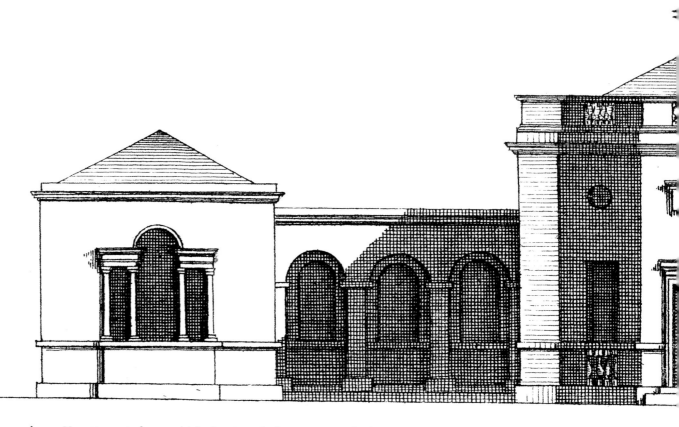

large Venetian windows which dominated the exterior of Chiswick House and the pavilions of Burlington House. Isaac Ware's comment in his *Complete Body of Architecture* of 1756 that Venetian windows were of 'a kind calculated for shew, and very pompous in their nature' neatly describes this novel English usage.

In exploring the aesthetic possibilities of the Venetian window, Palladian architects in Britain made extensive use of the relieving arch, a motif taken from Palladio (who in turn took it from Bramante) but which subsequently became one of the hallmarks of English Palladian design. Large Venetian windows spanned by relieving arches were first used in Britain by Colen Campbell, who inserted them into the façades of Wanstead (now demolished), Burlington House and Walpole's Houghton Hall. The Venetian window was also frequently arranged in isolated groups of three, a device which Burlington borrowed from Palladio. Kent used the motif at his Horse Guards of 1750, and from there it passed into the repertoire of the mid-century Palladians such as James Paine and Robert Taylor.

Another common Palladian motif was the Diocletian window: a semi-circular, lunette opening with two pronounced vertical glazing bars or mullions. Like the Venetian window, this was by no means a recent invention. Occurring originally in the Roman Baths of Diocletian in Split (hence

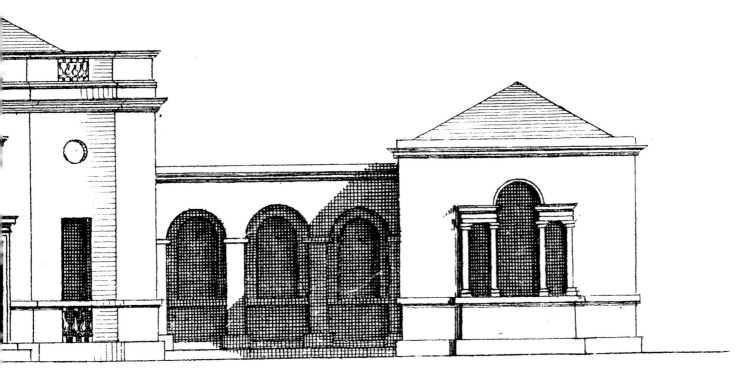

the unlikely name), the Diocletian window was transplanted by Palladio to a number of sixteenth-century designs, both domestic and ecclesiastical. However, while the motif was only sparingly employed by Palladio and his Italian contemporaries, over a century later Burlington and his disciples embraced it with enormous enthusiasm, the window becoming a key element in most of Burlington's buildings.

Similarly recurrent, and peculiarly English, was the use of the so-called 'Gibbs surround': block quoins superimposed on door or window jambs underneath a heavy mass of voussoirs. Following the spread of Gibbs' pattern-books across the Atlantic in the 1730s and '40s, this form became particularly popular in North America, where eighteenth- and nineteenth-century Gibbs surrounds still survive on many homes and churches.

English Palladianism also experimented with different shapes as well as with new motifs. The prevalence of simple cube shapes is at its most obvious in buildings such as Burlington's Tottenham Park, Kent's Horse Guards and Roger Morris' Combe Bank. More sophisticated than this rather unsubtle reliance on cubes, however, was the manner in which the Palladians used the classical vocabulary at their disposal to create an impression of clarity and isolation, where blank spaces and widely separated features emphasize the significance of each individual element of construction or decoration. In this

Cubic proportions abound in Robert Morris' design for a small villa with wings from *The Architectural Remembrancer* of 1751.

respect, English Palladian design was quite unlike the buildings of the Italian Renaissance: these buildings made no reference to the typically Italian restlessness of Palladio's façades, where the constant repetition of standard units was a common feature. Instead, the English – true, perhaps, to their aloof and uncommunicative natures – adopted the principles of space and isolation for even the largest buildings.

This principle particularly affected the provision of window openings. Large areas of fenestration had been distinct features of the Baroque houses of the late seventeenth and early eighteenth centuries: massive window openings closely packed between giant columns and pilasters had, for example, characterized the façades of Vanbrugh and Hawksmoor's celebrated palaces of Blenheim and Castle Howard. Such arrangements were denounced by Robert Morris, who ridiculed the modern architects who 'croud and fill the Spaces by some gay Dress'. In Palladian buildings, windows were instead largely employed as isolated elements on a blank wall. Morris declared that he much preferred '*Plainness* and *Utility* to *Gaiety* and *Ornament*': 'A Plain regular front', he asserted, 'without Dress or Ornament, if justly proportion'd, will better satisfy the taste of the Judicious.' One of his principal concerns was to retain the balance between wallspace and openings: 'Dress and Decoration', he noted, should be 'used to preserve and equal Space from Vacuity to Vacuity', while stipulating that the main purpose of exterior decoration was so that 'the spaces are preserved by breaking the Distances with Festoons or Drapery'. Twenty years later, Ware was still censuring those wall surfaces that were 'in a manner, all windows'.

Plainness and simplicity of form represented the basis of the Palladian style. The term 'plain', for example, recurs with Shaker-like emphasis throughout the pattern-books of Robert Morris, implicitly incorporating the ideals of accessibility and honesty which had been so loudly trumpeted by Shaftesbury and Campbell in calling for a national style devoid of foreign excess and licence. Simple adornments were considered permissible – 'Ornaments certainly give a noble Contrast to a Design', Morris reluctantly admitted – but in general the opinions of Robert Morris and his fellow-Palladians anticipated late eighteenth-century neoclassical antipathy to excessive ornamentation, as well as the Modern Movement's more recent exhortations concerning honesty of materials and clarity of function. Thus Portland Stone was recommended as preferable for 'Dress', while artificial stucco was definitely to be avoided. Decoration, Morris harrumphed, was often employed merely to disguise 'ill-proportion'd Fabricks – architects preferring to garnish the in-elegant Design, to atone for the Disproportion of Parts'. True elegance was a far more complicated matter.

Right The Palladian Bridge from Wilton House, built in 1736–7 by Roger Morris and John Deval, as copied at Stowe, Buckinghamshire (possibly, Timothy Mowl suggests, by Gibbs) in 1739. Morris' design was inspired by Palladio's scheme for a crossing of Venice's Grand Canal, and was mimicked not only at Stowe but at Prior Park, Bath in 1755 and, most exotically, in the gardens of Catherine the Great's St Petersburg palace of Tsarskoe Selo in 1774.

I KNOW OF NONE THAT ARE NOT MAD OR RIDICULOUS, AND I REALLY BELIEVE THAT ANYBODY THAT HAS SENSE, WITH THE BEST WORKMEN OF ALL SORTS, COULD MAKE A BETTER HOUSE WITHOUT AN ARCHITECT THAN ANY HAS BEEN BUILT THESE MANY YEARS. The Duchess of Marlborough, 1732

Left Detail of the entrance steps and loggia at Chiswick House. The fat stone balusters and weighty urn are very much in the manner of the rural villas of sixteenth-century Italy.

The purest expression of Palladian form was to be found in the rural or urban villa. The Italian-style villa was a new building type for Britain, its sophisticated neoclassical aspirations being offset by the relative modesty of its scale, Palladian villas both in Britain and North America being small enough to attract well-heeled professional patrons as well as aristocrats seeking an idyllic escape from the rigours of urban life. The services needed

Above The pediment of the ancient Temple of Castor and Pollux in Naples, as engraved for Palladio's *Quattro libri*. Burlington took this design as the model for the entrance to his villa at Chiswick.

for the great houses of the past had always been accommodated in separate blocks or wings; the same was also true of Palladio's own Italian villas. However, with numerous limits on both space and cost, many of the Palladian villas of the 1720s – and, indeed, the Palladian terraces of the 1730s – incorporated service areas within the main house.

Given the vagaries of the British climate, importing the Italian villa style was not always a great practical success. Elegantly classical the Palladian villa may have been; warm and comfortable it was not. As Pope famously wrote, many patrons were 'Proud to catch cold at a Venetian door;/ Conscious they act a true Palladian part,/ And if they starve, they starve by rules of art.'

The primary inspiration behind the revolutionary new Palladian villas of Augustan England was the Earl of Burlington. When he began work on his new villa at Chiswick in Middlesex in 1727, Burlington was already well established as the country's leading authority on architectural style – to say nothing of music, sculpture and art. As already seen, he used his influence with the government – in 1729 he was made a Privy Councillor, and the following year a Knight of the Garter – to secure Crown appointments for his protégés, and to exclude those outside the cosy Palladian sphere from any share in Robert Walpole's carve-up of government patronage.

Recently attempts have been made to brand Burlington as a Jacobite. However, the evidence pointing to the Earl's involvement with this most politically suicidal of causes is at best slender. Certainly Burlington was a leading Freemason; James Anderson's *Constitutions* of 1721 describes him as such, taking care to flatter a powerful land-owner 'who bids fair to be the best Architect of Britain (if he is not so already)'. And there is undoubtedly some masonic imagery in the sumptuous ceilings at Chiswick. But none of this makes Burlington a crypto-Jacobite; after all, members of the Hanoverian royal family were also Masons. When Burlington did resign from Walpole's government in 1733, he did so over an issue – the Excise Crisis – which had severely agitated most of the country and had almost caused the Prime Minister's downfall, and he did so in the company of some of the most eminent Whig aristocrats of the time, amongst them the Duke of Bolton, the Earl of Chesterfield and Lord Cobham, sponsor of the future Whig statesman William Pitt.

On resigning from Walpole's government, Burlington also formally retired from his Piccadilly mansion to his Middlesex retreat. All his best pictures were moved from Burlington House to Chiswick, which, despite its cramped nature, now became the Earl's principal home. To suffer in true Italian style was evidently preferable to living in West End opulence.

Right Peter Rysbrack's 1748 view of Chiswick House and its garden from the west. The old, pre-Palladian house can be seen behind the new villa.

Lord Burlington's Chiswick abounded in classical references. The columns of the portico on the entrance front were copied from those adorning the ancient Temple of Castor and Pollux in Naples, which Burlington had not seen but which Palladio had drawn and published in the *Quattro libri*. The shallow, stepped dome (later borrowed by Thomas Jefferson for his own house at Monticello) was taken by Burlington from the well-known model of the Roman Pantheon. The Diocletian window in the dome, as has already been noted, was borrowed from the ancient Baths of Diocletian on the Dalmatian coast, while the Venetian window was taken from Raphael and Giulio Romano, as reinterpreted by Serlio and, of course, by Jones. Even the tapering chimneystacks – a bizarre type of chimney never seen before in Britain – were designed to recall the obelisks of Ancient Rome.

The influence of Chiswick's
dome (*above*) is clearly seen
in Thomas Jefferson's
Virginia villa of Monticello
(*below*), completed to the
Third President's own
designs in 1809. The plan of
Jefferson's home is also
from an impeccably
English Palladian source:
the late pattern-books of
Robert Morris.

The small, two-storey pavilion erected by Burlington in the early 1730s to link his new villa at Chiswick with the old, seventeenth-century house. A splendidly proportioned cubic composition much in the manner of Palladio, Jones and the compact villas of Burlington's contemporary Roger Morris, the link building created a pleasant three-sided courtyard over which even the cynical Horace Walpole enthused, declaring that 'the classic scenery of the small court that unifies the old and the new house, are more worth seeing than many fragments of ancient grandeur'. The old house was demolished by Burlington's successors in 1788; the link building, though, happily survives.

Chiswick was undoubtedly a great improvement on Burlington's earlier architectural experiments. At Tottenham Park in Wiltshire, begun in 1721, the well-known Wilton towers were set either side of a cramped and rather naïve box, which later had to be completely rebuilt. Similarly, the façade of Burlington's house of 1723 for General Wade, in what is now Old Burlington Street in London's West End, was not only a direct transcript from an unpublished Palladio design, but was horribly claustrophobic inside.

However, this is not to say that Chiswick was especially spacious. In 1727 Sir John Clerk visited the site and pronounced the half-built house to be 'rather curious than convenient'. The plan of the villa was perfectly square, with the rooms taking their cue from the central octagonal saloon; yet even the octagon itself was oddly undersized. As Richard Hewlings has observed, the villa's plan 'is curious, unprecedented and not very clearly functional'. There was no room for preparing or eating food in the villa itself; these tasks had to be done in the old house or, once the latter had been demolished in 1788, in the small link building which remained to the east. Small wonder that Lord Hervey – with predictable rancour, and forgetting that the house had been designed more as a home for the Earl's art collection than as a habitation – immediately poured scorn on the new villa, proclaiming, 'House!

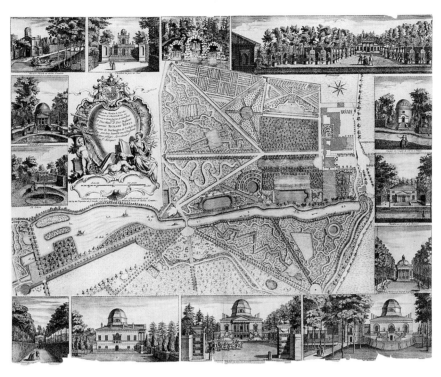

Left **The fabulous blue-and-gold ceiling of the Blue Velvet Room from Chiswick House. The blue in the ceiling was as much a status symbol as the gilding or William Kent's decorative panels; it is Prussian blue, made from a pigment invented in Germany in 1704 but only just being introduced into Britain in the 1720s – at which time it still remained prohibitively expensive.**

Do you call it a house? Why! it is too little to live in, and too large to hang on one's watch.'

As a realization of the Italian villa ideal in England, the Earl of Westmorland's Mereworth Castle in Kent was far more successful – and considerably more habitable – than Burlington's Chiswick. John Fane, who succeeded to the title of Seventh Earl of Westmorland in 1736, commissioned a large version of Palladio's Villa Rotonda from Colen Campbell. Work began on the villa in 1722, and was finished in three years; wings were added some 20 years later – ironically by Roger Morris, who had during the late 1720s supplanted Campbell in the affection of many of his Leicester House patrons.

Campbell was extremely pleased with his design for Mereworth. 'I shall not pretend to say', he began with false modesty, 'that I have made any Improvements in this Plan, from that of Palladio.' However, he then used the medium of *Vitruvius Britannicus* to list the numerous alterations he had actually made in order to adapt the concept of the Villa Rotonda to the English climate and to Westmorland's taste, giving more space to the description of Mereworth than to any other building in all of his three

Above centre **The 1736 map of the grounds at Chiswick House by John Rocque, showing all of Burlington and Kent's new garden buildings.** *Above left* **and** *right***, details from Chiswick: one of the Venetian windows and one of the garden terms.**

volumes. Mereworth was not the first Palladian villa to be built in Britain. William Benson had, of course, already built Wilbury, probably with Campbell's help. Campbell himself had attempted minor essays in the villa style at Shawfield, near Glasgow, in 1711–12, and at Ebberston Lodge, near Scarborough, in 1718, and had in 1720 begun work on two fully fledged Palladian villas: Newby Park in Yorkshire and Stourhead in Wiltshire. However, as a result of the inordinate amount of copy Campbell was able to devote to Mereworth in *Vitruvius Britannicus*, it became one of the best known of Palladian compositions.

Many actually preferred Chiswick and Mereworth to the real thing. In 1753 William Lee visited Vicenza and reported that 'I saw the Rotunda from whence Lord Westmorland's house in Kent is taken, and the hint of Lord Burlington's at Chiswick. The copies are different from the original and in external beauty exceed it.' In many respects, however, the villas at Chiswick and Mereworth represented stylistic dead-ends, interesting in their archae-ological precision but unwieldy as models for the future. In the event, it was the less obviously Italianate villas of Roger Morris and Lord Pembroke and

Colen Campbell's Mereworth Castle, Kent, built in 1722 for John Fane. Engraving from *Vitruvius Britannicus* (*above*) and portico detail (*right*). Mereworth was a close adaptation of the famous Villa Rotonda – although slightly bigger than Palladio's original. Burlington's essay on the same subject of a few years later, Chiswick House, dispensed with many of the features included in both Palladio's and Campbell's villas, most notably the four identical porticoes.

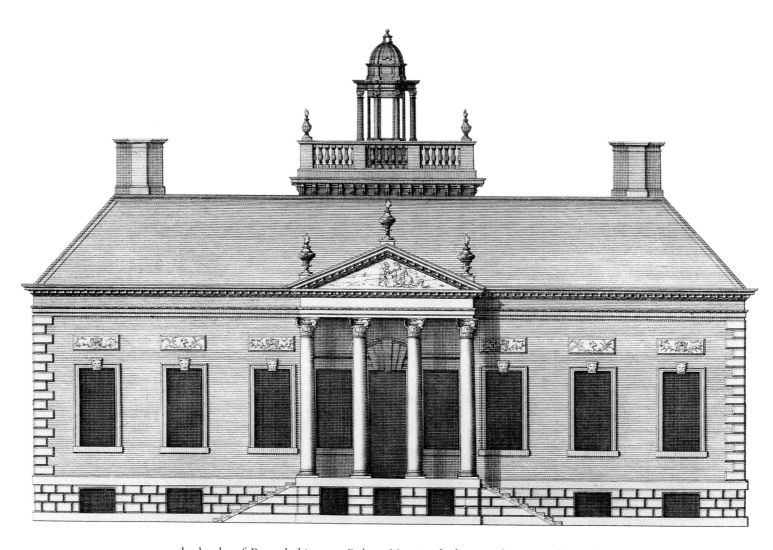

the books of Roger's kinsman Robert Morris which proved more influential on villa construction both in Britain and America.

Roger Morris' Marble Hill is in many senses the prototype for all subsequent villas of the eighteenth century. It was built for Henrietta Howard, Countess of Suffolk and long-suffering companion of one of the least appealing of British monarchs (and there are many to choose from), George II. Mrs Howard was no great beauty. As her friend and admirer Philip Stanhope wrote, damning with faint praise: 'Her face was not beautiful but pleasing. Her hair was extremely fair, and remarkably fine. Her arms were square and lean, that is, ugly. Her countenance was an undecided one.' Henrietta had only two acknowledged vices: hunting and beer-drinking. Such behaviour was in marked contrast to her husband: having while only a teenager married the Honourable Charles Howard, the rakish son of the Earl of Suffolk, Henrietta discovered too late that her charming spouse was in fact a drunken, violent

Left Elevation of Wilbury House, Wiltshire, from the first volume of *Vitruvius Britannicus* of 1715. The plan of Wilbury, begun in 1708, was a radical departure from the typical 'double pile' country house of the late seventeenth century. In good Jonesian fashion, both the Hall and Saloon in this rather undersized house were a cube and a half, while the flanking apartments were cubes. This scheme thus represents one of the first attempts to apply Palladian principles to a British home.

Early Palladian villas by Colen Campbell: *top,* the miniature Ebberston Lodge, Yorkshire, built for William Thompson in 1718, and *bottom,* Stourhead, Wiltshire, built for the banker Henry Hoare in 1720–4. The influence of the simple Veneto villas of Palladio and Scamozzi is clearly evident in these modest yet powerful compositions.

The quintessential Palladian villa: the south (river) front of Marble Hill House, Middlesex, built between 1724 and 1729.

Right The first occupant of Marble Hill: Henrietta Howard, Countess of Suffolk, painted by Charles Jervas shortly before the construction of the house.

liability, constantly in debt and a perennial embarrassment. Hervey recorded that Charles Howard was 'wrong-headed, ill-tempered, obstinate, drunken, extravagant, brutal', and after the birth of their only son in 1707 Henrietta lived apart from him. In 1714, however, she was elevated to a minor Court position in the household of the Princess of Wales, a post which brought her into daily contact with her husband as well as the heir to the throne, Prince George Augustus. Soon she was being regarded as the Prince's mistress; yet, as everyone acknowledged, she acted the part more of patient companion than of passionate lover. Hervey noted with his usual acute perception: 'She was forced to live in the constant subjection of a wife with all the reproach of a mistress, and to flatter and manage a man whom she must see and feel had...little inclination...to her advice.'

In 1731 her outrageous husband inherited the earldom of Suffolk. Fortunately for Henrietta, he died only two years later, worn out by his dissipations – but not before he had dragged the Queen bodily out of a moving carriage in a drunken rage and had attempted to blackmail the King (for which he was bought off with an exceedingly handsome pension of £1,200 a year). The following year the Countess – sick of the King's boorish behaviour – retired from Court service, and in 1735 she married the elderly, gouty but benevolent George Berkeley, with whom she passed many happy and blissfully uneventful years before his death in 1747.

Henrietta Howard was not a great intellectual; moreover, from the year of her retirement she grew increasingly deaf. Yet her memory and shrewdness were renowned – as was her ability to listen, her neutrality in

Right **Views of the Great Room at Marble Hill, a sumptuous composition in gilt and stone-colour paint. The carving is by James Richards, the royal Master Sculptor and Master Carver who subsequently worked with Morris on a number of other projects. Stripped of its original furniture in 1900, this magnificent room is now being restocked with what furniture the house's current owners, English Heritage, can trace and repurchase. The recovery by 1988 of the Panini overdoors (one of which can be seen on the left) and overmantel, which had been specially commissioned for this room in 1738, was the result of a particularly impressive piece of detective work, the paintings having been located as far afield as the South of France and New York.**

arguments earning her the nickname of 'the Swiss'. Her royal companionship bought her a Thames-side villa, where she surrounded herself with the greatest literary talents of the day, among them Swift, Pope and Defoe. Alexander Pope, Henrietta Howard's neighbour at Twickenham, even played a leading role in designing the garden at Marble Hill. In September 1724 the landscape gardener Charles Bridgeman was asked to provide a plan for the garden; within a year, however, Bridgeman appears to have been working under the direction of the poet. In 1727 Pope lavished sycophantic praise on the house: both John Gay and himself, he informed Mrs Howard, 'think your hall the most delightful room in the world except that where you are'. In the same year Jonathan Swift used Marble Hill and another of the new Palladian villas, Royal Lodge in Richmond Park, to illustrate his satire *A Pastoral Dialogue between Richmond-Lodge and Marble Hill*. Inevitably, though, Swift paid more attention to the fact that the taxpayer bore the cost of the two villas rather than to their innovatory architectural vocabulary:

> *My house was built but for a show,*
> *My Lady's empty pockets show;*
> *And now she will not have a shilling*
> *To raise the stairs, or build the ceiling...*

Unlike Chiswick House, Marble Hill was intended not as the wing of a larger, older house, nor as the home of an indulgent patron's art collection, but as the only home of a single woman – one who was not wedded to ostentation or an overt display of taste or wealth. The author of its design was Roger

Morris, then a little-known London craftsman. Morris was one of the new breed of highly professional, craft-trained architects. His models were not rich Renaissance amateurs such as Vanbrugh or dilettante dabblers such as Burlington but professional architects such as Nicholas Hawksmoor, who were as comfortable with directions for making bricks, sawing floor timbers or slaking lime as they were with the massing of villa blocks. Men such as Morris and Hawksmoor had helped to create a true architectural profession by the middle of the eighteenth century. As George Vertue wrote in 1749, 'the branch of the art of building in architecture is much improved and many men of that profession made greater fortunes…than any other branch of art whatever.'

The form of Marble Hill established the peculiarly simple, cubic villa style that was to become so characteristic of Morris' later villas. However, Morris could not have won this, his first major commission, alone. Trained as a lowly carpenter and bricklayer, he lacked the social graces and society contacts to penetrate the Prince of Wales' Court. In this instance, as on so many other occasions during his career, he was dependent on the help and advice of Henry, Lord Herbert, afterwards the Ninth Earl of Pembroke.

Pembroke was roughly the same age as Burlington – Pembroke was born around 1689, Burlington in 1694 – and, like Burlington, he had established his Palladian credentials early in his career. Having been an undergraduate at Christ Church, Oxford during the construction of Dean Aldrich's hugely influential Peckwater Quad, in 1712 he visited Italy – two years before Burlington. In 1722 he and William Stukeley jointly founded the Society of Antiquaries, and in 1743 he was elected a Fellow of the Royal Society. Pembroke retained close contact with Leicester House and, after 1727, with the Court of George II; although no politician he was, in Hervey's opinion, 'of great quality, of an extreme good character' and 'beloved by everybody who knew him'. He became a good friend of Queen Caroline, who declared him to be 'the best creature in the world', although in her opinion he was still 'as odd as his father was…and full as mad'. It was presumably this royal influence which helped him to capture the office of Surveyor-General for the Leicester House interest in 1726: following the death of Thomas Hewett in that year, Pembroke's half-brother Richard Arundell – and not Burlington's new discovery William Kent – was appointed in Hewett's stead. At the same time, Pembroke was notoriously eccentric. 'Often mad and always very odd' was the Dowager Duchess of Marlborough's opinion of him – and she herself was hardly the most congenial of companions. An inveterate boxer, swimmer and vegetarian, in an age when none of these interests were considered suitable for an aristocrat, he was also widely known for his appalling temper.

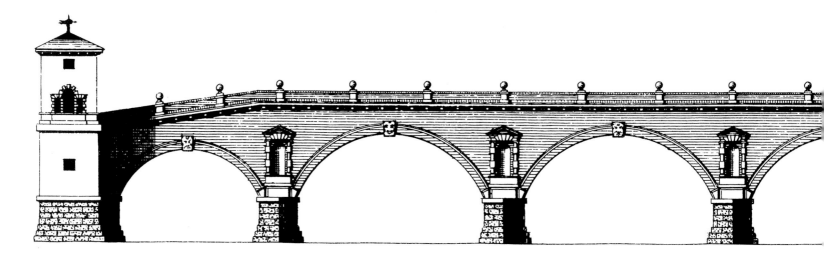

Pembroke's involvement at Marble Hill, and his close identification with Roger Morris' commissions over the next 20 years, has led many to credit the designs of Morris' villas to the rumbustious Earl rather than to the retiring architect. Horace Walpole, for example, described both Marble Hill and the Royal Lodge in Richmond Park of 1727–30 as 'incontestable proofs of Lord Pembroke's taste'. Morris and Pembroke were undoubtedly close; in 1734 the Earl presented Morris with a silver cup, engraved with a portrait of Inigo Jones and bearing the touching inscription, 'GIVEN by My Noble Patron HENRY EARL OF PEMBROKE By Whose favour alone I am Enabled to fill it R Morris'. However, in most cases it seems that, while Pembroke acted as aristocratic go-between linking architect and patron and even as architectural adviser, the final decision was Morris'. Pembroke is known to have designed some buildings, such as a Water House for Walpole's Houghton Hall and the Column of Victory in the park at Blenheim Palace. But even at his own home, Wilton House, Pembroke employed Morris when he needed major alterations or additions – most notably the Colonnade Room of 1735 and the much-quoted Palladian bridge of 1736–7.

Generally the 'Architect Earl' contented himself with guiding Morris in both architectural and political matters. And with clients such as the Duchess of Marlborough this was very necessary. In designing a house for her at Wimbledon, Pembroke and Morris (like Vanbrugh before them at Blenheim Palace) had to endure a succession of insults and rages. The embittered, cantankerous Dowager Duchess had already condemned their collaboration over the new villa at Westcombe Park in Kent as 'the most ridiculous thing that I ever saw in my life', and after only a few months' work on her own home at Wimbledon was flinging yet more invective at both Earl and architect. Refusing to enter her home via the customary flight of steps, she insisted (according to Horace Walpole) that Morris 'dug a saucer to put it in and levelled the first floor with the ground', only to complain that the architects

were 'setting the house in a pit'. She subsequently accused the Earl of overcharging for materials, and Morris for building features 'not only without having ever seen a plan of them, but after I had positively said that they shou'd not be done'. It was no doubt with great relief that Pembroke and Morris found themselves sacked from Wimbledon in 1733.

At Marble Hill, Morris and Pembroke publicly expressed their debt to Palladio – in particular to the latter's Villa Emo and his project for the Palazzo Capra. The simple 1–3–1 rhythm of the Villa Emo was indeed subsequently used by Morris as the basis for all his own villa designs, including those for Combe Bank, Kirby Hall, South Dalton, Westcombe, Richmond Park Lodge and even his own home at 61 Green Street, Mayfair. Yet the façade that Marble Hill's elevations most closely resembled was, significantly, the principal front of Pembroke Lodge, the Whitehall villa which Colen Campbell had erected for Pembroke himself in the year in which Marble Hill was begun, 1724. (Pembroke Lodge, although tragically demolished in 1913, was immortalized in Hogarth's satirical series *Marriage à la Mode*, where it was used to represent the pretentious and costly architectural ambitions which had been instilled in the 'nouveaux riches' of the 1740s.) Inside, Marble Hill not only quoted liberally from the attributed works of Inigo Jones, but also featured the very latest in interior decoration: a china closet with a ceiling specially painted by the French artist Andien de Clermont (all of which was demolished in 1903); a Chinese room, complete with japanned furniture; and masses of West Indian mahogany, 'liberated' from Spanish Honduras by the Royal Navy and presented to Henrietta Howard by a grateful monarch.

Burlington, Campbell, Roger Morris and Pembroke were not the only individuals who helped to define the classic Palladian villa format. Robert Morris, too, had an important part to play. As John Harris has written, in his two pattern-books of 1750 and 1751 Morris proved himself 'the undisputed

Colen Campbell's design for a bridge over the Thames, from *Vitruvius Britannicus*.

master of the neo-Palladian villa with models...nearly always small in scale and exquisite in execution'. Morris was the first to define exactly what the Palladian villa constituted. Villas were not, he explained, designed to be political centres or incarnations of financial success, but simply diminutive weekend or seasonal retreats where the patron could relax in a harmonious, natural setting, 'divested from Care, and the agonizing Pains of Gout, and of all other real and imaginary Maladies'. As such, not only was the design of the villa to be closely considered, but also its site, which should as far as possible exploit the calming and rejuvenating influence of Nature. Morris stated emphatically that 'a small Fabrick...gives the Mind nobler Ideas than one of twenty times the Bulk'. In particular, he advised that villas should always be positioned upon an eminence, 'for the more easily obtaining a Variety of Views': much of his *Essay upon Harmony* of 1728 was concerned with recommendation of exemplary sites (such as Shooter's Hill and Richmond Hill, both close to his native London) whilst in his *Lectures* of 1734 he pleaded for both convenience and 'uninterrupted Vistas and Avenues, an agreeable River, or some opening Lawn, or at least a distant Group of Hills and Vales diminishing from the Eye by a pleasing Gradation...'.

During the 1750s – after the deaths of Burlington and of Roger and Robert Morris – it was the architect Sir Robert Taylor who fully realized the Palladian ideal of the astylar villa. Taylor's great rival, James Paine, was conservative in approach and tended to specialize in larger houses. Taylor was more daring in design, and was responsible for the further development of the type of villa Morris had advocated in *Rural Architecture* and *The Architectural Remembrancer*. In his biography of Taylor, Marcus Binney merely emphasized the architect's 'ingenious and original development of the Palladian villa'; however, many of Taylor's plans and elevations do bear a remarkable affinity to Morris' designs, which were appearing in print just at the time that Taylor was beginning his first full-scale commissions. Not only does the plan of Asgill House in Richmond, for example, closely resemble Morris' printed models; in addition the elevation of the villa is in the form of a double pediment, a visual device favoured not only by Palladio but also by Morris. Similarly, Taylor's Surrey villa of Mount Clare not only possesses a plan based on that suggested by Morris in plate 30 of *Rural Architecture*, but also a garden front remarkably similar to that provided by Morris for the same design. Most significantly, Taylor's first major work – Harleyford Manor, near Marlow in Buckinghamshire, of 1755 – demonstrates that its author was well acquainted with Morris' recent publication. Undoubtedly many elements of the house were original, most notably the exceedingly compact plan, the single, asymmetrical canted bay, and particularly the novel and ingenious

Fireplace design from Abraham Swan's *The British Architect* of 1745. Swan financed this volume himself, but the gamble paid off, as it passed through four editions in 20 years – despite its premium price of 13 shillings a copy.

The principal front of
Drayton Hall, South Carolina,
of 1738–42. The unknown
architect of this remarkably
sophisticated villa evidently
drew his inspiration from
the villas and plates of
Palladio, from early
Palladian compositions
such as Marble Hill and
Pembroke's Whitehall house,
and from the pattern-books
of the late 1720s and early
:730s.

arrangement of rooms around a central staircase. Nevertheless, the general
conception of Harleyford owes much to Robert Morris, both in the planning
of the first floor, which strongly echoes plate 2 of *Rural Architecture*, and
particularly in the arrangement of the elevations, which distinctly resemble
the five-bay, astylar elevation of the 'house commanding a view of the Park
or Gardens, from the Arcade' engraved in plate 29 – even down to the
horizontal banding on the projecting, pedimented centre of three bays.

Pattern-books such as Robert Morris' two volumes also exercised
considerable influence on the villas appearing in the American colonies and,
later, in the new Republic. For example, George Washington's own home
of Mount Vernon, rebuilt in 1757–9 and again in 1773–8, incorporated a
large number of architectural details from contemporary British pattern-
books. The front door was based on plate 33 of Batty Langley's *Treasury of
Designs* of 1740, the library chimneypiece was taken from Abraham Swan's
The British Architect of 1745 – as was the chimneypiece in the west parlour –
while the internal doors were culled from Langley's *The City and Country
Builder*. Langley's *Treasury* also provided the source for the splendid plaster
ceilings in the library and drawing room at the otherwise highly Gibbsian villa
of Kenmore in Virginia, a house of 1752 possibly designed by the local
architect John Arris. The plan and the riverfront of nearby Mount Airy, built
in 1758–62 for Colonel John Tayloe, were also taken directly from plates in
Gibbs' *Book of Architecture*, while the entrance loggia was derived from plate
58 of Gibbs' volume. The north front, though, was based on a plate of Haddo

Far left **The front door from Westover, a Virginia villa of the early 1730s.** *Left*, **its mirror image – and, possibly, its source: plate xxvi of** *Palladio Londinensis* **of 1734.**

House in William Adam's *Vitruvius Scotius* of 1750. The architect of Mount Airy may once again have been John Arris, who consistently used Gibbs as his guide. His symmetrical villa, whose innate Palladian orthodoxy greatly appealed to the conservative Virginian planters, proved highly influential on other Virginian villas.

Gibbs and Langley were not of course the only sources for the prospective villa-owners of colonial America. William Salmon's bestselling *Palladio Londinensis* of 1734 provided the source for countless Palladian interiors, amongst them Thomas Lee's fine, H-plan villa of Stratford, Virginia. Salmon's book was also used for the front door of the Virginia villa of Westover; although this house was actually begun four years before Salmon's work appeared, it seems that in this instance the doorcase was bodily imported directly from London.

Other plantation owners preferred to turn to more fundamental Palladian influences. In South Carolina, John Drayton commissioned an unknown designer to build perhaps the purest expression of Palladianism in Colonial America. Drayton Hall, built between 1738 and 1742, not only borrowed directly from Marble Hill and from Campbell's Whitehall villa for Lord Pembroke, but also from Palladio's own villas of the sixteenth century. The result was a remarkably Neo-Palladian villa, one which has, fortunately, been well-preserved in the intervening centuries.

Palladian decoration was not brought to the colonies solely by the books of Gibbs, Langley and Salmon, nor even through the *Quattro libri* of

The principal front of
Stratford Hall, Virginia,
built in the 1730s for the
Lee family. The elevation is
dominated by the orthodox,
stone-coloured sash
windows and by the rather
un-Palladian, almost
Vanbrughian quadrupled
chimneystacks.

Palladio himself. It was also introduced by emigré craftsmen such as Peter
Harrison and William Buckland. Peter Harrison (1716–75) was the first true
Palladian architect in North America. Born in York in England, he emigrated
to Rhode Island in 1740, serving as a customs officer and a sea captain.
Amongst his most famous works is the Redwood Library at Newport, Rhode
Island of 1749 – a building which utilizes the classic Italian temple front – and
his Brick Market of 1761, also in Newport, which borrowed a Jones design
for Somerset House.

William Buckland was specifically brought over from England in the
mid-1750s as an indentured servant by George Mason, subsequently the
author of the Virginia Declaration of Rights and a prominent revolutionary.
Buckland, who appears to have trained as a carpenter and plasterer, was hired
by Mason to work on the interior of Gunston Hall, Mason's Virginia villa,
which was begun in 1755 and completed in 1759. Having introduced both
orthodox Palladian mouldings and the newer, more frivolous Chinese
Chippendale style into the house, Buckland was so taken with the colonies
that he stayed. In the 1770s he designed the interiors for Edward Lloyd's
handsome Annapolis villa (now known as the Chase-Lloyd House) and for
the villa of Whitehall, also in Maryland's capital. Whitehall's impressive
Corinthian portico had been taken from a plate in Halfpenny, Morris and
Lightoler's *Modern Builder's Assistant* of 1742; Buckland added plasterwork
inspired by the plates of Swan and Lightoler. His masterpiece, however, was
the Hammond-Harwood House in Annapolis, on which he was working when

The Carlyle House in Alexandria, Virginia. This splendid house – begun in 1752 – was, unusually for this area, faced in stone. The motifs are mostly culled from British pattern-books; the doorcase, for example, is taken from Gibbs or Salmon, while the fanlight – an early example of such a feature – borrows from Marble Hill.

he died in mysterious circumstances in 1774. It was partly due to Buckland that a visiting cleric of 1770 felt moved to call Annapolis 'the genteelest town in North America' and to proclaim, 'I hardly know a town in England as desirable to live in.'

Not everyone, of course, could afford a designer of the calibre of Buckland or Harrison. Nor could all Americans erect a Palladian villa in the newly settled colonies with the greatest of ease. Having, for example, begun work on a handsome, five-bay, stone-walled villa for himself in Alexandria, Virginia in 1752, John Carlyle soon found that:

> Its a Pleasure to build in England but here where we are obliged To Doe Everything With one's own Servants & thise Negros make it Require Constant Attendance & Care – & So much Trouble that If I had Suspected it woud have been What I have met with, I believe I Shoud made Shift with a Very Small House.

In fact, Carlyle's house was a very successful composition, one which constituted the quintessential colonial villa of the mid-eighteenth century. However, American Palladianism found its most imaginative expression after the Revolution in the works of Thomas Jefferson. Although executed some 50 years after Burlington's death, Jefferson's villas betray the strong influence of the Palladian pioneers. Disgusted with the contemporary architecture he

Left Detail of the principal
front of the Lady Pepperell
House in Kittery, Maine.
The house provides a fine
example of Palladian details
– sash windows, Ionic
pilasters, panelled front
door and pediment with
dentil mouldings – applied
to a weatherboarded
American home of 1760.

had seen on his visits to Britain in the 1780s, Jefferson turned for inspiration
to the solid, plainer and less fussy English Palladianism of Robert Taylor,
James Paine and, in particular, Robert Morris. Jefferson is known to have
owned a copy of Robert Morris' *Select Architecture* of 1755 – which 'had
been acquired in 1770 or 1771' – and used it continually. 'Jefferson's use of
the octagonal form in the planning of space', the architectural historian
W H Adams has noted, 'became a kind of Jeffersonian signature.' However,
as used at Monticello and other Jeffersonian houses, where it thrust through
the wall in dramatic fashion to form a three-sided canted bay, the large
octagonal saloon was very much an English Palladian motif, a projecting
octagon having been introduced by Kent and Morris 30 years before it
became a 'Jeffersonian signature'. Plans for a house at Poplar Forest in
Virginia both resemble plate 30 of Robert Morris' *Rural Architecture* and are
strikingly similar to the compact, octagon-dominated arrangement used by
Sir Robert Taylor at Asgill House. Indeed, as built, Poplar Forest, with its
four internal octagons and square central room, owes much to Kent and
particularly to Robert Morris in plan and elevation: the plan derives from
plate 17 in Book II of Kent's *Designs of Inigo Jones*; plate 30 of *Rural Architecture*
may have suggested the four octagons set round a square; while the elevation,
with its high attic over a pedimented portico, closely resembles a number of
Morris' other designs. At the same time, Jefferson's plans for the Governors
Houses at Williamsburg and Richmond are remarkably similar to various
examples of Morris' plates, his design for Barboursville closely follows the
plan of Taylor's Morris-inspired Asgill House, while his sketch for Edgemont
replicates the plan for Taylor's Purbrook. Only rarely, in his later drawings,
does Jefferson depart from the English Palladian pattern. Even his design for
a house for the President used the concept of the Villa Rotonda which had
been so famously reinterpreted by Campbell and Burlington in the 1720s.

Certainly Thomas Jefferson's most renowned design – the villa at
Monticello, Virginia, which he built for himself – is firmly rooted in the style
of Robert Morris and his fellow Palladians of the early eighteenth century.
Most of the early versions of the villa, as well as the plan of the house as
ultimately executed, are based on formulas originally evolved by Morris in
plates 2 and 30 of *Rural Architecture*. And the stepped octagonal dome of the
finished house distinctly resembles not only engravings in Morris' *Rural
Architecture* but also the roofline of the most famous Palladian villa of them
all, Burlington's Chiswick House – a building Jefferson is known to have
visited in 1786 (when, with some irony, he publicly condemned the dome
for contributing 'an ill effect'). Clearly, North America's first great native
architect found the appeal of English Palladianism hard to resist.

ALL THIS WE MUST DO, TO COMPLY WITH THE TASTE OF THE TOWN. John Gay, *The Beggar's Opera*, 1728

Left **Detail from Canaletto's**
The Thames and the City of
London from Richmond House
of 1746 contrasts an engaging
glimpse of everyday life in
the foreground with Wren's
dramatic city spires.
Canaletto's depiction of
St Paul's Cathedral is clearly
painted from memory, as the
architectural detailing is
notoriously inaccurate.

The rules and precepts of the Palladian style were not limited to the great houses of the rich. Palladian ideas filtered down to the average home, too. In fact the modern-day notion of the 'Georgian' house derives directly from the proportions, forms and manner of the great Palladian designers.

Few would, of course, have been lucky enough to have seen the latest Palladian mansions at first hand. Rather, architects, builders, masons and owners relied heavily on the new generation of pattern-books for ideas and inspiration that was entirely up to date in its classical correctness. As we have seen, the works of James Gibbs and Batty Langley were particularly important in this respect, proving very influential on the way the early Georgian house developed in respectful mimicry of the homes of the wealthy.

This is not to say that every builder or mason was immediately able to grasp the intricacies and complexities of Palladianism – particularly those who were well used to the building styles of their forefathers. Pope observed that even celebrated architects were at times apt to take 'random drawings' from Palladio or Jones, using the inspiration of Burlington to:

Reverse your Ornaments, and hang them all
On some patch'd dog-hole ek'd with ends of wall,
Then clap four slices of Pilaster on't,
That, lac'd with bits of rustic, makes a Front.

Above **Detail of the York**
House Water Gate, off
London's Strand, from
***Vitruvius Britannicus.* The**
engraving is captioned 'by
Inigo Jones 1621'; however,
the gate was probably the
work of the colourful
courtier, diplomat and
amateur architect Sir
Balthazar Gerbier, a Dutch
émigré who was employed
as artistic advisor to the
all-powerful Duke of
Buckingham – the owner of
York House – until the
Duke's assassination in 1628.

Swift, too, warned in his *Gulliver's Travels* of 1726 of the danger of expecting semi-literate builders and craftsmen to imbibe the lessons of Palladio at first go. Of the inhabitants of Laputa he wrote, in a thinly disguised attack on the building standards of the age:

> *Their houses are very ill built, the walls bevil, without one right angle in any apartment, and this defect ariseth from the contempt they bear for practical geometry, which they despise as vulgar and mechanic, those instructions they give being too refined for the intellectuals of their workmen, which occasions perpetual mistakes.*

However, by 1750 even the most doggedly traditional of builders found himself with a bewildering array of publications designed to help him understand and execute the most basic as well as the most complex of Palladian forms. As Eileen Harris has observed, this 'was an entirely English phenomenon: nowhere else in the world were so many books published'. It was a phenomenon which helped to spread the latest Palladian fashions into the farthest British provinces and the most remote American colonies.

For the more academically inclined, there was available a large variety of works on the Italian masters – although, oddly enough, Vitruvius himself did not appear in an English translation until William Newton's edition of 1771–91. Three separate editions of Palladio's *Quattro libri* were published between 1715 and 1742, for example, in addition to two editions of Book I alone, while Godfrey Richards' rather approximate 1668 version of Palladio's First Book had passed through as many as eight editions by 1733. Even more rarified was Robert Castell's *The Villas of the Ancients* of 1728, a guide to the classical villas described by Pliny. In marked contrast with the delicate and scholarly nature of the subject, the book's author was committed to the Fleet Prison for debt shortly after publication and died there of smallpox the following December.

More useful, as far as the average builder or craftsman was concerned, was the flood of basic guides which appeared from the mid-1720s onwards. Professional architectural commentaries and builders manuals had hitherto been rare in Britain, publishers having previously been content with translating and adapting continental texts, which themselves were only approximate versions of the original Italian works. Yet now pattern-books appeared in great profusion, compiled with evident enthusiasm by architect-writers such as Robert Morris, John and William Halfpenny and, most notably, the prolific Batty Langley.

The primary purpose of these volumes was to ensure that Palladian details were executed with professional exactness, helping local builders to

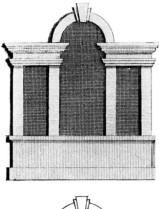

Designs for a Venetian window and a rustic door from William Halfpenny's *Practical Architecture* of 1724. Halfpenny's volume translated the designs of Palladio, Jones and the contemporary Palladians into simple, easy-to-read and precisely measured drawings.

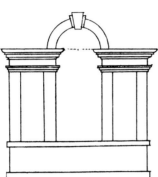

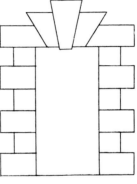

master a new style whose discipline often proved more technically demanding than the relative freedom of the vernacular or English Baroque styles with which they were familiar. Thus it was important that the new philosophy was not cloaked in confusing historical backgrounds or over-complex technical jargon. William Halfpenny's first guide, his aptly titled *Practical Architecture* of 1724, laid out the Ancient orders in a brief and accessible manner, and provided a large number of sample Palladian doors and windows, as devised by the great masters Jones and Campbell. The result was, in historian Eileen Harris' words, an exceptionally 'clear and convenient' manual which would have proved invaluable to contemporary architects and tradesmen. However, emboldened by the success of *Practical Architecure*, the following year Halfpenny included in his *Art of Sound Building* methods by which the new Palladian proportions could be applied to traditional Gothic architecture – an unfortunate marriage which resulted in a ludicrous travesty of contemporary design. Seventeen years later Batty Langley attempted much the same thing in his *Ancient Architecture*, with similarly hilarious consequences. It was not surprising to find the rather more academic theorist Robert Morris condemning in 1751 any variation from the Palladian norm which involved authors

Early Georgian London streetscapes: *left*, Spitalfields in the East End, with houses of the 1720s, and, *right*, Bedford Row, Bloomsbury of 1718. Note the highly visible frames of the sash windows; the Building Act of 1774 prohibited such generous displays of joinery as a precautionary measure against fire.

such as Langley or Halfpenny acting as Frankenstein to create Palladian hybrids of the Gothic manner or other exotic styles. The highly fashionable but 'improperly call'd' Chinese taste, so beloved of the Halfpennys, comprised in Morris' gruff opinion 'mere whims and chimera, without rules or order', which 'requires no fertility of genius to put in execution':

> *The principles are a good choice of chains and bells and different colours of paints. As to the serpents, dragons, monkeys, &c, they, like the rest of the beauties, may be cut in paper, and pasted any where, or in any manner.*

The most prolific of all pattern-book authors was undoubtedly Batty Langley. Trained as a gardener, he owed his architectural career to his masonic links. The Palladian world was riddled with Freemasonry: Burlington and Pembroke were fellow Masons (although Langley did dare to attack Burlington during the 1730s), and it is no coincidence that Langley's early work *Practical Geometry* of 1726 was dedicated to Lord Paisley, recently installed as the Masons' Grand Master.

Considering that he had a wife and 14 children to support, it was not surprising that Langley wrote so much. However, few of his books contained any astonishing insights. As Eileen Harris points out, 'Langley was monotonously restricted to two themes: geometry and the orders', and 'With the exception of *Ancient Architecture*, Langley's architectural books are unoriginal, repetitive, slap-dash productions.' Like his contemporary William Hogarth, Batty Langley was a passionate nationalist, railing against foreign styles and foreign craftsmen while conveniently forgetting the Italian origin of the Palladian manner to which he owed his livelihood. He even attempted to cut Inigo Jones down to size, boldly declaring that the great architect 'was subject to error as any other man'. But, however unoriginal and rushed-out his works, they sold extremely well. By 1750 Langley was claiming with considerable justification that his books had helped British craftsmen to become 'the best proficients in the world'– despite the 'great disregard shown to English Artists and Industry' throughout Britain.

Even more successful than any of Langley's numerous volumes was William Salmon's *Palladio Londinensis* of 1734. As Eileen Harris has written, for 40 years his work 'remained a standard builder's manual and in that time saw more editions than any of the several other books of its kind'. This was despite the fact that 'Salmon himself had virtually nothing new to offer'; the book's only innovatory aspect was the publication of the prices of building materials and of labour costs – a service provided by Salmon so as to 'prevent Gentlemen from being imposed upon by fraudulent, crafty workmen'.

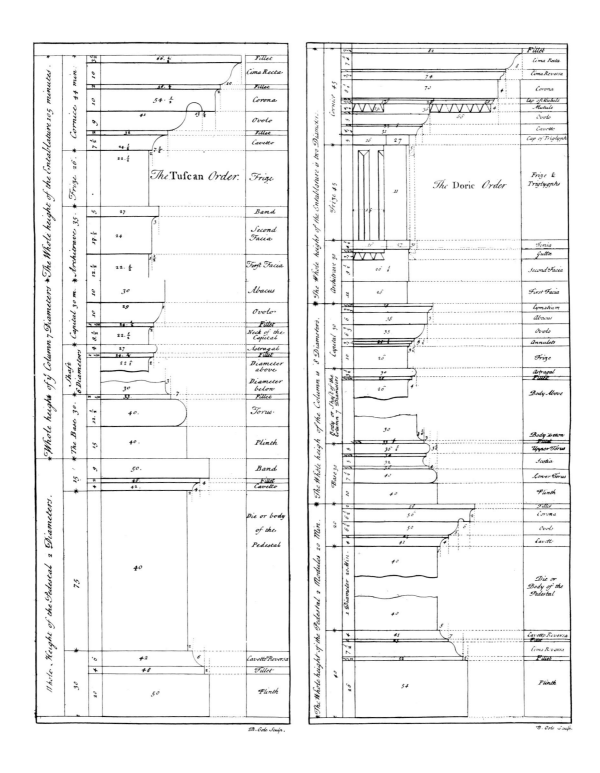

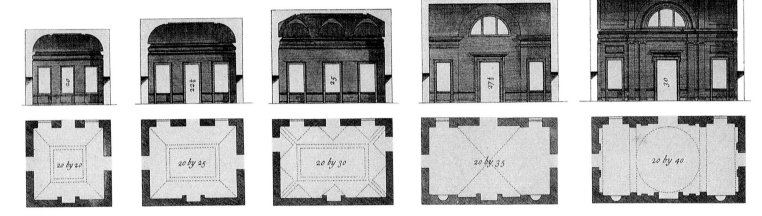

Ironically, perhaps the best-known of all the numerous pattern-books of the Palladian era – if not a work as financially successful as any of Salmon's or Langley's publications – was a book penned not by an intimate of Burlington, nor even by a Palladian architect, but by an isolated and lonely figure who remained shunned by the Palladian establishment: James Gibbs. His *Book of Architecture* of 1728 was designed, like the works of the hack architects Langley and Halfpenny, not for the glitterati of Burlington House but for the provincial builder, 'especially in the remote parts of the Country, where little or no assistance for Designs can be procured'. Using 'the Instructions of the greatest Masters in Italy', Gibbs had produced a work which, he hoped, could be comprehended by any builder 'who understands lines'. The first British work entirely to comprise a native architect's own designs, the *Book of Architecture* influenced the form of buildings not only in the British Isles but also in America, where its designs became the templates for buildings from the average Philadelphia terrace to the White House. However, British and American workmen rarely acquired Gibbs' advice from the pages of the *Book of Architecture* itself. As Eileen Harris has remarked, at '4 guineas in sheets, or even at the reduced price of 3 guineas asked for the second edition in 1739, it was out of reach to ordinary builders'. It was left to less gifted jobbing writers such as Batty Langley and William Salmon to recycle and reinterpret Gibbs' ideas in their own, cheaper and thus more accessible volumes – even on occasion stealing Gibbs' original drawings without acknowledgement. When, in 1732, Gibbs brought out an even more basic work – *Rules for Drawing the Several Parts of Architecture*, aimed at 'Beginners and such [who] are but little skilled in Architecture' – the plagiarists were once more out in force. It was in this way, however, that good building practice was communicated to the farthest parts of Britain and her colonies.

Five room plans from James Gibbs' *Rules for Drawing the Several Parts of Architecture* of 1732. Gibbs sought to make Palladian proportions comprehensible to the average builder by eliminating complex fractions from the proportional equations and, instead, subdividing each design into five parts. His attempt to copyright this novel idea failed, however, and the concept was swiftly borrowed by Langley, Hoppus, Salmon and other pattern-book authors of the 1730s.

'Night', from Hogarth's *The Four Times of the Day* of 1738. Hogarth's original paintings were commissioned to decorate the fashionable Vauxhall Gardens on London's south bank, with the everyday disasters and endemic drunkenness depicted here – all overseen by Le Sueur's equestrian statue of Charles I – being intended to contrast with the refined pleasures available at Vauxhall.

Right Elfreth's Alley, a tiny Philadelphia street which, although now much restored, has been continuously inhabited since 1702. The oldest surviving houses in this passageway date from the mid-1720s.

Pattern-books also helped to regulate the often all too variable methods of building. Poorly built cottages and terraces were a familiar sight in early Georgian Britain; in 1738 Samuel Johnson remarked that 'falling houses' were apt to 'thunder on your head'. Even the most derelict properties, however, were exploited by the unscrupulous. An observer wrote of London in 1753:

> *There have within a few years arisen in the outskirts of this town a kind of traffic in old ruinous houses which the occupiers fill up with straw and flock beds, which they nightly let out for twopence for a*

single person or threepence for a couple...Four or five beds are often in one room, and what with the nastiness of these wretches and their numbers such an inconceivable stench has arose from them that I have been hardly able to bear it...

All too often even new buildings were designed to last no longer than the period of the first leasehold. Whether that was 42 or 99 years, this still did not augur well for the long-term prospects of the building. It is thus quite astonishing that some of the frankly jerry-built terraces of the early eighteenth century have actually survived into the twentieth.

Not all new developments were poorly built. In the more fashionable districts of cities such as London, Bath and Philadelphia, land values soared as peers, architects and builder-speculators all vied with each other in erecting the most sought-after terraces. By 1736 the poet James Thomson was celebrating 'Lo! stately streets, lo! squares that court the breeze.'

Early eighteenth-century houses in Albury Street, Deptford. Substituting glass for the top two panels of an old door is a commonly executed and wholly reversible way of admitting more light to the common entrance hall.
Left Samuel Scott's view of Charing Cross, London of c.1750, with pale-coloured windows and green shutters.

For the successful entrepreneur the rewards were considerable. The Duke of Bedford, whose ancestors had hired Inigo Jones to design the brick and stone streets of Covent Garden and who now looked to develop the area of Bloomsbury to the east, took an enormous £3,700 in rents in the year 1732 alone. However, not all profited as handsomely as Bedford. Many a speculator was ruined by ill-advised developments in which it took years to dispose of all the leases.

To regulate the quality of such developments, an increasing number of explicit Building Acts were passed. The first of these had been the celebrated Act of 1667, designed to ensure that the Great Fire of London never happened again. The provisions of the Act strictly limited the external use of external woodwork in house construction, stipulating instead the employment of more resilient masonry materials such as stone and brick. In 1707 a new measure banned the use of prominent wooden eaves (a form which had been exceedingly common for the past three centuries) and dictated that henceforth all roofs were to be at least partly hidden behind parapet walls constructed not of timber but of masonry. Thus was born the rectangular-fronted house that became such a characteristic symbol of the Georgian period.

The Building Act of 1709 went even further, stating that the wooden weight boxes of the new sash windows – which up till now had been completely exposed on the outside wall – should be recessed at least 4½ inches from the face of the brick or stonework. This measure, as well as affording better fire protection, gave buildings a degree of visual solidity and three-dimensionality that is only now being eroded by inappropriate replacement windows placed flush with the masonry. (Thirty years later Robert Morris deemed this reform to be not only eminently practical but also philosophically correct: 'I have often reflected on the useless Frames of the Windows, which our Moderns shew, to convince the Thoughtless that they are necessary to be seen, to inform them that they are made for Concavities for the Weights.') And in 1739 an Act was passed regulating the average brick size at 8¾ by 4⅛ by 2½ inches.

Although most of this legislation was initially designed to apply only to London, in a few years the provisions of the various Building Acts had been generally accepted by towns and cities on both sides of the Atlantic. At the turn of the century, the indefatigable traveller Celia Fiennes was already noting that towns all over the country were beginning to emulate London's new housing developments. Nottingham, she had observed in her diary, was 'built of stone and delicate and large and long Streetes much like London and the houses lofty and well built', two 'very large streetes' running from its

Above A house from Spitalfields' Fournier Street, of the 1720s. By 1750 dark green was often used for front doors, although the door surrounds were usually painted in a contrasting stone colour.

A stone-fronted development of the 1730s in Bath's Beauford Square. Note the prominent triglyph frieze below the cornice, the uniform doors surmounted by rather over-large segmented pediments, and the unusual paired windows.

Right Elevations and plans of two three-storey homes from *The Modern Builder's Assistant*, a 1757 volume which unashamedly pillaged designs from the works of Robert Morris and William Halfpenny.

Market Place, 'much like Holborn'. Of Liverpool, which comprised 'mostly new built houses of brick and stone after the London fashion', she noted 'the streetes are faire and long, its London in miniature as much as I ever saw anything' and that 'there is a very pretty Exchange stands on 8 pillars besides the corners which are each treble pillars all of stone'. Newcastle, Fiennes judged, 'most resembles London of any place in England, its buildings lofty and large of brick mostly or stone; the streetes are very broad and handsome and very well pitch'd and many of them with very fine conduits of water in each'. Even in the sleepy Welsh town of Hawarden she noticed, 'a very fine new built house of brick and in the exact form of the London architecture' – the home of a 'Mr Major'.

The average middle-class, urban home of the 1720s usually comprised two simple rooms per floor, at right angles to the street, with a yard at the back. Light would thus enter the two, three or even four storeys from both front and back, and possibly via a top-lit staircase. Robert Morris' economical £480 house featured in the *Modern Builder's Assistant* of 1742 was much in this vein, with two rooms front and back on both ground and first floors and a top-lit stair. Most of the services would be housed in the basement, described by de Saussure in 1727: 'in all the newly built quarters the houses have one floor made in the earth, containing the kitchen, offices and the servants rooms. This floor is well lighted, and has as much air as the others have…and is called the "area".'

Behind the front wall of neat, presentable 'place' bricks was often an inner skin of poor-quality brickwork, bound by ill-fitting timbers and often bolstered by settling rubble. All too often, the thin outer veneer was only

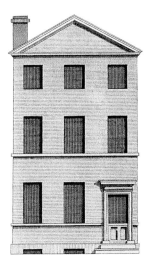

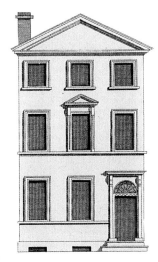

anchored to the inner skin by a few 'headers', bricks placed at right-angles to the two walls with only the short, 'header' face showing on the exterior.

As for the decorative finishing of the exterior of the house, while many of the developments of the late seventeenth century or early eighteenth century were undoubtedly impressive in their use of brick and stone, not until the 1720s was any attempt made to introduce the grandeur and, most importantly, the proportion of Italian façades into the humble terrace by uniting the entire row of houses as a symmetrical and even pedimented composition. As already noted, Henry Aldrich's Peckwater Quad at Christ Church, Oxford, begun in 1707, daringly experimented with the revolutionary 'palace front', converting a modest college quadrangle into an Italianate mansion. Yet outside the rarified atmosphere of Oxford, builder-speculators were reluctant to import such novelties. Colen Campbell's 1725 design for London's Grosvenor Square (a square which has suffered much since Campbell's day) was never executed, although Edward Shepherd did manage to build three houses of his ambitious palace-fronted scheme, which was at least punctuated by a pedimented projection with engaged columns. In the event it was in Bath, not London, that the Palladian terrace made its first true appearance.

John Wood was one of the more colourful architects of the period. His architectural theory was a bizarre 'mishmash' of Old Testament, Egyptian, Druidic and masonic influences, all of which were tacked on to the latest Palladian orthodoxy. Finding Vitruvius and his Roman contemporaries distastefully vulgar or dull, he turned his attention to ancient history that was closer to home, writing lengthy volumes which purported to prove, amongst other things, that Stonehenge was built by the Druids and copied from the Jews, and that Bath, his home, had been founded not by the detestable Romans but by the Druids as a Druidic university – their splendid if rather intangible achievements having been deliberately razed by the jealous Roman legions. Although his beliefs were undoubtedly eccentric, it is worth remembering that the great Inigo Jones had also ascribed Stonehenge to the Druids. While his architectural theories tended to the historically obscure, Wood's executed buildings were of the very latest and most innovative kind – none more so than Britain's first grandly scaled square. The north side of Bath's Queen Square, begun in 1728, owed something to Jones' Covent Garden terraces and much to Aldrich's Peckwater Quad, not only in its palace front but also in its rusticated ground floor, its alternating window pediments – first triangular, then curved (or 'segmental') – and its giant order of pilasters. It was also a strangely flat composition; as Wood's biographers Mowl and Earnshaw have observed, 'Wood rarely indulged in deep articulaton of parts.'

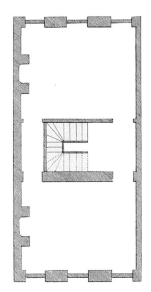

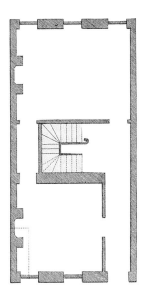

Palladian Bath: *left*, one of the villas on the west side of Queen Square and *right*, the centrepiece to the square, begun in 1728. During the nineteenth century the original multi-paned Georgian windows were replaced by plate glass examples which needed no internal glazing.

And, most disappointingly, the completed square was not symmetrical: obstruction from the landlords on the west side necessitated the erection not of another palace-fronted terrace but of three small Palladian villas. Nevertheless, Queen Square was a daring step forward, a bold leap which, in Dan Cruickshank's words, provided the world with 'a textbook example of Neo-Palladian urban design' that was to prove highly influential on subsequent development. While the squares and terraces which sprang up in towns and cities across Britain and North America after 1730 may have lacked the grandeur (and expense) of Wood's stone-built façades, they looked to Queen Square and its immediate progeny for lessons on the basic disposition of the Palladian terraced house.

After Queen Square, Wood himself proceeded to build the basis of what is now the World Heritage Site of Georgian Bath. Having created in Queen Square a home for the wealthy and fashionable, he constructed terraces in the surrounding streets that were for humbler, middle-class families. Palace fronts were still occasionally in evidence, but developments of the 1730s and '40s such as Beaufort Square and South and North Parades ('uniform, wellmannered and dull' in Timothy Mowl's opinion) were far more restrained in their use of theatrical ornament. There was no place here for ostentatious expenditure.

Wood's new terraces helped to make Bath the most fashionable resort in the country by the middle of the century. In 1750 the city's population had quadrupled since 1660, with thousands of British and foreign tourists swelling the numbers during the 'Season'. As one of the many visitors said of Bath in 1745, 'this is the place in all England to enjoy good health and to turn it to account.' Yet Bath was not the only city to witness substantial growth during this period. The Palladian era was a time of unprecedented urban expansion throughout Britain: the populations of Manchester, Leeds and Nottingham doubled between the beginning of the century and 1750;

Palladian sash windows at Blandford Forum (*far left*) and from a terraced house in Montpelier Row, Twickenham (*left*). Both windows incorporate glazed window guards, designed to stop the room's inhabitants plummeting from an open window yet cleverly integrated with the rest of the window composition. The lower Blandford window has the heavy glazing bars and rusticated surround characteristic of the early 1730s.

that of Sheffield rose from 3,500 in 1700 to 12,000 in 1750, whilst that of Birmingham grew from 4,400 in 1676 to 23,000 in 1750.

The principal materials required to build these new Palladian districts were invariably brick or local stone. External timberwork, which had been so prevalent in houses before the end of the seventeenth century, was kept to a minimum. The reason, as already seen, was the need to combat the risk of fire. Large-scale fires were often the catalyst which promoted the wholesale rebuilding of a town in the latest Palladian manner, complete with rows of carefully proportioned brick or stone façades. In 1731, for example, the picturesque Dorset town of Blandford Forum was razed to the ground, and the opportunity was subsequently seized to rebuild what had been a largely timber-built medieval town in brick and Portland stone – an extremely hard and highly expensive material, but quarried only a few miles away on the Dorset coast. Portland stone had been extensively used by Wren in rebuilding the principal monuments of the capital after the Great Fire; in Blandford it was used to construct key public buildings such as the new church and town hall. In the absence of similarly dramatic acts of God, existing homes were often simply refronted in brick or stone. This not only gave added protection against fire, but provided a veneer of costly metropolitan sophistication.

In 1715 the popularity of red bricks was at its height. The most common type of masonry brick was the 'place' or 'stock' brick, 'made in a Place prepared on purpose for them, near the Building they are to be used in', as Langley noted in 1734. Stocks were so named after the stock-board on which they were moulded; after moulding, they were stacked to dry in 'hacks', and

Left **Principal elevation of a town house of the 1730s or '40s for the Third Earl of Cholmondeley. This elevation is part of a rare find: a complete set of drawings for an average terraced house. The author of the design remains unknown.**

Doors from Uley, Gloucestershire of 1734 (*above left*) and Thaxted, Essex of 1718 (*above*).

when dry were burned – usually in clamps made of the bricks themselves, which were fired with wood or, if it was available, with sea-coal. Burning was an exact science; as Langley recorded: 'a Kiln of Bricks may be burnt so equally, that those on the Top shall be burnt as hard as those at the Bottom; So that an expert Burner affirms, he has burnt several Kilns of Tiles and Bricks, together, about three thousand Bricks, and ten or eleven thousand of Tiles, and has not had above fifty waste…'.

Particularly sought after were 'rubbed' bricks, which were not fired to such high temperatures as the average place bricks and which were as a result both softer and redder in colour than the average place or stock brick. Rubbed bricks were then literally rubbed on a circular rubbing stone to create a product that was exactly sized. They could be used for precision work – particularly window and door arches, where erratically sized bricks would not only look awkward but would also cause structural difficulties. The mortar joints between them – coloured white, to emphasize the unusual precision of the work – were as thin as possible. To achieve this, the mortar was not laid on with a trowel or a key; the bricks were simply dipped in unadulterated white lime putty and placed in position. The excess mortar would then be rubbed off after setting, at which time the whole rubbed brick arch would be rubbed down with stones of increasing flatness to attain a uniform finish. Such quality work was in marked contrast to the rapidly laid, darker-coloured brick courses which surrounded it, and was usually reserved for window dressings. (In early Georgian homes the brick piers between the windows were often as wide as the windows themselves, allowing plenty of room for rubbed brick dressings on both sides of the pier.) It was also very expensive: in 1748 rubbed bricks cost 60 shillings per hundred, compared to 30 shillings for red stocks and 14 shillings for simple place bricks.

Brightly coloured brickwork was a fashion which had been all the rage since the late seventeenth century. Wholly new, however, was the use of an Italian finish to disguise humble bricks as stone. Stucco was in essence a thin lime plaster, applied in three or more coats to an exterior of poor-quality brickwork and then painted and incised to resemble blocks of ashlar. During the reigns of George I and George II, however, it was only taken up by the most enthusiastic adherents of Italian taste: the villa-owners of Palladian Britain. Rokeby, a Yorkshire villa of 1725–30 built by Burlington's friend Sir Thomas Robinson much in the manner of Morris' Marble Hill, was, as oil paintings of the 1750s show, finished in plaster, which was then painted a light stone colour. The walls of Burlington's Chiswick House were also treated in this manner, as shown in a painting of the west front of 1742 by George Lambert. The fashion for stucco had spread sufficiently by 1744 for

An anonymous view of Sir Thomas Robinson's impeccably Palladian Rokeby Park, Yorkshire. Designed by Robinson himself (probably with the help of his friend and neighbour Burlington) and built in 1725–30, its construction was symptomatic of the extravagance which subsequently brought Robinson to the brink of ruin. The offer of the lucrative post of Governor of Barbados – and his marriage to a wealthy widow whilst in the West Indies – helped temporarily to restore his fortunes; however, renewed financial difficulties forced Robinson to sell Rokeby in 1769.

Right Colour contrasts in a house on Montpelier Row, Twickenham: white-painted sash, red brickwork and black iron railings. The ironwork would originally have been painted grey, stone-colour or (if the owner could run to the expense) blue; black as the accepted colour for railings is very much a modern innovation.

paint merchant Joseph Emerton to instruct how to imitate Portland stone with painted plaster, the wet paint being strewn with sand to give an even more stone-like character to the surface. This treatment seems to have become increasingly common on middle-class façades; clearly, not all could afford to adhere to the Palladian aristocrats' high-minded doctrine of truth to materials.

While stucco was not employed for middle-class housing until the last decades of the eighteenth century, the provision of another relatively new material, cast ironwork, did increase substantially in and around the Palladian home. The use of cast iron was pioneered by the prolifically fertile Bristolian inventor and engineer Abraham Darby. In 1708 Darby had been granted a patent for his new, more effective method of casting iron pots in sand beds. The following year he moved to what was to become the birthplace of the Industrial Revolution, Coalbrookdale in Shropshire, to take over a primitive blast furnace, and rapidly succeeded where others had failed in smelting iron using coked coal. The significance of Darby's triumph was immediately apparent. Coal was relatively cheap and far more plentiful than wood, which was now in alarmingly short supply; it could also, most importantly, attain a far higher temperature in the furnace than charcoaled wood. It was some years before a reliable method of converting cast-iron 'pigs' (so-called because the line of moulds feeding off the main supply of molten iron resembled a row of suckling piglets) into wrought iron could be perfected, but with Darby's success cast iron could be adapted to a wide variety of structural and

American Palladian (*clockwise from top left*): a massive, Jonesian doorcase and a Venetian (or, in North America, a Palladian) window at the Samuel Ely House in Lyme, Connecticut of 1739; a dominant Venetian window at Sheldon's Tavern in Litchfield, Connecticut, built in 1760 (though considerably restored after 1876); the Mission House in Stockbridge, Massachusetts; and a mid-eighteenth-century house with prominent Palladian overdoor, also from Lyme, Connecticut. The Stockbridge Mission House was begun by the Rev John Serjeant in 1739 as the base for his missionary work with the Housatonic Indians; now open to the public, it has been moved to its present site from its original location on nearby Eden Hill.

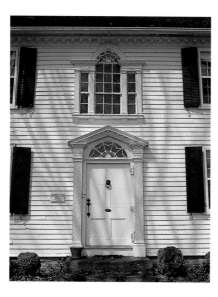

Right The Temple of Echo at Rousham. The garden at Rousham remains largely as Kent devised it between 1737 and 1741, with sculptures and temples set in a contrived landscape of grassy slopes, trees, pools, cascades and a tiny, winding stream. This octagonal temple, built by local architect-mason William Townesend after a design by Kent, houses an antique Roman tombstone. It is thus a perfect example of the marriage of ancient and modern that the Palladians sought to create.

decorative purposes. Cast-iron railings, manufactured in Sussex, were first used to provide a boundary fence to Wren's magnificent St Paul's Cathedral in 1714; 12 years later (and nine years after Darby's death) James Gibbs, always looking to utilize new materials, specified cast-iron railings around his new church of St Martin-in-the-Fields. And in 1735 London's Lincoln's Inn Fields became the first square to replace its wooden fence with cast-iron boundary railings.

Not all of the raw materials used for homes after 1715 were so novel. Indeed, many of the materials used in even the most radically new housing developments were the same as had been used a century before. Lead was still an important component of the house, used for cisterns and rainwater heads (which were on occasion painted or gilded), roof and wall flashings and

Irish Palladian: the front entrance to Ledwithstown, County Longford – a small country house of 1746, probably by Richard Cassels.

for water piping; lead was also a key ingredient in window glass and, of course, in lead paint for joinery. In 1740 Batty Langley wrote that lead was 'the most beautiful' of roof coverings, 'but the Expence being the greatest, it is therefore never used, but for to cover magnificent Buildings.' Exposed leadwork could be given added protection from a layer of 'tinning' (thin tin foil melted on the surface of the lead, which was then rubbed with resin) and could be decorated with a stencilled pattern executed in lamp-black. The manufacture of lead, however, was fraught with danger: a report of 1747 warned that leadworkers 'are sure in a few years to become paralytic by the mercurial fumes of the lead'.

Timber was by no means banished from house construction. While the Great Fire of London and similar conflagrations had instilled in the population a far greater awareness of the dangers of using highly inflammable materials for the external finish of a building, timber-framed construction was still very much the rule for most houses. To keep up with the vastly increased demand for structural timber after 1715, a new timber market was developed in the American colonies – the import of American softwoods helping to reduce

Britain's often politically embarrassing dependency on the Baltic for timber for both naval and building uses. Stone was, however, widely used in place of timber and external plaster where it was locally available. Blocks of freshly quarried stone – then called 'ashlar', a label now reserved only for squared and dressed blocks – were, according to Batty Langley, usually cut to a standard size of 9 inches thick if required for facing houses; subsequently stone lintels, sills and cornices were, adds Langley, often given a protective coat of white oil paint to preserve them from the weather. By 1740 even pre-Georgian brick or timber houses were being refaced in stone, the proportions of the new façades being painstakingly altered in order to reflect the new Palladian proportional ideals and, more specifically, to accommodate the newly fashionable sash windows.

Early Georgian window glass could be had in a variety of forms. The highest quality was crown glass, whose production Langley declared had been learned from the French by an English glassmaker who 'came over again into England, and set up the Making of Crown Glass, and in the Performance, outstripp'd the French his Teachers, as Englishmen usually do'. English window-glass manufacture was, Langley asserts, first attempted 'at the Bear-Garden, on the Bank-side, in Southwark, in the Year 1691' – a site close to the old Globe and Rose theatres which was owned by the Duke of Buckingham, who accordingly had his ducal insignia stamped on the centre of each table. By the 1730s crown glass could be obtained in tables 'of a circular Form about three Foot, six, seven or eight Inches in Diameter', either in the form of Ratcliff crown (which was blueish in hue) or Lambeth crown (which tended to be green in colour).

Early in the seventeenth century James I had banned the use of timber for glassmaking, encouraging the glass trade to turn to coal a century before the rest of industrial Britain. Accordingly, most of the new window-glass factories were to be found in coal-mining areas such as Newcastle or coal-importing cities such as Bristol. Batty Langley noted that French and German glass could be imported, but that most households in Britain had to put up with poor-quality Newcastle glass – a cylinder glass (blown into a cylinder, which was then opened out over sand) which was 'of an Ash Colour, and subject to Specks, Streaks, and other Blemishes, and besides, is frequently warp'd and crooked'. Bristol glass appears to have been of slightly better quality: at Dyrham Park in Gloucestershire William Blathwayt had foot-wide panes of local Bristol glass 'of the whitest mettle they make here', and costing a hefty 6d a pane, inserted into his new sash windows. How products such as Newcastle and Bristol glass were used to glaze windows such as these can be found in the next chapter.

Early eighteenth-century window details: *above*, **thick glazing bars and original crown glass remaining in the left-hand panes;** *above left*, **a comparable window viewed from the street, partly veiled by superbly detailed ironwork of c.1713.**

DOORS, WINDOWS ARE CONDEMNED BY PASSING FOOLS, WHO KNOW NOT THAT THEY DAMN PALLADIO'S RULES.

John Gay, *Epistle to Paul Methuen,* **1720**

Left **Detail from 'Chairing the Member', from Hogarth's four-painting satire** *An Election* **of 1754. The defeated Whigs can be seen jeering from a stone-coloured Venetian window, a symbol of their wealth and of their cultural pretensions. Below the window, the doorcase is surmounted by an improbable confection in the latest chinoiserie style – a comment by Hogarth on how contemporary good taste could be corrupted by the vagaries of momentary fashion.**

O ne of the most characteristic features of the Palladian house was the double-hung sash window. Two-part sash windows appear to have been invented (possibly in Britain) in the middle of the seventeenth century, and were definitely in use by the early 1650s. These early windows were not necessarily operated by the familiar system of cords and balanced weights, but were often merely propped up by wooden pegs or blocks.

By 1700 sash windows were de rigueur in any home with pretensions to artistic sophistication: Celia Fiennes damned even the grand pile of Euston Hall in Suffolk for the fact that 'the windows are low and not sashes'. Early sashes were made of oak or occasionally mahogany; it was not until the Georgian period that painted softwood became the rule for window joinery. Even oak windows, however, were generally given a coat or two of paint, at least on the external joinery. The most pretentious sash windows were not just painted but gilded, a treatment which produced a brilliant, glittering visual effect, provided good protection from the weather and told passers-by exactly how wealthy the owner was. At Chatsworth in Derbyshire, home of the socially pre-eminent and fabulously rich Dukes of Devonshire, even the surrounding box frames were gilded. On occasion, the whole of the window

Above **Detail of the roof balustrade and octagonal lantern from Campbell's Ebberston Lodge, Yorkshire of 1718.**

Early Georgian sash windows from Queen Square in Bath, of c.1730. The addition of pilasters and heavy pediments gives these otherwise unremarkable six-over-six paired openings an air of weighty grandeur.

frame was executed in metal. James Gibbs, for example, used copper windows at his Bank Hall in Warrington of 1750. It was not until the end of the eighteenth century, however, that metal windows became commonplace in domestic buildings.

The provision and form of early Georgian windows was greatly affected by two iniquitous taxes, on windows and on glass. The notorious window tax was first levied in 1696, and not repealed until 1851 (aptly enough, the year in which the glass Crystal Palace was opened to house the Great Exhibition). This measure did little to promote sanitary conditions within homes, encouraging house-owners to keep their rooms dark and poorly ventilated. Dummy windows were often painted onto recessed brick panels instead – keeping the Palladian proportions of the façade intact while escaping the tax burden of another real window. Alternatively, two windows could be combined into one; if the division between them was less than 12 inches, they counted as one unit for tax purposes.

The mid-Georgian glass tax was based on weight, not size or frequency of use. As a result, Georgian window glass was often as thin as possible, its inherent weakness requiring a strong frame, with much internal glazing, to support it. Early Georgian glazing bars were necessarily thick and chunky; they could, as Ivan Hall has discovered, be as wide as $2\frac{1}{4}$ inches. The internal profile was usually in the form of a robust combination of two ovolo or quarter-circle mouldings, a solution adopted not because Georgian joiners

An engraving of 1743, after Francis Hayman, showing home-grown entertainment – a game of blind man's buff – at Vauxhall Gardens on the south bank of the River Thames. The original was one of a series specially commissioned from Hayman for Vauxhall. The contrived, rustic nature of the scene has been emphasized by equipping the thatched cottage with an old-fashioned, pre-Georgian cross-framed leaded window.

could not construct anything more delicate, but because the thin and fragile glass needed considerable structural support.

To help reduce the tax burden further, indented 'bull's-eye' panes were often used for windows on unseen elevations, such as the kitchen window at the rear of the house. These unsightly panes were a by-product of the crown manufacturing process, originating from the centre of the glass table, where the blower's rod or 'pontil' had been disengaged. Most importantly, though, they were untaxed. On the higher floors of the front façade, expensive crown glass was again often dispensed with – though this time not to avoid taxation. Householders would install cheaper and inferior cylinder glass in the openings on those storeys which could not be seen by passers-by, and whose interiors were generally the preserve of children, servants or lodgers. On the more important and more visible ground and first floors, however, it was a different story. Sometimes even plain crown glass did not suffice. Batty Langley notes in his *Builder's Dictionary* of 1734 that mirror glass 'is commonly used in and about London, to put into the lower Lights of Sash-Windows, &c, where the Windows are low next the Streets, to hinder People who pass by from seeing what is done in the Room'. Mirrored windows are thus revealed not as a modern invention but as an idea which originated in the early eighteenth century.

The size of the window itself was, like the choice of window glass, largely governed by the relative social importance of the floor on which it

was sited. The largest windows were on the ground and first floors, since these housed the most important rooms. While most first floor windows of the 1720s were built as a double-square, the square-and-a-half and square-and-two-thirds were also accepted as good Palladian proportions for windows elsewhere on the front elevation, while many attic windows were reduced to simple squares. In turn, the windows constituted essential reference points for the proportional system of the Palladian façade as a whole – the urban terraced unit being generally framed as a square and a half.

Palladian sash windows were typically square-headed, unless grouped in the form of a tri-partite Venetian window. (The Venetian window found particular favour not only with Lord Burlington and William Kent but also with those who could afford large amounts of glass but who looked to save money on annual maintenance, since in the context of a Venetian window three openings were taxed as one.) Swept-head windows were not only associated with the outmoded Baroque houses of the preceding decades but were also more expensive to construct, since the bent top rail required more skill and time to make.

As characteristic of the new Palladian house as the sash window was the panelled door. By 1720 multi-panelled doors, of a roughly double-square proportion and with six or eight recessed or raised and fielded panels, were replacing the traditional ledged forms. Some doors were constructed from the complex proportional systems advocated by the pattern-book authors; other joiners turned directly to Palladio, who recommended a system by which the door's breadth could be calculated by dividing the distance from the floor to the underside of the joist beneath by $3\frac{1}{3}$, and the height of the door by taking a double-square shape and subtracting one-twelfth of this area.

Left **The mid-eighteenth-century Palladian staircase at Ledwithstown in Ireland. Note the splendid swooping dado on the left.**

Above **Venetian windows from William Kent's** *Designs of Inigo Jones* **of 1727.**

Doorways from Bath's South
Parade (*top left*) and
Peckover House, Wisbech
(*top right*) with, below, two
designs for doors from *The
Designs of Inigo Jones* of 1727
– the right-hand example
by Jones, the left-hand by
Burlington.

Above left Early nineteenth-century door furniture on an early Georgian door. *Above*, a rare Irish rim lock of c.1750.

The substantial appearance of these doors was often enhanced by fusing the lower panels together, to create a more effective barrier against boots and shoes. A further refinement was the introduction in the 1720s of a fanlight above the door, which for the first time allowed daylight to enter the hallway. One of the first fanlights was introduced by Roger Morris at Marble Hill House in the mid-1720s; soon afterwards sophisticated house-owners were installing similar features above their panelled doors. By 1740 fanlights were commonplace, and the thick, tapered wooden glazing bars of the early examples had given way to more elaborate confections in wood, lead or wrought iron.

Above the fanlight projected the canopy or pediment of the doorcase. Doorcases were no longer the vast, heavily scrolled and bracketed compositions of the Baroque age. Gone were the curved hoods and oversized columns; in their place were sedate, square-headed projecting canopies supported by relatively restrained columns or pilasters. By 1730 the typically Palladian door-case had become well established, with a simple, barely projecting triangular pediment replacing the canopy. This classic design was to last throughout the next two centuries, long enough to be revived – in a hideously bastardized form – to adorn the neo-Georgian estates of brave new postwar Britain.

Door furniture was minimal in the early Georgian period. Front doors would have been provided with little more than a black-painted cast-iron doorknob, if that. According to John Wood, internal doors of the 1720s – at least those in Bath – were equipped with varnished iron locks. Twenty years later, Wood alleges that 'Doors in general…had the best sort of Brass locks put on them' – heavy rim locks with hefty keys to go with them. However, this type of expense would once again have been limited to the principal rooms of the house. When Samuel Richardson's revolutionary working-class heroine Pamela, in the eponymous novel of 1740, attempted to escape from the awful Mrs Jewkes, the garden door was equipped with 'a lock, which was a great wooden one'.

The average room of the early Georgian period would have been fitted out with wooden panelling or 'wainscot', plaster ceilings and solid floors. It was only in the 1740s, with the growing popularity of wallpaper, that wooden panelling was abandoned above the dado in favour of flat plaster – a better surface on which to hang paper. As early as 1724, John Bold has recorded, the specification for a wealthy Bristol merchant's house included the firm stipulation, 'There will be no occasion of wainscotting any Chamber at least not higher than the Sells of the Windows,' although it did also suggest, 'Eating Rooms should be wainscotted for as bare Walls are not tolerable in this Age.' The retention of wood panelling below the dado, the architect-

Right View of the hall floor at Abbot Hall in Kendal. The small squares of dark grey slate are interset with flags of local 'fossiliferous' limestone – stone in which the fossil content can clearly be seen. *Far right,* excellent oak boarding in the dining room at Pallant House, Chichester. Only the grander homes of the period would have been able to afford good oak boards such as these; most households had to use cheaper deal, which was waxed, painted or covered by carpets or floorcloths.

Right The drawing room at Drayton Hall, South Carolina, built in 1738–42. The villa's current owners, The National Trust for Historic Preservation, have sensibly opted not to recreate a fanciful 'Palladian' scheme for the interiors, but have largely left the rooms as found. The Victorian paint-work is just as much a part of the history of the house as the Palladian portico.

mason declared, was done for eminently practical reasons: 'to prevent the breaking the Plastering with Mopps or Brushes in cleaning the Room'.

Palladian wainscot was most commonly in the form of simple 'square panelling', with vertical stiles and horizontal rails bordering recessed panels; there was also the even less sophisticated 'post and panel' variant, with vertical stiles reaching from floor to ceiling. Neither of these types had bolection mouldings, which linked raised and recessed members; raised and fielded panelling was only to be found in the grander homes. The only wall mouldings in middle-class households were located on the cornice, dado rail and skirting or baseboard. The size and decoration of each of these elements related directly to their role in the social and architectural hierarchy of the Palladian house: the more important the room, the more elaborate the mouldings. In the case of the wall, the hierarchy was directly derived from the notion of the classical orders: the ancient pedestal corresponded to the domestic dado, the column shaft to the length of wall above the dado rail, and the classical entablature to the domestic frieze and cornice.

At the dado and cornice, the type of decorative mouldings to be found in the 1720s, '30s and '40s were heavy and pronounced – a far cry from the delicate fripperies of the later eighteenth century or the low-relief, architectural forms of the Regency period. Most common were the family of ovolo or 'echinus' mouldings, based on the quadrant or quarter circle. These were developed into perhaps the most characteristic moulding of the Palladian era: the 'egg-and-dart' moulding which, as the name implies, resembled a row of

Plaster detailing of the 1720s from Peckover House in Wisbech, Cambridgeshire. *Right*, the dining room, with the prominent use of a Greek key motif on the overmantel; *far right*, Vitruvian scroll moulding featured on the staircase string.

Right A scheme by William Kent for a grandiose Roman interior at his projected new House of Commons. Kent liked to enliven even his most solemn drawings with sketches or caricatures of the likely inhabitants; in this instance he depicts the most famous episode in Parliament's opening ceremony, during which the King arrives at the Commons and is refused entry – as was the case with Charles I in 1642. Despite such delightful additions, however, Kent's ambitious designs for a new, Palladian Palace of Westminster, submitted to Parliament for inspection in 1739, were never executed.

half-spheres or eggs separated by small leaves, darts or, to Isaac Ware, anchors. Burlington himself helped to popularize two of the continuous, low-relief decorative mouldings most often found in the pages of Vitruvius and Palladio: the interlinked 'S' pattern known as 'guilloche', and the wave ornament inevitably known as 'Vitruvian scroll'. Both of these rhythmic forms were most often found on dado rails. In contrast, the simple dentil (a plain, square-sectioned, projecting tooth), the more complex modillion (a scroll-shaped bracket) and the rope-like torus were, given their relatively high relief and bold profile, usually found decorating the cornice.

Most early dados and cornices were of wood. Increasingly, however, plaster mouldings were used for the cornice, if not for the dado rail or skirting, which needed to be resistant to everyday wear and tear. In the early Georgian period both lime and gypsum plasters were employed for internal ornament, whereas by the second half of the eighteenth century only gypsum plaster (plaster of Paris) was used for interiors. The choice of plaster had a profound effect on the character of the moulding or ornament being created. Gypsum plaster, as a viscous liquid, could be poured smoothly into even quite complex moulds. Raw lime putty, in contrast, was a stiff paste and thus could not always be pushed into every crevice of the mould. As a result, lime plaster mouldings often had a rougher, more handmade appearance to them.

By 1750 more elaborate plaster decoration was being applied between the dado and the frieze or cornice in the larger homes. This type of virtuoso plasterwork often incorporated the latest Kentian motifs or mimicked the ambitious compositions of the immigrant Italian and Swiss *stuccatori* employed

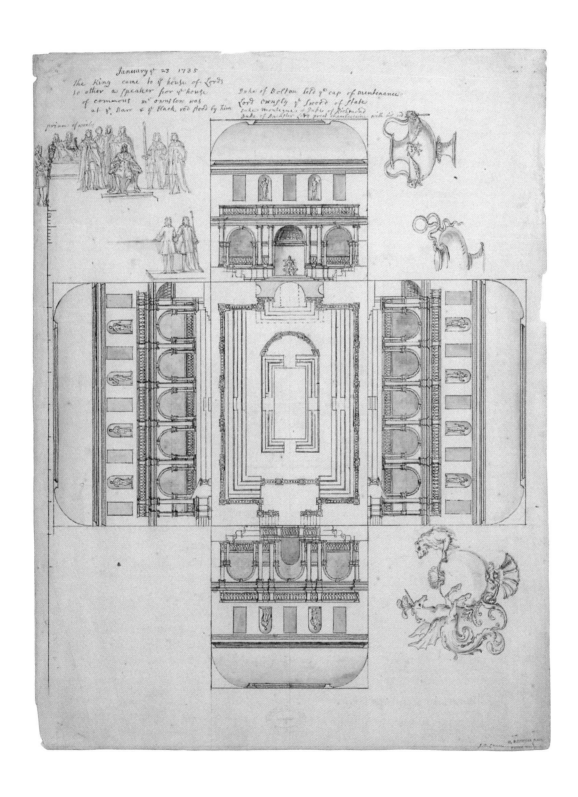

to decorate the great houses of the land. Indeed, by 1751 the architect James Paine was boasting of his recently completed Mansion House at Doncaster that the banqueting room decoration was 'of stucco (executed by Mr Rose and Mr Thomas Perritt) inferior to none of the best Performances of the best *Italians* that ever work'd in this Kingdom'.

For most, however, specially moulded plaster ornament – especially when it was partially worked on site – was far too expensive. Instead, cheap fabric hangings or, after 1730, wallpaper, had to suffice above the dado, while ceilings, invariably painted white, were left plain. By the mid-1740s, a cheap alternative to moulded lime or gypsum plaster was available. John Cornforth has discovered the first reference to papier-mâché decoration in a letter of 1742, in which Lady Hertford boasts that the walls and ceiling of a pavilion at her home of Percy Lodge has been 'fitted within with paper in imitation of stucco'. Papier-mâché was not only less expensive but also far lighter than plaster, and thus could be used with far greater flexibility. By the mid-1750s 'chew'd Paper', as William Shenstone called it in 1752, was being used for wall ornaments and for complete ceilings in the most fashionable homes, and was being regarded by woodcarvers as a serious threat to their livelihood. Applied papier-mâché ornament was, according to Shenstone, habitually painted white and 'washed over Oker'. It could, like plaster mouldings, also be gilded if resources allowed.

In most middle-class homes, where Kentian ceiling decoration or even papier-mâché wall designs were an unheard-of luxury, the decorative as well as the social centrepiece of any important room was invariably the chimney-piece. Early eighteenth-century chimney surrounds were flat and relatively unadorned. Yet under the influence of stylistic arbiters such as Kent and Gibbs – and particularly works such as Kent's *Designs of Inigo Jones* and Gibbs' *Book of Architecture*, both of 1728 and both featuring an enormous variety of chimneypiece designs – boldly projecting and highly decorated marble, plaster or painted wood fireplace surrounds became increasingly common in the more well-to-do households. The more ambitious designs featured Kentian masks or shells in place of the usual plain central tablet, and Vitruvian caryatids in place of the supporting pilasters or piers at the sides. These could be copied by any skilled woodcarver or stonemason from one of the numerous pattern-books which by 1750 offered the craftsman and his client a vast range of decorative solutions.

Palladian chimneypieces, like windows and doors, theoretically adhered to what was often a decidedly over-complicated system of proportions. In 1734 Batty Langley briefly summarized Palladio's rules for the proportions of chimney surrounds. Surrounds in halls, he directed, should ideally be 6 to

Variants on the classic Palladian chimneypiece: chimneypiece details from Peckover House, Chichester and 22 Arlington Street, London. *Clockwise from top left*: the chimney surround from the anteroom at Peckover, with its heavy egg-and-dart moulding and emphasized motif of three acanthus buds (elements that were continually to recur in Palladian designs of the next 40 years); Kent's surround for the Great Room at Arlington Street, featuring an elaborate cornucopia; a detail of the acanthus leaf decoration on the imposing marble chimneypiece in the hall at Arlington Street; and the simpler, more robust design of the drawing room chimneypiece at Peckover.

8 feet broad and 4½ to 5 feet high, and should project 2½ or 3 feet; those in major rooms should measure between 5½ and 7 feet by 4 to 4½ feet, and so on. Equally confusing was Robert Morris' simple rule of thumb for chimneypieces, also first published in 1734: 'To find the height of the opening of the chimney from any given magnitude of a room, add the length and height of that room together, and extract the square root of that sum, and half that root will be the height of the chimney.'

More usefully, Langley also compared the price of chimney surrounds. These ranged from 10 to 20 shillings for painted wood (and wooden chimneypieces were always painted, never left bare or stripped) to as much as £2 for stone and a sizeable £10–£12 for marble surrounds. For those who could afford the latter, there was a sumptuous array of native and foreign marbles on offer, from red-veined English White to Auvergne marble (which Langley describes as an exciting, even shocking 'pale red, mingled with violet, green and yellow'), and including pure-white Carrara marble from Genoa (a favourite for grand chimneypieces), terracotta-coloured Sicilian marble ('stain'd with oblong Squares of white and Isabella, like strip'd Taffetas'),

Fireplace designs 'borrowed' from James Gibbs by Batty Langley for his *The City and Country Builder's and Workman's Treasury of Designs* of 1740.

blue-grey Namur marble (comparatively cheap, and often used for floors) and black Dinan marble (also much used for floors). Not all marble was quite as high-quality as it seemed, however. Given the expense of the material, it was not surprising that unscrupulous suppliers attempted to deceive their customers. Henry Purefoy spent many months in 1739 and 1740 having a handsome red and white marble fireplace fitted at great expense, only to find out it was a fake: after a few weeks of use, the thin marble veneer blistered and cracked, revealing underneath coarse stone pieces bound with iron cramps to stop them disintegrating.

Inset within the chimney surround were, on occasion, blue-and-white tin-glazed Delftware tiles, copied from Dutch examples but made (at least since the beginning of the eighteenth century) in England or Scotland. Until the 1750s the subjects depicted on these charming ceramics were very much in the Dutch manner, with flowers, biblical quotations or countryside scenes being the most commonly found decorations.

Within the tiled inset was the fireplace opening, containing the grate. While the fireback was invariably of cast iron, the splayed cheeks of the opening were occasionally made of brass rather than of brick, stone or iron, an innovation designed not to retain heat (the energy-efficient fireplace did not appear until the end of the century) but to reflect the light from a blazing fire around the dimly lit room. Typically, the socially ambitious and immensely wealthy Duke of Chandos had to go one better than this, installing

Francis Hayman's *Rev. Dr John Hoadly and Dr Maurice Green* of 1747. In 1747 the composer Greene published a pastoral opera, *Phœbe*, which he had written jointly with Hoadly, a poet, dramatist and chaplain to the Prince of Wales; this painting was presumably commissioned to mark the event. The interior is very much an average one of the period: the wood-coloured door, green walls and bare floorboards are very modest, and the only evidence of any sizeable financial outlay on the room is to be found in the marble chimneypiece and accompanying firescreen.

silver fireplace cheeks at his Cannons mansion in the 1720s. Grates were invariably made of iron; other items of fireplace furniture were more lustrous, andirons, shovels and tongs being made of brass, polished steel or even, in the wealthier households, of silver. Andirons, however, gradually became employed more for display than to support logs, since the introduction of the basket grate made this latter function superfluous. Gradually the simple, free-standing iron basket grate, with two or three bars at the front and a grid at the bottom to dispose of loose ash, developed into the more advanced 'hob' or 'stove' grate, equipped with iron cheeks, decorated front bars of iron and steel with perhaps some brass ornamentation, and permanent or movable iron plates or hobs at either side of the fire-basket to warm kettles and pots. Brass fenders were also increasingly common by 1750; indeed, some mid-century grates made entirely of cast brass have been found.

When the fire was not in use, the fireplace could be filled with a vase of flowers, a paper fan or a chimneyboard. These were painted with *trompe l'œil* scenes – flowers were very popular – or, by 1750, with one of the increasingly fashionable 'Chinese' designs. Temple Newsam's fireplace exhibition catalogue cites, for example, 11 chimneyboards being stored in a coal closet at Kiveton in 1727, as well as an order for Ham House of 1730 for 'a white board for a Chimney grownded for Japaning'.

Charles Grignion's 1743 engraving of Francis Hayman's *Sir John Falstaff in the Buck-Basket*, painted in c.1741 for one of the supper-boxes at the highly popular Vauxhall Gardens. Falstaff was one of Hayman's favourite characters; as his biographer Brian Allen has remarked, 'Hayman seems to have developed a particular affinity with Shakespeare's bawdy and boastful glutton', and indeed came physically to resemble the fat knight. The original painting from which this engraving was taken has since been lost. Note the wide uncovered deal floorboards.

Right Firescreens like this exemplary floral design of 1700 remained popular throughout the eighteenth century. This superb example even includes a *trompe l'œil* inset comprising blue-and-white Delftware tiles.

Floors in poorer, rural households were usually made of simple brick paviours or, more likely, of an earth-based plaster or 'stucco'. This was usually coloured brown – a colour which, as John Wood observed, was designed 'to hide the Dirt, as well as their own Imperfections' – and could be made from anything that was easily available, from loam and lime to 'Anvil-Dust from the forge'. Langley's *Builder's Dictionary* of 1734 gives a typical recipe for an earth floor:

> Take two Thirds of Lime, and one of Coal Ashes well-fitted, with a small Quantity of loamy Clay; mix the Whole that you intend to use together; and temper it well with Water; making it into a Heap, let it lie a Week or ten Days, in which Time it will mellow and digest...till it becomes smooth and yielding, tough and glewy. Then the Ground being levelled, lay your Floor therewith about two and a half, or three Inches thick, making it smooth with a Trowel...

Grander homes had floors of deal (pine or fir softwood) or of oak, if this could be afforded and the floor was not to be almost entirely covered with a carpet. White deal, says the anonymous specifier for the Bristol merchant's house of 1724, was 'much in vogue' in the mid-1720s; indeed, he recommends oak or deal rather than more expensive stone or marble alternatives, for the eminently practical reason that costly flooring materials have to be 'constantly coverd by painted or Outer Clothes' – that is, by

Right Floorboards painted as black-and-white marble blocks, contrasted (*far right*) with the real thing: a stone-and-slate floor from Peckover House. Painted floorboards were very common in middle-class households of the eighteenth century, yet few survive. This impressive recreation, complemented by a reproduction pillar-and-arch wallpaper, is from Kittery, Maine.

painted floorcloths or druggets – 'to preserve them so that [the householders] seldom or never enjoy that beauty they purchase at excessive prices'. Wooden floors were built of wide, but not standardized, boards; *Chambers' Cyclopaedia* of 1738 recommended that boards were not 'more than 6 inches broad, and in the best floors [should] not exceed 3 or 4 inches'. These boards were then either partially covered by expensive imported carpets or, more commonly, were waxed or limed. Once again, though, the anonymous Bristol builder warns against the practice of waxing floors, for reasons that will be all too familiar today: 'I would not have these Oak floors rubd with Wax and other practices to make them shine for that renders them so sleek and slippery there is no walking on them but at the hazard of your neck…'.

Parquetry floors, constructed from tessellated blocks of different woods, were still much in demand in the grandest homes, and could even be extended to the staircase treads and landings. But the most expensive flooring material – and one apparently immune to the vagaries of fashion – remained marble. Marble floors, first introduced into England by Inigo Jones at the Queen's House in Greenwich, were usually to be found in entrance halls and large ground-floor reception rooms, being too heavy for the important chambers of the first floor. Different marbles could be used in conjunction with other expensive stones to create a complex geometrical pattern, usually involving tessellated polygons in white, black or grey. In his *Ancient Masonry* of 1736, Batty Langley devised a particularly intricate design of his own, 'which being made with White, Black and Dove colour'd Marble, represents so many Tetrahedrons, or Pyraments, with their vertical Angles, seemingly perpendicular to their Bases…which in the Dusk of an Evening appear as so many solid bodies not to be walked on.' At Hawksmoor's Castle Howard Mausoleum of 1731–42 brass ornament was inlaid into the marble.

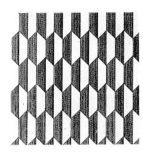

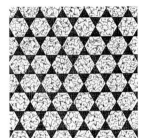

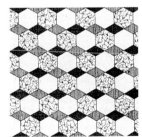

However, marble was not always structurally appropriate. In 1747, for example, James Gibbs found that 'Portland Stone, intermixed with red Swedish or Bremen stone', was more suitable than marble for the floor of his new Radcliffe Camera in Oxford: 'This Floor was at first proposed to be of black and white Marble polished, but was rejected, being thought improper for the Place, because the Air condensing upon it, occasioned by its hardness...makes the Place damp, especially where no fire is kept.'

If marble proved too expensive or too heavy, then the sham marble known as scagliola could be used in its place. *Chambers' Cyclopaedia* gives a detailed recipe for making this versatile, plaster-based material, which could be used for floors, walls or chimneypieces, any location in which marble could be expected:

> Now to prepare the sifted gypsum to be applied on this ground, they dissolve it and boil it with the best English glue, and after mixing it with the colour it is to bear, the whole is worked up together into the ordinary consistence of plaister; and then taken or spread upon the ground, five or six inches thick...'Tis on this plaister, thus coloured like marble or precious stone...that the design to be represented is drawn... The cavities...made in the ground, are filled up with the same gypsum boiled in glue, only differently coloured; and thus are the several colours of the original represented. To have the necessary colours and tints at hand, they temper quantities of the gypsum with the several colours, in little pots. When the design is thus filled, and rendered visible, by half polishing it with brick or soft stone; they go over it again, cutting such places as are either to be weaker, or more shadowed, and filling them with gypsum; which is repeated till all the colours... represent the original to the life.

In 1756 Isaac Ware commented that scagliola 'when well worked and laid makes a very beautiful floor, some of it looking like porphiry'. However, he also remarked: 'We see these miserably executed in the country...and in good houses in London, where there are stucco floors it is too common to see frightful cracks across them.'

Whatever the type of solid flooring on the ground floor, downstairs in the basement it was a different story. Here paved floors, using brick paviours or coarse stone flags, were the rule. *Chambers' Cyclopaedia* advised that kitchens 'are paved with tiles, bricks, flags, or fire-stone...and rag-stone'. And at the other end of the house, upstairs beyond the important entertaining rooms, any oak boarding installed at ground or first floor level inevitably gave way to cheaper deal floors.

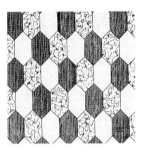

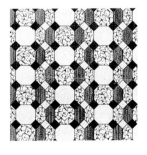

Floor designs from Batty Langley's *Treasury of Designs* of 1740.

Details from the principal staircases at Pallant House, Chichester (*right*) and Peckover House, Wisbech (*far right*). Although that at Pallant House is earlier in date, its twisted balusters, grouped three to a tread, are more in the vanguard of fashion than the bulbous supports at Peckover, built ten years later. Each of the oak tread ends at Pallant House carries a different set of motifs.

The staircase was one of the most attractive features of the early Georgian house. The heavy, bulbous wooden balusters of the late seventeenth century had by 1730 given way to delightfully delicate turned or twisted forms, grouped two or even three to a tread. At least, this was the case with stairs which linked the principal floors of the house. Once again, the social hierarchy of the house dictated how intricate and how expensive the fixtures and decoration were to be on each floor of the Georgian home. Thus the higher the stair rose, the simpler was the baluster design. By the time the stair reached the attic storey, where the servants dwelt, the balusters may have become no more than plain, square-section sticks. Even the dimensions of the risers and treads were reduced as the stair ascended to less salubrious heights. John Bold's Bristol house specification of 1724, for example, includes the provision for a staircase: 'Five foot wide, a foot broad and Six Inches high from the Parlour to the Principal Chamber [ie the first] Floor, and from thence to the Upper Chamber Floor to be only four foot wide, and 5 Inches and a half high.'

Even plainer and narrower than the attic stairs were those rear, servants' staircases found in the larger homes. The primary purpose of these back stairs was to allow servants to go about their daily (or indeed nightly) business without bothering or even meeting the family. They were not, though, exclusively for servants' use; as the anonymous architect responsible

for the new middle-class Bristol home in the mid-1720s observed, they also ensured that 'the young Men may at night go to their Beds and in the morning come to their business without disturbing or dirtying the best part of the House'. These rear stairs were naturally of the simplest construction, with square sticks and a rudimentary handrail. In this, as in so many other aspects of their lives, servants were not expected to require more.

Staircase design from William Halfpenny's *The Art of Sound Building* **of 1725.**

BRUSH NOT THY SWEEPING SKIRT TOO NEAR THE WALL; THY HEEDLESS SLEEVE WILL DRINK THE COLOUR'D OIL AND SPOT INDELIBLE THY POCKET SOIL. John Gay, *On Walking the Streets By Night*, 1714

Left **A surprisingly colourful wallpaper design of the 1730s. Patterns such as these still relied heavily on the influence of Chinese design.**

Above **Detail from a 1721 edition of *The Architecture of A. Palladio*, by Giacomo Leoni.**

Virtually every element of the Palladian interior, and every piece of exposed external joinery or ironwork, was painted. As William Salmon wrote in 1734, in words which many modern home-owners would do well to remember:

> *Sash-Frames, Sashes, Window-Shutters, Doors, and Door-Cases, for want of Painting, in a very few Years, are so much decayed, that were those Buildings to be made tenantable, most of the outside Timber-Work must be renewed. Iron-work, though of a much stronger Nature than Timber, if not well secured by painting, is likewise subject to the same Misfortune. On the contrary, where Timber-Work is often painted, it will endure many Ages; no Weather being able to penetrate through it.*

The Palladian taste was for simple, bold colours – not the pallid, anaemic pastel shades so often associated with the early Georgians by modern commentators. The principal guide for the early eighteenth-century decorator, John Smith's *The Art of Painting in Oyl* of 1687 (new editions were brought out in 1705, 1723 and 1753, and it was even reissued in 1821) listed not only

Scenes from a 1757 edition of Pope's *Dunciad*, a satire on contemporary individuals and mores, originally published in 1728.

the darker wood colours so popular in the seventeenth century ('walnut', 'oak', 'mahogany' and so on) but also striking tones of pea green, sky blue and straw yellow. The brown-coloured walls of the last scene of Hogarth's *Marriage à la Mode* of 1743–5 were designed to illustrate the financial as well as the moral depths to which the doomed family had sunk – brown being both cheap and old-fashioned, and a marked contrast to the vibrant green walls of the redecorated family mansion shown in scene II. Reds and greens (especially the drab or olive tones seen in the paintings of Hogarth and his contemporaries) were particularly prevalent by 1740, being widely regarded as excellent foils to the gilt frames of wall-hung pictures. As Ian Bristow has pointed out, a dull olive green can be seen on the walls of Hogarth's *Wanstead Assembly* of c.1729, while the term 'green room' can be found as early as 1740, in Samuel Richardson's substantial novel *Pamela*: '"I will then," resumed my lady, "lie in the best room, as it is called; and Jackey shall lie in the little green-room. Hast thou got the keys of those, Fat-face?"'

Yellows were also frequently used. Ian Bristow records that, for Gibbs' addition to King's College, Cambridge of 1731, while most of the rooms were painted olive or pearl, one panelled room's walls were painted 'brim Stone' (presumably a sulphurous yellow) and another a 'fair Blew'. By this time, too, the more daring house-owners were painting the recessed panels on their walls a subtly different colour to that of the surrounding rails and stiles, and

Hogarth's evocation of one of the most fashionable Palladian interiors of the day: *The Assembly at Wanstead House* of 1729–30. Wanstead in Essex, begun at the time of George I's accession in 1714, was Colen Campbell's first large-scale commission, and the first sizeable mansion in Britain to encapsulate the precepts of the new Palladian style.

shadowing dado and especially cornice mouldings in grey so as to make them appear even more three-dimensional.

For those who could afford it, wall mouldings were not just shadowed but also gilded. Most architectural woodwork or plasterwork was oil gilded, a process by which the ground was painted and provided with a layer of oil size (often tinted to obtain the required shade of gilt) before the gold leaf was painstakingly applied from small books of wafer-thin gold sheets. Water gilding, a more time-consuming and intricate, and inevitably more expensive, method – involving the creation of a ground of many layers of smoothed gesso before the coloured bole primer and watered glue were applied – was largely limited to items of furniture. Today far too much gilding is reworked with gold paint, a medium which dulls and fades very quickly, and which soon looks nothing like the real thing. The Palladians had a better way of economizing. Batty Langley's *Builder's Dictionary* of 1734 noted that 'the common Painters do now generally, in gilding, use more Silver than Gold, in most works that are not much exposed to the Air, to which they afterwards give the Colour of Gold, by means of the Lacker Varnish'.

While gilding was perennially popular with those who could afford it (and even in a great house such as Dyrham Park only three rooms had any gilded decoration in 1710), other paint techniques such as graining and marbling appear to have become less fashionable as the eighteenth century wore on. Dyrham's Great Hall, for example, was in 1710 still panelled with deal grained a cedar colour, while the staircase panelling was grained in imitation of Virginia walnut; but 20 years later this sort of dark wall finish had given way to stronger, brighter tones. Chocolate brown, though, survived well into the eighteenth century as a finish for internal joinery. The graining of internal doors had by 1720 generally given way to the practice of painting them a chocolate colour, a tone which was also applied to the skirting board. And while marbling had been all the rage at the turn of the century (in 1697 Celia Fiennes had admired Newby Park in Yorkshire for the fact that 'the Best Room was painted just like marble'), by 1750 the practice was usually confined to the decoration of wooden or plaster chimneypieces.

Another fashion which had evaporated by 1740 was the predilection for the semi-gloss finish that oil-based lead paints naturally produced. Increasingly, oil paint was given a matt appearance by the addition of a flattening coat of turpentine; alternatively, the paint itself could be 'flatted' with turpentine, which, when mixed with white lead, produced the dead, white 'stone colour' so popular with Palladian designers.

All oil paints were based on white lead. In Vitruvius' day this vital ingredient had been made by putting sheets of lead in covered jars filled with vinegar, and extracting the oxide. By the early eighteenth century the methods of extraction were on a larger scale, but had not become much more sophisticated. White lead, stated Langley in 1734, was almost invariably used 'for every Kind' of external timberwork. Inside, however, was far greater variety. Even the poorer households could afford simple 'common colours' such as lead-colour, chocolate brown, the 'timber colours', made with earth pigments such as umber, and ochre, and 'stone colour'. Lead colour and stone colour, which could vary from an off-white (designed to resemble pale Portland stone) to a yellowish-brown, were particularly popular. Dan Cruickshank has discovered that the panelled interior of his Palladian terraced house in Spitalfields, east London, was almost entirely painted either in a stone colour or a lead colour made from indigo, white lead and a small proportion of black.

In poorer homes, and especially in cottages in rural areas, green and not white was frequently used for joinery both inside and outside the house. Only windows in more sophisticated urban and country districts appear to have been painted with a white or stone oil colour. (The white used was always, of course, what we would now call an 'off-white'; the searing, bleached brilliant whites so popular today are very much a recent creation, and are totally inappropriate for Georgian homes.) Doors appear to have been painted a dark colour, within a pale, white or stone-coloured doorcase. Black and red-brown seem to have been the most popular colours for front doors.

Paint pigments varied enormously in cost, based on the time needed and the difficulty encountered in extracting them from their source. Thus some oil paints were far more expensive, and far more rarely and sparingly used, than others. The wealthier the household, the wider the range of oil and distemper paint available to the aspirant decorator. The seriously rich could afford paints such as verdigris, the bluish-green oil paint pigmented with oxidized copper which, as Langley put it, 'makes the delicatest Grass-green in the World'. The fabulously rich could afford luxurious blues such as smalt, not really a paint pigment at all but a covering of powdered blue glass. Smalt was strewn onto a base of white lead while the paint was still wet, and then, according to Langley, stroked 'with the Feather edge of a Goose Quill, that it may lie even and alike thick in all Places'; the result was a glittering finish considered highly appropriate for internal and some external ironwork. The most expensive type of smalt was ground extremely fine, and could actually be added to white lead to form a proper oil paint. However, Langley observed that this paint 'does not bear a good Body, nor does it work but with much Difficulty'. A cheaper alternative to ultramarine or smalt was Prussian blue, a powerful pigment made from animal bones and alum which was invented in Germany in 1704. By the 1720s it was being used in Britain; given its expense, however, it was employed only by rich patrons such as Burlington, who used a flamboyant combination of Prussian blue oil paint together with rich blue velvet, copious gilding and decorative painting by William Kent to create the most sumptuous and ostentatious room at Chiswick House. By 1750, the price of Prussian blue had fallen considerably, providing the middle classes with a far stronger and brighter blue than they had been able to achieve using cheap and cheerful indigo. As late as 1805, however, Prussian blue still remained twice the price of indigo.

William Salmon's *Palladio Londinensis* of 1734 includes a useful table of oil paint prices which helps to indicate which colours would have been widely used in the 1730s and which would have been limited to the great houses. Pure white lead and 'Pearl', 'Lead', 'Cream', 'Stone' and 'Wainscot' or 'Oak' colours were all cheap, at 4d or 5d a pound. Other wood colours – 'Chocolate', 'Mahogany', 'Cedar' and 'Walnut-tree colour' – were slightly more expensive, at 6d a pound. Costing between 8d and a shilling were gold, olive, pea and 'Fine Sky Blue'; at a shilling a pound were orange, lemon, straw, pink and 'Blossom Colour'. Verdigris – 'Fine deep Green' – was, predictably, the most expensive of all: at 2s 6d a pound, it was six times more costly than the common colours.

The green-painted dining room at Abbot Hall in Kendal, Cumbria (*right*), and (*far right*) looking into the first-floor hall at Pallant House in Chichester. Built in 1759 under the supervision of the Yorkshire architect John Carr for Colonel George Wilson, the interior decoration of Abbot Hall is strongly reminiscent of metropolitan homes of 20 years earlier. The Pallant House room features a recently recreated floorcloth, painted in imitation of a complex marble floor.

Right A range of typical – though by no means exhaustive – Palladian house-paint colours, matched by Patrick Baty from original samples and recipes. These colours would have ranged considerably in price.

The pigments used to create these colours were ground in a mill, like flour. In 1718, as Ian Bristow has observed, one Marshall Smith took out a patent for a 'machine or engine for the grinding of colours, to be used in all kinds of paintings'. These mills were usually powered by horse, the advantages of which were testified to by Robert Campbell's *The London Tradesman* of 1747, which noted that some of the 'Colour-Shops' or paint retailers 'have set up Horse-Mills to grind the Colours, and sell them to Noblemen & Gentlemen ready mixed at a low price, & by the help of a few printed Directions, a house may be painted by any common Labourer at one Third of the Expense it would have cost before the Mystery was made public.'

Not all pigments could be used both in oil paints and in distempers. Distemper, made from chalk and glue, was entirely different, and often could not accommodate the sort of pigments regularly ground with oil. As a softer finish, and one that was easier to remove, distemper was frequently used on plaster walls and ceilings, whose mouldings would have been quickly clogged if thick, hard-to-shift oil paints had been employed. Oils were generally restricted to internal and external woodwork.

Those who had money to burn did not have to be content with just painted walls. Fabric hangings – in plain, watered or damask cloth, or in the form of tapestries from France, the newly created Austrian Netherlands (present-day Belgium) or from London factories such as the Royal Tapestry Factory in Soho – were still as fashionable in 1715 as they had been in 1615. By 1730, however, the passion for fabric wall-hangings was on the wane even in the grandest households (although black cloth was still routinely hung

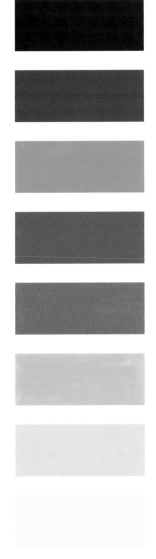

about a room in the event of the death of the master of the house). The poet James Thomson was deliberately evoking an old-fashioned air when he wrote of his 'Castle of Indolence' in 1748, 'The rooms with costly tapestry were hung.' For fabric wall-hangings were not only popularly regarded as unduly expensive, but also as homes for dust and dirt. As an anonymous architect wrote in 1724, 'hangings of all Stuffs are apt to be impregnated by the Fumes of Victuals, or Tobacco if smoking is frequently used, and the smell will not be easily got out.' Since hanging tended to weaken their top edges, even the most expensive tapestries had a surprisingly short life.

Fabric hangings were fixed to the wall much in the manner of the early wallpapers. Canvas was tacked to a wooden frame attached to the wall, and covered first with lining paper and then with the fabric or wallpaper itself. By 1750, however, wallpaper had far outstripped wall-hangings for convenience of use, with many papers being glued directly onto the bare wall. To hide the rows of tacks above the dado rail and below the frieze or entablature, narrow borders or 'fillets' of wood, papier-mâché, paper (often printed in mimicry of stamped lead or some other exotic material) or even cast lead or brass were employed. In 1743 Charlotte Fermor used costly dyed lace as a border for her wall hangings, writing that her 'new apartment is now furnishing with crimson velvet doubly bordered with a broad gold lace, and set in carved and gilt frames'.

Leather hangings were still used for the walls of old-fashioned mansions. The Dyrham inventory of 1710 records the survival of gilt leather hangings, put up eight years earlier in the vestibule. This expensive covering was, as Karin Walton has noted, 'made up of rectangles or "skins" of leather, faced with foil, embossed with a pattern of putti and painted in colours', and was provided with a frieze of vine leaves and grapes and with narrow leather strips to cover the joins between the skins. Dyrham's gilt leather closet still retained its pre-Georgian leather hangings in 1742; indeed, this covering still survives today.

Early wallpapers often imitated the patterns of contemporary fabric or leather hangings, but were far cheaper than either textiles or leather. This remained the case even after the wallpaper tax of 1712 imposed a duty of 1d per yard of paper. (This measure, introduced by the Tory government to pay for the War of the Spanish Succession which ended the following year, was not actually repealed until 1836.) By 1740 papers which mimicked architectural forms – columns, pediments, temples, pillar and arch designs – were widespread, as were designs resembling blocks of marble or other fine stone.

English wallpaper manufacture, so often in the shadow of the French industry, was given a terrific boost in 1746 with the return from Italy of John

Baptist Jackson, the charismatic designer. Although the success of his oil-coloured papers proved to be short-lived, the trade reverting to the traditional distemper colours after oils had proved unreliable and unwieldy, Jackson established new standards of quality and greater ambitions in the fledgling English industry. His engraved versions of Italian Old Master paintings, designed to be used in combination with a paper background and paper borders, were especially popular. In 1753 Horace Walpole, always in the vanguard of taste, was hanging one of the parlours at his Hollywood-Gothick retreat of Strawberry Hill 'with a stone-coloured Gothic paper and Jackson's Venetian prints'. In the same year Edward Dighton was granted a patent to produce hand-coloured papers printed by copper and brass plates operated by a rolling press. No examples of Dighton's papers have so far surfaced; nor indeed were continuous roller presses in general use until the end of the eighteenth century. However, Dighton's invention neatly demonstrated how rapid the pace of industrial advance was becoming in Georgian Britain.

Partly as a result of Jackson's indefatigable self-promotion, by the mid-1750s English wallpapers – especially flocks, made from wool clippings applied to glued patterns – were all the rage in France, and were being widely

Hogarth's intimate *Family Party* of c.1740, one of a number of delightful middle-class interiors Hogarth depicted during the 1740s.

Right This early eighteenth-century wallpaper from Wickenford Court, Worcestershire, with its lively pattern of flowers, foliage and pine cones, shows how colourful English wallpapers of the period could be. The modern impression of eighteenth-century interiors being couched in reticent, pale colours is, as this detail shows, often quite misplaced.

used to replace old fabric hangings. No less an arbiter of style than the celebrated mistress of Louis XV, Madame de Pompadour, chose English flock papers for her redecoration project at Versailles. In England, in the same year, Lady de Grey actually took down her expensive and prestigious but now sadly old-fashioned stamped leather hangings from the pavilion walls at Wrest Park and hung wallpaper in their place. Using the most expensive flock papers, however, could prove as expensive as buying the textiles these papers were designed to mimic. Lady Mary Wortley Montagu wrote in 1749, 'I have heard the fame of paperhangings, and had some thoughts of sending for a suit but was informed that they are as dear as damask here which put an end to my curiosity.' If flocks were too costly, then mock flocks – papers using two or more paint colours in a combination designed to give the impression (at least from a distance) of a raised pile – would do.

In North America wallpapers were imported from Britain from the turn of the century – the earliest reference to wallpapers being found in the 1700 inventory of a Boston stationer. (The best fabrics were also imported from Britain, although these were often copied by resourceful local textile workshops.) However, during the first half of the eighteenth century papers in North America were, on account of their high cost, largely limited to use in the wealthier homes. Those who could not afford imported wallpapers turned instead to the practice of stencilling simple patterns onto plaster or even onto panelled walls, using bright distemper colours – an American tradition which has continued to this day.

Wallpapers were sold in 12-yard lengths or 'pieces', made by glueing together individual sheets of hand-made paper, which were then separately hand-blocked or hand-coloured. The paper was made not from wood pulp but from soiled rags, the sorting of which was a detestable job inevitably given to working-class women, who ran the risk of succumbing to the fatal diseases spread by the fleas and lice in the rotten fabric.

The earliest printed papers were in black and white, and often called 'domino' papers after the French 'dominotiers' who specialized in this kind of product. These monochrome papers could subsequently be coloured by hand, a lengthy process which made the end product excessively expensive. By 1730 most coloured papers were in fact hand-blocked using distemper colours. The blocks used for this process were made from two layers of cheap softwood, stuck together with their grains running at right angles, topped with a layer of more costly, grainless hardwood such as pear or sycamore – a wood which could take elaborate carving well. This laminated construction method was designed so that the block would not warp too much after being in contact with the paint, or the water used to wash it off, for some time. The piece of paper was passed along a table, and each section block-printed by hand, using locating pins at the corners to make sure the next block's pattern would be correctly aligned with the last one. Yet while the patterns may have been reasonably accurate, the quality of the paint colour itself was highly variable. As wallpaper historian Treve Rosoman has noted, 'if one looks closely at the paint on old wallpaper using a magnifying glass, it is possible to see granules of colour and the bubbles left behind as the colour dried.'

Window curtains, unheard of in most households before 1700, were beginning to be regarded as an affordable luxury by 1730. In 1728 Philip Dormer, the Fourth Earl of Chesterfield wrote to Henrietta Howard at Marble Hill that ships of the East India Company had just brought with them 'an extreme fine Chinese bed', and chintz bed and window curtains to match. These window curtains would probably have been disposed in the 'festoon' manner, drawn vertically from a pelmet above. At Dyrham Park in 1710 most of the rooms were provided with festoon curtains in red and white, although the Great Hall and Parlour had paired curtains; by 1742, however, the house's best bedchamber boasted 'Two Pair of Yellow silk Damask Window Curtains Vallens [valances] & Cornishes wth rods', with '2 Pair of stufe Window Curtains & rods' hanging in front of the expensive damask. By the middle of the century paired curtains could also be arranged in the 'drapery' manner, drawn up towards the two upper corners of the window architrave. More modest households, however, would have probably hung only a single piece of material, nailed to the architrave or to a wooden lath which

These fabric designs of the 1730s and '40s are all English, but their Chinese-derived patterns clearly demonstrate that Palladian influence on furnishing fabrics was, by 1750, still minimal.
Top Design by Anna Maria Garthwaite for silk material to be woven at Spitalfields, 1744; *bottom right*, a chinoiserie silk of the 1730s; *bottom left*, a Spitalfields silk of 1738. By 1740 the Spitalfields silk industry had begun its terminal decline, demand for silk having been cut by the new availability of cheaper cotton fabrics.

Right and *far right*
Embroidered chair-seat
covers of c.1730, made in
London and showing scenes
from Gay's *Fables*. The
example opposite depicts a
middle-class interior in
incredible detail.

projected over the window. By 1730, references to paired curtains, drawn horizontally rather than vertically, were becoming increasingly common.

The purpose of these early curtains was not to keep neighbours' curiosity out and warmth in; wooden window shutters already fulfilled these functions. Curtains were primarily intended to exclude direct light during the day, saving valuable pictures or furnishings from irreparable damage. They were therefore usually made of a lightweight material. Indian or cheap British calicoes, or the new, more refined cotton chintzes, were particularly suited to this purpose; alternatively, the more prosperous households could use silk. In 1735 the curtains at Temple Newsam House near Leeds were described as being of crimson 'In Grain [ie reversible] Silk'. Even more ostentatious than the silk curtains were the gilded brass pulley rods with their gilded hooks.

Elaborate curtain displays such as those at Temple Newsam were generally hung by a professional, rather than the householder. An upholsterer commented in 1747: 'This Tradesman's Genius must be universal in every Branch of Furniture; though his proper Craft is to fit up Beds, Window-Curtains, Hangings, and to cover Chairs that have stuffed Bottoms.'

The methods of production used to manufacture furnishing fabrics such as curtains and upholstery improved tremendously during the Palladian period. The single most important step forward was John Kay's invention in 1733 of the flying shuttle, an ingenious device which allowed cloths to be woven that were far wider than the previous 3 feet limit – the maximum distance a weaver could reach with the hand-held shuttle. Kay's invention ran

on wheels and wooden rails, and could be easily manipulated by means of a cord. In the same year John Wyatt perfected a method by which several threads could be wound at once, using rollers rather than the human hand. Eight years later he built the first modern textile mill, in Birmingham, and by 1755 water-driven textile mills, using Wyatt's rollers, were appearing throughout the Midlands and the North – the first of the dark, satanic mills that were to revolutionize Georgian society.

Industrial and mercantile progress such as this inevitably brought anger and violence in its wake, as textile workers feared – with considerable justification – the loss of their livelihoods through the use of machines or by the import of foreign goods. In 1719 there were riots in London and Norwich in protest at the import of plain or printed calicoes (cottons used for clothes, curtains and as simple covers for beds and seat furniture) while the British textile industry was slumped in a recession. Those unlucky women who went out in public wearing calicoes had them ripped from their backs in the street by the mob. (Curtains, of course, were more difficult to reach.) The weavers of Norwich presented a petition to Parliament, declaring 'that of late yeares this most valuable part of our Trade hath been gradually decreasing till it is almost entirely lost' because of 'the prevailing Use of printed Callicoes & linnen'; the result was that they were 'noe longer able to find the poore sufficient Imployment'.

The violence that followed these protests was bitter. A victim wrote to the Norwich *Mist's Journal* in August 1719 that 'We are oppressed and insulted here in the open streets,' and that 'we are abused, frighted, stript, our clothes torn off our backs every day by Rabbles.' On 5 July the Norwich *Saturday Post* reported:

> *Last night a Parcel of Fellows got together in a Mobbish Manner and tore Peoples' calico Gowns and Petticoats off their backs...This day they assembled again in great numbers and cut and tore all the Calicos they met with...carrying in a triumphing Manner the Callicos they get upon the Top of Poles and Sticks.*

The result of the so-called 'Calico War' was a victory for the mob. An Act of 1721 forbade the sale, use or wearing of calicoes – the vendor being fined £20 for each offence and the buyer £5. By November 1722, for example, Thomas Nash, a London upholsterer, was advertising in the *Post Boy* in a desperate effort to get rid of all his calico-covered furniture. Only in 1736 did Parliament pass a measure designed to help Nash and his fellow upholsterers, exempting cotton goods which had a linen warp.

The Calico War was by no means the only instance of violent disturbances connected with the early Georgian textile trade. In 1736 the silkworkers of Spitalfields, whose industry had been built up from nothing by the refugee French Huguenots fleeing to England after 1685, rioted in protest at the recently arrived Irish immigrants who were settling locally and undercutting their prices. In 1753 even John Kay found himself besieged in his home by a baying mob of furious clothworkers. To escape from this treatment he fled to France, where he died impoverished.

Even by the mid-eighteenth century there was still considerable suspicion about imported cotton cloths. Newly fashionable cotton chintzes from India – light cottons with colourful floral or geometric patterns – were still being impounded at the dockside, a prejudice which did much to encourage the native cotton industry. However, whether Indian or British, these new cotton cloths had two enormous advantages over more traditional furnishing fabrics. Not only were they lighter than most woollen cloths; they were also washable. In an age when soot, smoke and candlewax were ubiquitous in every household, this was an important consideration. When buying new chintz curtains in the 1740s, Mrs Purefoy thought to ask her London agent, 'I suppose you will warrant its standing ye colour when it is washed.'

A useful addition to curtains were window blinds. Venetian blinds (which do not appear to have originated from Venice) were beginning to be used by 1720, as were a variety of other forms of mechanical cloth, wood or metal blind. Pamela Clabburn cites a London upholsterer of 1729 advertising that he 'made and sold Window Blinds of all Sorts, Painted in Wier, Canvas,

Far left A needlework carpet made for Aston Hall, near Birmingham, in the 1750s, with the Holte family arms stitched into the centre. *Left*, a rare, green-painted snob screen at Peckover House. Removable blinds such as this, made of fabric or wood and set in a robust wooden frame, were designed not to keep out the sun but to shield the inhabitants from the gaze of curious passers-by.

Cloth and Sarcenet, after the best and most lasting manner so that if ever so dull and dirty they will clean with sope and sand and be like new' – a solution which, she comments, 'sounds very drastic'.

Window blinds spread as households bought increasing quantities of valuable furnishings which needed to be protected from direct light. Carpets, for example, had been rare even in the grandest homes in 1700, but within 40 years were appearing in countless middle-class homes. An advert in the Opposition newspaper *The Craftsman* of August 1740 offered 'many fine carpets from three to four yards square, and others from six to seven yards long and proportionable Weadths, extremely useful for Dining-Rooms etc with Hearth and Bed-side Carpets of excellent Patterns and Fineness'. The 1710 inventory for Dyrham Park, though, lists only three rooms as having carpets; rush or straw mats were placed in principal entrances and coarse cloth coverings were used to cover the stairs.

Luxury carpets were also used as table coverings, a practice which persisted in America for two centuries but which had died out in Britain by 1750. As Pamela Clabburn has noted, 'As late as 1727 *Chambers' Cyclopaedia* defines the word ["carpet"] as "a sort of covering to be spread on a table, trunk, an astrade [dais] or even a passage or floor", implying that its use on floors was minimal.'

The carpets used to cover both tables and floorboards in the early eighteenth century would invariably have been the highly expensive and brightly coloured flat-weave or knotted examples imported from the Ottoman or Persian Empires. These carpets were extremely expensive, and would only have been used in the best rooms of the house. Only fabulous creations such as James Thomson's luxurious 'Castle of Indolence' could boast 'halls, where, who can tell/What elegance and grandeur wide expand/The pride of Turkey and of Persia land'. Most households were by the middle of the eighteenth century turning instead to native alternatives.

British production of hand-knotted carpets had ceased altogether by 1700. However, by 1720 many women were making their own needlework coverings, some of which deliberately mimicked the colours and patterns of the oriental knotted carpets. One ambitious but anonymous needleworker even reproduced the Roman mosaic pavement excavated with great fanfare at Littlecote in Oxfordshire in 1732. Such complex patterns were often, as is the case with needlepoint today, roughed out by a professional on paper and then worked by the (invariably female) customer. In the late 1740s Wright and Elwick of Wakefield were advertising 'draws for all Sorts of Needle Work for Carpets, Beds, Chairs, Fire Screens etc'. The results were not, though, always as impressive as the Littlecote carpet. In 1751 the diarist and bluestocking Mrs Delany wrote that a friend of hers was working on 'a *fright* of a carpet' in needlepoint.

By 1755 the first experiments in reviving the English hand-knotted carpet industry were being conducted in London (at Fulham and Moorfields), in Axminster and in Exeter. For 20 years, however, a native industry specializing in the production of pile carpets had been prospering. In 1735 a factory had been set up at Kidderminster in Worcestershire to produce pile carpets, a form in which the worsted warp was brought to the surface in a loop. This practice was said to have originated in Brussels; hence looped pile carpets were generally called 'Brussels' carpets. When the loops were cut, to produce an effect rather like velvet, the carpet was known as a 'Wilton', after the second great pile carpet factory, set up in Wilton, Wiltshire in about 1740 at the behest of the Architect Earl of Pembroke himself. By 1750 native Brussels and Wilton carpets were all the rage; Wiltons were even being supplied to the household of King George II.

Kidderminster also produced coarse, reversible flat-weave carpets known as 'ingrains', and close relatives of these called 'list' carpets, both of which were often used for stairs, hallways and other areas which saw much traffic but where marble or stone was either too expensive or for structural reasons was impossible to install. By 1755 ingrains were also being manufactured at Kilmarnock in Scotland, a town which soon became the world centre of utilitarian carpet production. One of the Kilmarnock factory's most popular products was that rudimentary alternative to the ingrain, the horsehair carpet. In 1747 the household sage Hannah Glasse – the Georgian precursor of Mrs Beeton – advised that 'If you lay a Stair-cloth on, let it be a Hair-cloth.'

Detail from The Breakfast
Scene', the second painting
from Hogarth's bitingly
satirical series *Marriage à
la Mode* of 1743–5. Lady
Squanderfield is taking tea
after giving a card and music
party which has lasted all
night (the chandelier's
candles having only just
been extinguished), while
her new husband has
returned from a house of ill
repute (testified by the dog's
smelling of another woman's
handkerchief). The steward
– a godly Methodist, as
evidenced by the copy of
Wesley's *Regeneration* in his
pocket – is horrified by the
pile of bills, which are
accompanied by only one
receipt. The scene not only
demonstrates the type of
expensive fittings bought by
the *nouveaux riches* of the
time, but also ridicules the
antique pretensions of the
Palladian style.

Costly carpets, like seat furniture, were often protected by even cheaper
fabric covers or 'druggets' (a term which in the early eighteenth century also
applied to coarse wool or linen hangings). As soon as house-owners were
able to buy an expensive carpet, they realized the need to protect it from
accidental wear or damage – hence the provision of cheap brown or green
protective cloths. Bare boards might also be laid with oilcloths or floorcloths,
ancestors of linoleum which were painted in imitation of luxury carpets or
marble flooring, successive layers of oil paint making them durable and
resilient. The manufacture of floorcloths had to be carried out by specialists;
in 1747 Robert Campbell noted that 'In the Turner's Shop we generally meet
with Floor-Cloths, painted in Oil Colours, which is performed by a Class of
Painters who do little else.' The most popular floorcloth patterns appear to
have been those which suggested tessellated, black-and-white marble blocks.
However, many of those which have survived in North America are of a
block-printed design based on the patterns of oriental or pile carpets.

The earliest reference to a floorcloth in use in the English-speaking
world is, as Peter Thornton tells us, to be found in the inventory of the
possessions of the Governor of New York and Massachusetts, who died in
1728. The description of 'Two old checkered canvas's to lay under a table'
seems to fit; certainly eight years later imported English floorcloths were being
advertised in a Charleston (SC) newspaper. As was so often the case the
colonists had to make do with what the mother country saw fit to mark up
and export. By the middle of the eighteenth century, however, this tiresome
custom was beginning to gall the increasingly restive colonial population.

AND NOW, UNVEIL'D, THE TOILET STANDS DISPLAY'D

Alexander Pope, *The Rape of the Lock*, I, 1714

Left **Tapestry from the cheval firescreen at Peckover House, Wisbech, embroidered by Jane Jessup (who later married the owner of Peckover) in c.1750. The seventeenth-century building depicted with great clarity is possibly old Wisbech Castle.**

Not every aspect of the Palladian home was brightly coloured or spacious. Many of the rooms that the visitors did not see were cramped and insanitary; inevitably, these constituted the preserve of the servants or the lodgers. Many households, especially in urban areas, took in young working men as lodgers. In 1725 Benjamin Franklin, newly arrived in London and training as a printer, lodged with a widow in Duke Street in St James's; 12 years later another new arrival in the capital, Samuel Johnson, was told that 'A man might live in a garret at eighteen-pence a week', and that 'few people would inquire where he lodged', a coffee-house sufficing for his ostensible address.

Young Benjamin or Samuel may have lived in what they considered to be comparative poverty, but the servants generally had a far harder time of it. They were, in Dan Cruickshank's words, 'parcelled around the house in a most ad hoc manner to suit the convenience of the family'. This could involve sleeping in corridors, or even under the kitchen table. Those servants that slept in bedrooms in the attic – the coldest part of the house in the winter and the hottest in the summer – were the lucky ones. Others were provided with beds that let down from the walls in the hallways, store-rooms or kitchen. In most cases the servants' accommodation was kept well away from that of the family or families who lived there; as the specifier for the Bristol merchant's house of 1724 advised, it was always best for the family to eat far from the 'Common Servants from whom they seldom learn any good'.

Above **Design for a fireplace from Abraham Swan's** *The British Architect* **of 1745.**

Detail from 'The Death of the Countess', the last scene from Hogarth's series *Marriage à la Mode*, engraved in 1745. The decoration of the room is indicative of the Countess' financial plight: the floorboards are bare, uncovered by carpets or floorcloths and not even painted, while the basic, stile-and-rail panelling of the walls has been finished with the cheapest of all oil paints, a simple, brown wood colour. Even the food – about to be stolen by the emaciated dog – is poor fare: a pig's head. The silverware on the table is almost the only reminder of the family's former wealth.

The kitchen, on account of its warmth as well as its role as the provider of sustenance, was often the centre of the house for the servants. Few were of the Brobdingnagian order described by Jonathan Swift in his *Gulliver's Travels* of 1726:

> *The King's kitchen is indeed a noble building, vaulted at top, and about six hundred foot high. The great oven is not so wide by ten paces as the cupola at St Paul's: for I measured the latter on purpose on my return. But if I should describe the kitchen-grate, the prodigious pots and kettles, the joints of meat turning on the spits, with many other particulars, perhaps I should be hardly believed...*

Yet many kitchens were surprisingly sophisticated. By 1740 fashionable kitchens in the great urban centres may have had ball-valves to control the mains water supply, a feature which allowed the cook and kitchen maid to draw off only as much water as they required for each task. The kitchen may also have had one of the first cast-iron kitchen ranges, with a cradle-grate on legs, movable cheeks (operated from side to side by a rack-and-pinion system), swinging trivets to support a kettle or pot over the fire, and possibly a 'fall bar' at the top of the grate basket which could fold down to act as a further support for pots and pans. Clockwork mechanisms could, in the larger kitchens, be harnessed to rotate the joint over the fire. By 1750 the updraught in the chimney was sometimes exploited by an ingenious smoke

Far left **A cast-iron kitchen range with firebars, sliding cheeks and spit-racks, made for Seaton Delaval, Northumberland, between 1718 and 1729 and now in York Castle Museum.**
Left **Bread ovens of the late 1740s from the kitchen at 10 Upper Ormonde Quay, Dublin.**

jack, tin vanes in the flue being rotated by the draught to provide the power for the spit, relayed by a series of pulleys and chains. At the same time, 'perpetual ovens' (iron ovens with a grate underneath) were beginning to appear; in 1750 the Reverend John Lister paid over 4 guineas for a perpetual oven for his Halifax home.

Not all new kitchen equipment was necessarily a step forward. The new fashion for copper pans in the Georgian kitchen, for example, was potentially lethal. One cookery writer of the 1750s pointed out that acid fruit and vegetable juices and even butter could produce 'Verdigrease, a rank caustic Salt; in plain Terms, a Poison!'. Yet wholesalers and cooks still clung to the dangerous habit of adding copper salts to vegetables and pickles 'to give them a more enticing Green Colour by various fraudulent arts'.

Even the meanest kitchen would have been constructed largely out of stone, as a sensible precaution against the ever-present risk of fire, which invariably started in the kitchen. The Bristol specifier of 1724 advised that even 'the Windows should also have Stones instead of Window Boards', adding rather optimistically that 'if their Dressers and Shelves could be of stone they would be desireable, for fear of Fire'. Like most of his class, the author was quick to blame the servants for most house fires: 'There is scarce a Family', he declared, 'that do not often find themselves exposd to that hazard by the carelessness of Servants putting their Candles very often under Shelves and against Wanescot Partitions; and being called suddenly to other business often forget the place where they left their light.' The most advanced parishes even maintained their own fire service – preferring not to rely on rescue by the insurance companies' machines, which even if they arrived on time were scrupulous in dealing only with fires in homes bearing the lead insignia of the appropriate company prominently on their front elevations. The 1753 parish minutes for Spitalfields, unearthed by Mark Girouard, directed 'Mr Day to

Engraving of a typical kitchen scene of the 1720s from the title page of the twelfth (1744) edition of Eliza Smith's highly successful *The Compleat Housewife*, which first appeared in 1727. The spit which has impaled the chicken is being turned by a clockwork jack, while the open hearth has been fitted with a decidedly superior Palladian surround. Hannah Glasse's renowned *The Art of Cookery made Plain and Easy* of 1747 pirated many of its recipes from Smith's ground-breaking volume.

be engineer of the parish, to take out the [fire] engines twice a quarter and play them'. Day was to be paid 2 guineas a year, and 10s 6d per fire – a remuneration which surely offered him a good incentive for arson.

If the house was not burned down by fire, it could be flooded by bursting pipes. By 1740 water reached the homes in the more sophisticated towns and cites by means of iron pipes; yet, as Neil Burton has pointed out, iron pipes 'were an expensive capital item and all the water companies shied away from wholesale installation'. Those who did not enjoy such modern amenities had to make do with wooden pipes, literally no more than hollowed-out elm tree trunks, with perhaps a lining of lead. Larger junctions in these pipes were actually created from the original junction of trunk and branch, while smaller, tributary lead pipes – destined for the ground floors of the wealthiest households – were let in to the trunks via bronze ferrules. Yet even though the joints in these elm pipes were sealed with pitch, tallow and resin, and the trunks themselves were bound with canvas or cord or even iron rings to prevent splitting, leaks were unsurprisingly common.

As cast-iron pipes were gradually introduced, so drainage improved, too. An Act of 1724 made it compulsory for London homes to have down-pipes on the front of the house connected to a parapet gutter, which would either drain rainwater onto the street or direct it into a tank for storage. Whilst this measure only applied to the capital, like most building regulations of the time it was being followed in the provinces – and indeed in the colonies – within a decade or two.

Inside, water was rarely used for bathing. The celebrated early eighteenth-century marble baths at the Duke of Devonshire's stately pile of Chatsworth and the Duke of Chandos' Middlesex palace of Cannons were regarded as aristocratic eccentricities. Most householders washed in wooden tubs filled from jugs filled from the kitchen's water supply – if, that is, they washed at all: most shared the view of the mid-century Sussex grocer Thomas Turner, recorded by Derek Jarrett, that 'a bath should be taken every spring, along with the annual blood-letting'.

No less insanitary was the lack of provision for proper lavatories. Privies, also aptly known as 'necessary houses', were occasionally erected at the end of the garden, over a cesspit. These privies would have incorporated two or three differently shaped holes – not to encourage communal excretion, but so the children did not fall through. However, not every home possessed a garden. (Perhaps this was a benefit: privies were notorious sources of disease.) Inside the house, the inhabitants used chamber pots – emptied, naturally, by the servants – often hidden in 'close stools', early commodes made of sweet-smelling cedarwood. At No 2 Fournier Street in London's

The flowers of March and November and, *right*, title page, from Robin Furber's *The Flower Garden Display'd* of 1734. This work was a cheaper, more accessible version of Furber's *The Twelve Months of Flowers* of 1730, and demonstrates that there was already a ready market for down-to-earth garden advice.

Spitalfields district there were close stools situated in small closets beside the staircase at the first and second floors, both of which were lit by external windows. Such civilized provision was, though, extremely rare. More usually, chamber pots were sited in the dining room – for quick recourse during a meal – as well as in bedroom cupboards.

Chamber pots did not have to be the only solution. As far back as 1596 Sir John Harrington had installed the world's first flushing lavatory in his house at Kelston, outside Bath. Yet it was two centuries before this marvellous invention was taken up by anyone else. In the 1720s, as Alan Hardiman has noted, the enormously wealthy Duke of Chandos – a man who gave 'conspicuous display' a new meaning, and who was obsessed with possessing the very latest accessory for his palatial home of Cannons in Middlesex – attempted to coax John Wood to design ten lavatories for the new St John's Hospital in Bath. The result was a complete failure. Although they were provided with 'Scots marble basons' and 'lead pipes to let in and out the water', Chandos observed that the lavatories conveyed 'an abominable smell from the sewer', and ordered that they be replaced with the more traditional solution of close stools inside the building and privies in the yard.

In addition to the paved yard at the rear, the middle-class Palladian house was on occasion fortunate enough to be provided with a small garden. Some homes may even have had a front garden of sorts – or at least some type of front yard, probably paved but equipped with a flowerpot or two. In Richardson's novel *Pamela* of 1740, the eponymous heroine, once more contemplating flight from Mrs Jewkes, observed that 'seeing it was no matter to get out of the window, into the front-yard, the parlour floor being almost even with the yard, I resolved to attempt it.'

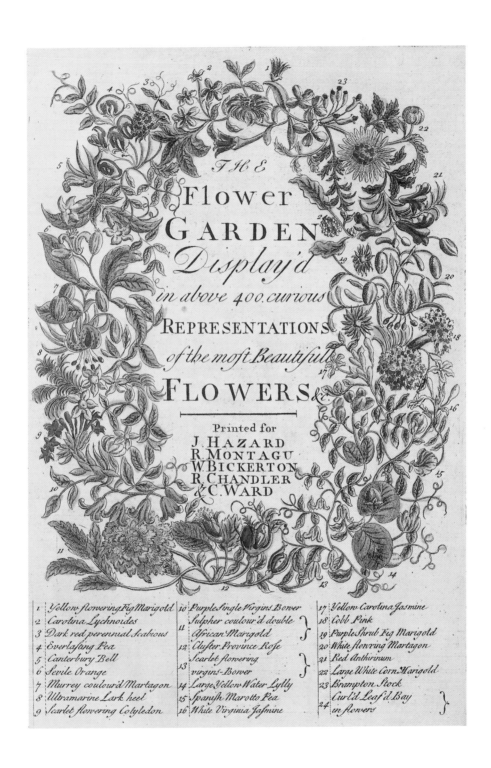

THE
Flower
GARDEN
Display'd
in above 400. curious
REPRESENTATIONS
of the most Beautifull
FLOWERS &c.

Printed for
J. HAZARD
R. MONTAGU
W. BICKERTON
R. CHANDLER
& C. WARD

1	Yellow flowering Fig Marigold	10	Purple fingle Virgins Bower	17	Yellow Carolina Jasmine
2	Carolina Lychnoides		Sulpher coulour'd double	18	Cobb Pink
3	Dark red perennial Scabious	11	African Marigold	19	Purple Shrub Fig Marigold
4	Everlafting Pea	12	Cluster Province Rose	20	White flowring Martagon
5	Canterbury Bell		Scarlet flowering	21	Red Anthirinum
6	Sevile Orange	13	virgins-Bower	22	Large White Corn Marigold
7	Murrey coulour'd Martagon	14	Large Yellow Water Lylly	23	Brampton Stock
8	Ultramarine Lark heel	15	Spanish Marotto Pea		Curl'd Leaf'd Bay
9	Scarlet flowering Cotyledon	16	White Virginia Jasmine	24	in flowers

Sutton Nicholls' view of London's Grosvenor Square, published in 1754 (but, Neil Burton believes, 'drawn somewhat earlier'), shows back gardens divided by brick walls. These gardens comprised large, presumably gravelled paths with borders of grass and flowers, and perhaps some shrubs or even topiary. Although the town garden remained, in Neil Burton's words, 'an upper-class innovation' during the 1720s, within a decade or two it was a fashion that had spread to the middle classes. As Burton has noted:

> *The garrulous Mrs Delany wrote to her sister in 1734 from her house at No 48 Upper Brook Street in Mayfair: 'You may think madam that I have no garden perhaps, but thats a mistake. I have one as big as your parlour in Gloucester and in it groweth damask roses, stocks variegated and plain, some purple, some red, pinks, philaria, some dead and some alive, and honeysuckles that never blow'. And in 1748 Mrs Edward Boscawen of No 14 South Audley Street, Mayfair, was boasting that 'My garden is in the best order imaginable, and planted with a hundred shrubs and flowers.'*

There was, however, little to guide the brave early Georgian gardener. The latest patrician landscapes of Kent or Bridgeman were of little use to the gardening enthusiast who lived in an urban terrace or rural cottage. Thomas Fairchild's *City Gardener* of 1722 was the only gardening book of the period specifically directed at the middle- or working-class household with only a small rear or front garden to dispose. Fairchild was well aware of the limitations of most of his readership. Not for them the rolling expanses of Blenheim or the carefully wrought acres of Chiswick. Fairchild's readers cultivated small rear gardens, back yards or perhaps just a balcony or windowbox. For the latter, Fairchild heartily recommended the use of a verdant covering whose popularity has never waned: Virginia creeper, a plant 'excellent for the ornament of balconies and windows and will grow so well in pots and cases that it will soon cover the walls and shade the windows if they lie exposed to the sun'. There was, Fairchild alleged, 'hardly a street, court or alley in London without some example' of Virginia creeper in 1722. Thirty years later, however, Isaac Ware was not as optimistic as Fairchild about the general chances of survival for the urban rear garden: 'Some attempt to make flower gardens of these little plots, but 'tis very idle: plants require a purer air than animals, and…they cannot live where there is so much smoake and confinement'. Instead, Ware recommended a solution horribly similar to that employed by countless modern-day city dwellers: 'to lay the whole with good sound stone pavement'. The only difference today is that modern apathetics use concrete rather than natural stone.

Title-page engraving from
Fairchild's revolutionary
The City Gardener of 1722.

Gardens were also used to site the household cesspit. But, as already noted, not every home had a garden. In 1715 those households without cesspits would have tipped their sewage into the road or thrown it over handy city walls. This detritus collected with the rainwater in the channel in the centre of the road; without pavements or gutters, it was all too easy for the pedestrian to end up there, too.

In the more sophisticated urban areas there was some provision for the removal of street waste. The flourishing, silk-weaving London parish of Spitalfields, for example, employed two 'rakers' ('that can neither read, nor write, nor speak English') at £160 a year to remove general waste – although not night soil, which remained the responsibility of the householders, who had to negotiate with the 'night men and rubbish carters'. Yet most streets and lanes remained filthy. A report of 1706 had declared of London that 'everybody knows that for a mile or two about this City, the [roads] and the ditches hard by are commonly so full of nastiness and stinking dirt, that often-times many persons…are forced to stop their noses to avoid the ill-smell.' Small wonder, then, that John Gay felt moved to pray in his 'On Walking the Streets By Night' of 1714, 'Oh! may thy Silver Lamp in Heav'n's high Bow'r/Direct my Footsteps in the Midnight Hour'.

Steps were, however, soon being taken to remedy this situation. By 1735, 16 major towns, including Liverpool and Birmingham, had introduced oil-lamps to at least some of their central streets. Liverpool erected 45 lamps as early as 1718; five years later York, not to be outdone by its Lancastrian rival, installed 50. In the capital, improvements came even sooner. An Act of 1716 required London householders to hang out lights on dark winter nights, while the 1736 City of London Lighting Act provided for the rating of Londoners in order to pay for comprehensive new street lighting. In Spitalfields in 1743 one Moses Smith was hired according to this Act to light the parish lamps at 27 shillings a year. Eighteen years earlier the Frenchman César de Saussure had been very impressed by London's new streetlamps:

> *Most of the streets are wonderfully well-lighted, for in front of each house hangs a lantern or a large globe of glass, inside of which is placed a lamp which burns all night. Large houses have two of these lamps suspended outside their door by iron supports, and some houses even four.*

Yet few streets outside London and the major cities of Britain and North America could boast such luxury. Usually the night-time street was the habitat of the thief, the burglar – and, of course, the night-soil man. In 1748 the German visitor Peter Kalm was, as Derek Jarrett has recorded, 'impressed with the care with which Londoners gathered up night soil and sold it, rather than flinging it at one another in a coprophiliac orgy'.

The street not only witnessed the disposal of household waste, but also the arrival of household fuel. As the eighteenth century progressed, the supply of coal, the fuel of the Industrial Revolution, became more common – at least in the streets of urban centres such as London and Philadelphia.

Silver candlesticks of the Palladian era, showing the development of this most prestigious of table decorations during the 40 years after George I's accession. *From the left*, a squat, fluted candlestick made in Exeter in 1717 by John Elston; a snuffer stand of the mid-1720s, made by James Gould; a chamber candlestick of 1720 by the Huguenot refugee Augustin Courtauld; and a sophisticated John Cafe design of 1749.

Coal cellars were sited under the pavement (if one existed) or directly under the street itself; they were accessed through a hole in the road, and covered with a cast-iron manhole.

Inside the home, coal or wood fires often provided one of the principal sources of light once dusk had fallen. Few households could afford more than a few rushlights or a handful of candles. Rushlights were the cheapest solution, yet the light they provided was dim and erratic. More expensive and reliable, and thus more socially respectable, were candles. Tallow candles were three or four times cheaper than those made of wax or spermaceti (the raw material most often used by New England households), but they burnt far quicker – even more rapidly than the cotton wick, which accordingly had to be constantly trimmed. Tallow candles also guttered constantly and smelt of the animals from whose fat the tallow had been rendered. However, when a tax on candles was imposed in 1709 tallow products were taxed at only one-eighth the rate of wax. This duty, levied once again to pay for the War of the Spanish Succession but not repealed until 1832, did much to ensure that the Georgian interior remained dimly lit and gloomy.

In most homes candlesticks of brass or china were used. Silver candle-sticks, one of the most eloquent symbols of taste and wealth, were only employed for wax candles, and exclusively by the well-to-do. Those seeking truly to impress the visitor, and able to afford the latest word in home lighting, used an even more extravagant candle-holder, the chandelier. The brilliance and expense of chandeliers, whether of wood, glass, brass or silver, constituted an extremely useful social indicator, one whose significance was immediately grasped by all. Conspicuous display was the order of the day when money was no object. Thus when Robert Walpole entertained the Duke of Lorraine at Houghton in 1731, in the words of Peter Thornton, 'They dined in the hall...lighted by 130 wax candles, and the saloon with 50; the

Right A characteristically architectural giltwood Palladian mirror of c.1735 from Colen Campbell's Stourhead; *far right*, an elaborate mirror of 1730, complete with shell motif and integral clock.

Right This stunning piece of Palladian furniture, the Askew Cabinet, was built in the form of a Palladian villa during the 1730s but incorporates Italian reliefs by Francesco Franelli carved a century earlier. Unfortunately, little is known about the piece, neither its maker (there is no signature or maker's mark), original location, nor subsequent provenance. In 1986, following its discovery, the cabinet was bought at auction by the National Art Collections Fund. It is currently housed at Pallant House. *Far right*, temple design from Palladio's *Quattro libri* of 1570.

whole expense in that article being computed at fifteen pounds a night'. Burlington's York Assembly Rooms, built in the same year, featured eight massive chandeliers, each provided with 14 wax candles.

Given the immense expense of candle-laden chandeliers, their owners were careful to keep them properly cleaned and maintained. In 1735 Lady Burlington directed her compliant husband that the chandelier in the Green Velvet Room at Chiswick was 'to be covered with Green silk of the same colour as the room' when not in use. To brighten the room still further, wealthy householders such as the Burlingtons would have installed multi-branched girandoles on the walls and attached candles to mirrors and even to items of furniture.

The designs even of grand items such as pier-glasses and girandoles could not, as was the case later in the century, be culled directly from engraved plates published by the leading craftsmen of the day. The pattern-books of Palladian architects contained no designs for furniture; unlike Robert Adam and his contemporaries, most Palladian designers eschewed furniture in favour of strictly architectural subjects. As a result, furniture-makers tended to turn to the English Baroque tradition they knew best. There were notable exceptions to this rule such as John Channon, a gifted designer well aware of continental predilections for brass and tortoiseshell inlays and similar refinements. However, Channon was a rarity. Thus, while British architecture progressed to new forms and new philosophies, with an emphasis on clarity,

rationality and lightness, the furniture of the period remained stuck in a time-warp. The resulting heaviness of Palladian furniture not only ensured it retained the imposing nature of seventeenth-century designs; it also precluded any serious attempt to revive Palladian furniture in later decades. It took the genius of men such as Thomas Chippendale and Robert Adam to break free of this weighty Baroque legacy. And while their furniture designs have remained perennially popular throughout the nineteenth and twentieth centuries, Palladian furniture has remained an acquired – and thus a fairly expensive – taste. 'Chippendale' and 'Sheraton' furniture abound today, but few popular reproductions have ever been made of the furniture designs of William Kent or John Channon.

What *was* new about Palladian furniture was its architectural emphasis – a tendency which was hardly surprising given the background of the most influential furniture designer of the Palladian era, William Kent. Kent's furniture was as massively three-dimensional as the masonry of his buildings. Crammed with favourite motifs such as scallop shells, dolphins, masks, heavy floral swags, huge brackets and weighty scrolls, his tables and chairs dominated any interior they graced. Kent was particularly fond of side and pier tables which, although small in size, were usually provided with massive scrolled legs or a single support in the shape of an eagle or another suitably classical element. In proper Italian style, most of his small table tops were not of wood but of marble or scagliola, while most of his grand tables and seat furniture were heavily gilded. Although Kent's furniture seems excessively demonstrative today, it did serve as a useful example to those designers

Left Characteristically heavy
and architectural seat
furniture by William Kent,
adorned with Kent's
favoured shell motif. These
designs were engraved for
John Vardy's *Some Designs of
Mr Inigo Jones and Wm Kent*
of 1744, a publication which
was primarily designed not
as a monument to Jones but
as a public showcase for
Kent's many talents. This
lavish tribute seems to have
paid off; as Eileen Harris
has pointed out, on Kent's
death in 1748 it was Vardy
who was appointed to erect
the Kent-designed Horse
Guards building.

Left A marble-topped side
table in typically heavy
Palladian fashion, by
Benjamin Goodison; *far left*,
a parcel-gilt console table of
roughly 20 years later, with
prominent mouldings and
shell motif.

who followed him. As Michael Wilson has observed, by the 1750s and '60s,
'men such as Benjamin Goodison and Matthias Lock created "Kent" furniture
of quality, adding to it fresh characteristics of their own. Lock in particular
was not afraid to mix the pomposities of Kent with the frivolities of the
true Rococo.'

Kent's furniture was largely limited to the great houses of the rich,
whose large rooms could accommodate the ostentatious theatricality of his
designs. (It is this individuality, and the absence of any popular market for
his work, that has perhaps made Kent's furniture designs so impervious to
reproduction or revival.) Yet, outside the charmed circle of patrons who
could afford William Kent's elaborate confections, chairs of the Palladian era
were still definably different from their contemporaries of Louis XV's France.
French examples were more rounded; British chairs were more architectural
in form, with squared frames and squared upholstery. British upholstery was
formed using stitched edges and visible tufts; edges were often nailed, with
large and widely spaced brass nails.

More humble Palladian chairs either mimicked the latest French or
Dutch styles or, more commonly, relied on traditional, seventeenth-century
patterns – a typical example of the latter being the plain but ubiquitous
'Dutch' ladder-back chair. Such modest seat furniture was generally either
caned, provided with a rush seat, upholstered in leather or in fabric, or
painted – usually in green if the furniture was for a middle- or working-class
home. Backs could be laddered or given a single, broad splat. Cabriole legs
were, from about 1715, often fitted with ball-and-claw feet – the invention
of which is, like so many other aspects of eighteenth-century furniture, often
erroneously attributed to Chippendale.

Francis Hayman's *Grosvenor Bedford with his Wife Jane and Son Charles* of c.1747–8 portrays a modest but fashionable interior of the time, which includes a modern chair and circular table and a costly marble fireplace (complete with requisite Jonesian face mask) on which has been placed tasteful blue-and-white china. Grosvenor Bedford was a close ally of the Walpole family, and received a number of sinecures from the Prime Minister, Robert Walpole, prior to the latter's fall in 1742 – most notably that of the Collectorship of Customs at Philadelphia.

One chair form that was wholly new was the Windsor chair. A cheap, simple and highly versatile form, which needed no upholstery or caning, the Windsor proved instantly popular both at home and abroad. It was soon being widely exported to Europe and sent in bulk to the colonies, where it was quickly copied and adapted. The original design for the Windsor chair may have been borrowed from Regency France: the first recorded use of the term occurs in 1724, when Lord Percival's wife was carried around the grounds of Hall Barn, Buckinghamshire (close by the source of the chairs' manufacture) 'in a Windsor chair like those at Versailles'. Ivan Sparkes has noted that three years later the London cabinetmaker John Brown was advertising 'All sorts of Windsor Garden chairs of all sizes painted green or in the wood'. Windsors were made wholly of wood, with the legs and back separated by the thick seat, into which all the principal members were anchored. The turned spindles and legs were made of beechwood by the itinerant chair 'bodgers' of Buckinghamshire's Chiltern Hills, and then taken to a nearby town, where they were incorporated into the finished chair. By 1800 High Wycombe had emerged as the furniture-making capital of the Chilterns, and indeed of the country. Windsors are first recorded as having

Furniture of the 1720s, '30s and '40s. *Clockwise from top left*, a baluster-splat armchair of c.1730, with fashionable mahogany veneer and prominently featuring one of the hallmarks of Palladian interior design – the shell motif; a walnut wing chair of c.1720 with contemporary needlework upholstery, cabriole legs and claw and ball feet; a classic beechwood Windsor chair, now in Gloucestershire; an ebonized armchair with decorated splat from Edenton, North Carolina; an Irish, red-upholstered walnut dining room chair of c.1740; and a tall fruitwood hall chair.

been made in High Wycombe in 1732; the name 'Windsor' may either refer to the nearby town of Windsor, from where they were sent by river to London, or may simply have been a piece of astute marketing, associating this most utilitarian of chairs with the sovereign's seat.

Windsor chairs could be made in a variety of ways. The 'comb-back', with its straight sticks thrusting up from the seat in the manner of a rake or comb, was particularly popular in the early eighteenth century. (It was while sitting on a revolving comb-back from Philadelphia that Thomas Jefferson penned the Declaration of Independence.) However, it is the bow-back, with its single, curved arm and rounded back bow, which proved the most enduring form. This chair – a version of which was on offer in Chippendale's *Director* of 1754 – first appeared around 1740, and offered a stronger and more comfortable back than the straight-backed varieties already being produced. A further variant of this was the 'Philadelphia low-back', a lower chair common in the City of Brotherly Love by 1750; this in turn became the inspiration for the ubiquitous 'smoker's bow' of the Victorian era.

Sometimes attempts were made to drag the humble Windsor chair into the fashionable salon. More pretentious examples were provided not with turned but with somewhat inappropriate curved cabriole legs; some even had ball-and-claw feet, in the fashion of the French seat furniture of the day. Others were even grander: Ivan Sparkes cites the instances of 'the seven japanned Windsor chairs which the Duke of Chandos had made for his library at Cannons in 1725 and the carved mahogany chairs reported to have been made for the library of the Prince of Wales about 1730'. The virtue of the Windsor chair, however, was its sturdy simplicity and resilient construction. It was these qualities which immediately endeared the form to the American colonies and which ensured its longevity.

Cabinets and bureaux of the Palladian era still retained much of the bulk and weight of their seventeenth-century ancestors. (In Britain, incidentally, the term 'bureau' signifies a desk with drawers and a hinged writing-flap, concealing pigeonholes and more, tiny drawers; in North America it indicates a straightforward chest of drawers.) They were, however, now more architectural in form, often with weighty urns or broken pediments surmounting the cornice, and without the marquetry inlay which had been so popular in the preceding century.

For those with more sophisticated tastes and larger purses, chests, cabinets and writing desks in walnut were very popular. By 1720 these were often decorated with an inlaid sunburst – a motif borrowed from Holland – and were being set on stands with curved cabriole legs. In the quest for architecturally derived design, chests and cabinets were often provided with

Right Architecturally modelled English and American cabinets and desks of the Palladian era. *Clockwise from top left,* a splendid corner cabinet from Salem, Massachusetts; a rectilinear writing desk of c.1720; a tall writing desk of 1726, now at Winterthur, Maryland; an English walnut kneehold desk of c.1720; a charming bookcase of 1765–75 from Charleston, South Carolina, with two types of glazing for the shelves; and a walnut burr cabinet of the 1720s. All of this sophisticated furniture has surprisingly clean, vertical lines and little evidence of fussy decoration.

columns or pilasters at their front corners, while the drawers were given additional architectural emphasis by way of a bead moulding. The 'bachelor chest' (a narrow chest of drawers with a hinged top which folded forward for writing) was introduced, as was the French 'commode', a small chest whose drawers were hidden by two doors. By 1750 commodes were beginning to depart from the staunchly squared form typical of previous decades and were being made with French, Rococo-style serpentine fronts.

By the middle of the eighteenth century the most fashionable item of furniture was the 'japanned' cabinet or chest of drawers, a lacquered piece either imported by the East India Company from the Far East or imitated by native cabinetmakers. By 1800 the term 'japanned' referred not to genuine oriental work but to English lacquering; in 1720, however, the distinction was blurred.

For those who preferred their furniture unlacquered and unpainted, by 1730 West Indian mahogany was fast replacing walnut as the most fashionable wood for large items. In addition to its rich colour, mahogany was both harder than walnut and less liable to warp, and could be obtained in larger pieces than walnut, box or other woods fashionable in the Stuart era. (Although walnut is also a 'hardwood', this term can be misleading. Beech, for example, although a hardwood, is actually softer and more at risk from infestation than softwoods such as Douglas fir.) Following the abolition of the duty on imported timber in 1721 – an unusual instance in the Palladian period of the removal, rather than the imposition, of a tax on constructional materials – the use of mahogany for furniture-making, if not yet for interior decoration, soared.

Expensive woods such as walnut and mahogany were invariably used for the traditional four-poster bed, equipped with rich bed-hangings and a valance or cornice. By 1715 a cheaper variant of the well-known four-poster form had appeared: the 'angel' bed, with no posts but a large tester suspended by chains from the ceiling or wall. Grand beds such as these would have been provided with 'case-curtains', simple wool hangings wrapped around the bed to protect the valuable bed-hangings underneath. Increasingly, though, grand Palladian beds tended to dispense with heavy, Baroque hangings in order to emphasize the architectural woodwork of the cornice and back. At the other end of the social scale, beds for children or for servants doubled as tables – when they were known, for fairly obvious reasons, as 'table beds' – or even as part of the wall panelling, from which they were let down to a horizontal position by pulley.

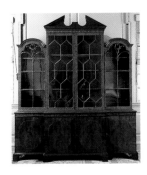

Library writing tables, with kneeholes and supports fitted with drawers or cupboards, grew in size after 1720. Some were fitted with hinged tops,

The Damask Bedchamber (*right*) and Lady Suffolk's Bedchamber (*far right*) at Marble Hill. The Damask Bedchamber was originally provided not only with red damask curtains but also with crimson flock wallpaper. Scraps of the 1720s flock were discovered recently; however, they were too small to enable exact reproduction, so an equivalent paper of the same period, with a large pomegranate pattern, has been hung here. The bed itself – again, not original to this room, but similar to the bed described in the house's inventory of 1767 – is of carved mahogany, rather than the traditional walnut, and features a prominent band of Vitruvian scroll ornamentation on the cornice. Lady Suffolk's Bedchamber, with another imported Palladian bed, is bisected by an Ionic screen similar to the one installed by Roger Morris in the Colonnade Room at Wilton House in 1735.

Right This detail from the fourth scene of Hogarth's *Marriage à la Mode*, begun in 1743, shows the Countess at her levee, being attended to by her hairdresser – and her lawyer, Silvertongue – in front of a suitably fashionable mirror, complete with Earl's coronet and Kentian shell decoration. In the foreground are various trivial *objets d'art*, bought at the auction of the effects of one Sir Timothy Babyhouse. The page, in pointing to Actaeon's horns, is emphasizing the adulterous affair that is clearly brewing between the Countess and her advisor.

which could be raised to support a hefty book. The weighty English library writing tables of the 1740s – a classic form that was to culminate in William Vile's and Thomas Chippendale's sumptuous tables of the 1750s – were decorated in pompously Kentian manner, with ovals of ribbon, heavy brass rings, pilasters and terms, masks and shells. In contrast, the dining tables of the time were simple rectangular compositions with stout, turned legs; the D-ended, multi-leaved table did not come into general use until the end of the eighteenth century.

While the dining table was still made from native walnut or other English hardwoods, the crockery used in households sophisticated enough to prefer porcelain to earthenware was invariably imported. The great English porcelain factories were only in their infancy in 1750. What we now know as the 'Potteries' region around Stoke-on-Trent was known not for the delicate Wedgwood wares with which it was intimately associated after 1760 but for rough-and-ready white, salt-glazed Staffordshire stoneware and for oddly variegated 'tortoiseshell' earthenware. (In the mid-1750s the *Boston Gazette* advertised 'new fashioned Turtle-shell tureens' and 'Tortoise Shell Teapots' recently imported from England.) The middle classes who sought more delicate dinnerware purchased porcelain from continental Europe – or, if funds were sufficient, from China itself. Particularly popular during this period was the tin-glazed Dutch earthenware known as 'Delftware', which was usually found coloured in blue and white (in imitation of genuine Chinese porcelain) but could also be found in brown or red. Also popular for both dining services and vases was the more colourful tin-glazed ware

A Colonial dining room from East Derry, New Hampshire, recreated at Winterthur, Maryland. The splendid bowl in the centre, imported from England, is dated 1732; the furniture dates from 1725 and is in the Albany Queen Anne style.

Right Silverware by Paul de Lamerie, the most outstanding silversmith of the day; *right*, a castor dated 1743 and, *far right*, a sauce-ladle with shell bowl of c.1735. The crest on the castor is that of the Earls of Essex; that on the handle of the sauce-ladle is of the Jacksons of Kelwoold's Grove, Yorkshire.

which had traditionally been traded from the Balearic islands of Majorca and Minorca, and which had as a consequence earned the name of 'majolica'.

By the 1720s the middle and upper classes were eating their dinner – the main meal of the day – at about 2pm, breakfast having been taken at around 9 or 10am. Gradually, however, the dinner hour crept ever later, with the result that supper (generally a selection of cold left-overs) got so late that, as the *Tatler* was warning as early as 1710, supper was 'now in Danger of being entirely confounded and lost in Breakfast'. The food consumed at dinner was, outside the homes of the wealthy and fashionable, relatively plain fare which avoided what were perceived to be the unhealthy excesses of the French diet. 'So much is the blind Folly of this Age', wrote the pioneering cookery author Hannah Glasse in 1747, 'that would rather be impos'd on by a French Booby, than give Encouragement to a good *English* Cook'. Nevertheless, an examination of Hannah Glasse's ground-breaking and hugely successful *The Art of Cookery Made Plain and Easy* shows how far domestic cookery has come in the past 250 years. As J C Drummond and Anne Wilbraham put it in their classic study of the historic diet, *The Englishman's Food*, 'The recipes which Mrs Glasse prepared are suited to an era when a quart of the best cream, the yolks of two dozen eggs and a quart of the best Madeira were incidental items on the kitchen list.'

In the poorer households, cabbages and onions were always welcome. Root vegetables grew enormously in popularity during the Palladian era: by 1740 the turnip was not being used merely as cattle feed but also to grace the dinner tables of working- and even middle-class homes, a development which, after 1755, encouraged the import from Holland of the swede or rutabaga. Potatoes, however, were still regarded with much suspicion in most rural areas. Bradley's *Dictionary of Plants* of 1747 noted that potatoes 'are cultivated pretty plentifully about *London*, but are not I think got enough into the Notion of our Country People, considering their Profit'. In urban areas, milk often came from the town cows kept in frightfully insanitary conditions. Most cheese, however, was distributed around the country, and exported abroad, from Cheshire.

Even in relatively modest middle-class homes mealtimes were attended with a high degree of formality. Dishes were arranged symmetrically on the table, and followed a certain pattern. As Jennifer Stead describes:

> *The first course to be arranged on the table always consisted mainly of meats, roasted, boiled, stewed and fried; some with sauces. Vegetables do not generally appear except as garnish to the meat. Bread was handed round. Soup…was served and eaten first, then removed, and a fish dish put in its place. After fish, the meat, which must have by then cooled considerably, was served.*

After that came lighter dishes of fish and meat – always during this period carved by the mistress of the house – intermixed with sweet puddings; then dessert of fruit, nuts and cheese. What vegetables there were would have been liberally sauced with butter. By 1740, roast beef – invariably served with batter pudding and a suet pudding with dried fruit – had become so popular as to be immortalized by Hogarth, in his famous *Calais Gate* of 1749, as epitomizing the best of British virtues. A Swedish visitor of 1748 sagely observed that 'The Englishmen understand almost better than any other people the art of properly roasting a joint, which also is not to be wondered at; because the art of cooking as practised by most Englishmen does not extend much beyond roast beef and plum pudding.' This commentary is, sadly, almost as true today as it was two and a half centuries ago.

If wine or ale was had with dinner, it would, in the best homes, have been drunk from a 'baluster' glass – a superbly proportioned vessel, resembling a stair baluster, with a conical or tulip-shaped bowl and a thick stem with a single, heavy 'knop' or swelling. Since glass was taxed by weight (the 1745 Excise Act imposed a duty of 1d a pound on all flint-derived glass), these heavy early eighteenth-century glasses inevitably became thinner and lighter,

with three or four small knops gradually replacing the heavy, single punctuation. Many of these drinking glasses were made in Newcastle upon Tyne, a city also, as we have seen, known for its window glass. The best glass-engraving, however, was found not in Britain but in Holland, and special orders of glass were shipped from Newcastle and other eastern ports to be engraved by the Dutch specialists. By 1750 the tears which punctuated the knops were being reheated and drawn out by the glassmaker to produce spectacular filaments ('air twists') just below the surface of the knop or stem.

After dinner, foreigners were astounded to see the women leave. During his visit to England of 1727 de Saussure watched in amazement as 'the women rise and leave the room, the men paying them no attention or asking them to stay'. The purpose of this odd ceremony was not, as had become the custom by the middle of the nineteenth century, in order to leave the men to port, cigars and 'masculine' conversation. It was so that the mistress of the house could prepare after-dinner tea. Tea halved in price between 1690 and 1760 (after 1715 the country was flooded with green Chinese tea) and consequently became more widely available as the century progressed. In 1717 Thomas Twining opened the first 'Tea Shop' in London – a venture specifically directed at women, as coffee-houses had been designed for men – and by 1730 tea was regularly on sale at Vauxhall Gardens. Indeed, as Drummond and Wilbraham noted, 'The growing popularity of tea was a source of considerable anxiety to the brewers who were obliged, in order to compete with it, to brew weaker beer and to keep their prices as low as possible.' However, by 1750 tea was still a relatively precious commodity. Not only were tea-caddies made in costly silver and usually locked; it would also have been unsuitable for a mere servant to handle this most sought-after of social stimulants. Tea was initially drunk in shallow tea dishes without handles, and was drunk with sugar and with or without milk, which was believed to weaken the effect of the caffeine.

One of the few hot, non-alcoholic alternatives to tea was chocolate. Coffee was, during this period, very expensive – and difficult to fake. Chocolate, originally grated into wine, was now mixed with hot water and sugar, a commodity which itself had fallen considerably in price since the colonial gains of the 1713 peace settlement and the subsequent exploitation of the West Indian sugar plantations. In 1744 Duncan Forbes wrote that '*Sugar*, the inseparable Companion of *Tea*' had come 'to be in the Possession of the very *poorest* Housewife, where formerly it had been a great Rarity'.

Wines, of course, were regularly imported from France, Germany and, since the War of the Spanish Succession (when merchants sought an alternative to imports from France), from Portugal. Once in Britain, though, they could suffer horribly. Cheap, crude wine was 'mollified' by the addition of alum or by a judicious mixture of plaster of Paris and chalk, while lead preparations were added to make the wine sweeter and clearer – an adulteration which caused countless instances of lead poisoning. Life was clearly hazardous for the average citizen of Palladian Britain. Thankfully, there were many compensations – not all of them alcoholic.

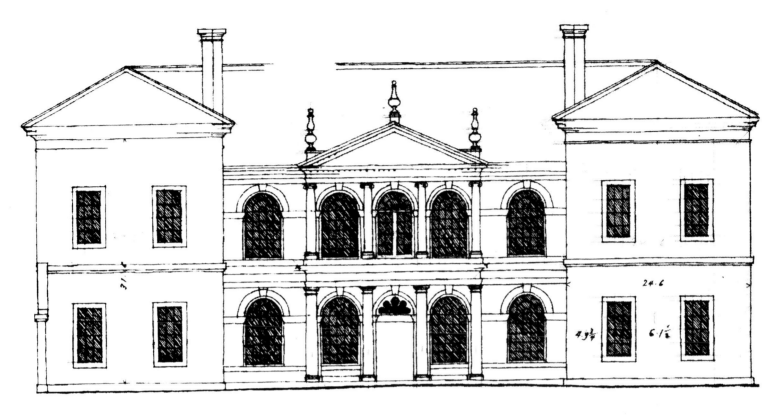

AS FOR WHAT YOU AND I DO, IT MAY BE ESTEEM'D A HUNDRED YEARS HENCE, BUT AT PRESENT DOES NOT LOOK LIKE IT, BY WHAT I SEE DOING IN THE ARCADES OF CONVENT GARDING. William Kent to the Earl of Burlington, 16 November 1732

Left Neo-Palladian façades at Richmond Riverside of the 1980s, by Quinlan Terry.

Above An Erith and Terry sketch by for Kings Walden Bury, Hertfordshire, a modern villa built for the glass magnate Sir Thomas Pilkington.

When the eclectic interior decorators of the late nineteenth century looked into the past for inspiration, they alighted not on the Palladian style but on more versatile and malleable historic forms. Owen Jones' vastly influential *Grammar of Ornament* of 1856 contained a bewildering cornucopia of decorative styles, ranging from Greek and Pompeiian to Arabian and Indian. Culled from Britain's own past were medieval, Elizabethan and even Celtic forms. But English Palladianism was wholly absent. Even the 'Renaissance' section drew on French decoration of the sixteenth century, while all of the 'Italian Ornament' was pre-Palladian.

Particularly popular by the 1870s was the 'Free Renaissance' style, a loose amalgam of fifteenth- and sixteenth-century forms from Italy and France mingled with the latest in Victorian technology. At the same time, French furniture of the eighteenth century, and English furniture of the Adam and Regency periods, were growing increasingly popular. Almost everything from the early modern era was culled – everything except Palladian design. While the publication in North America of Edith Wharton and Ogden Codman's *Decoration of Houses* of 1897 energetically promoted the French styles of the Ancien Régime, Palladianism won no similar champion there. Compared with the light, delicate designs of Louis XV's France, English Palladian furniture was deemed heavy and crude. And compared with the fashionable airiness of the Rococo and neoclassical styles, Palladian architecture was both too pompous and too restrained. Thus Palladianism missed out in the late nineteenth-century scramble for style.

The 'Queen Anne' style espoused by Norman Shaw and others in the last decades of the Victorian era had, of course, little to do with the reign of Anne, but looked instead to Wren and his late seventeenth-century contemporaries, and even to earlier Jacobean and Tudor inspirations. As Mark Girouard has pointed out, whereas those who pined for the elegance and simplicities of the Augustan age dreamed of the land of Walpole and Pope, 'Architecturally, this meant Wren and red brick rather than porticoes and Palladio.' The multi-paned sash window made a welcome return to many urban and rural streets; in the context of the red brick façades of 'Queen Anne' homes, however, they were invariably painted cream or off-white, engendering a belief which still persists today that these were the only suitable colours for Georgian sashes.

Across the Atlantic, stylistic revivals were developing along similar lines. The American Colonial Revival was initially sparked off by the Philadelphia Centennial Exposition of 1876, at which room sets 'from Olden Times' could be seen equipped with colonial tables, Windsor chairs and early kitchen ranges, and staffed by hostesses in colonial costume. The new enthusiasm for colonial design coincided with the new 'fad' for antique collecting, and for the concept of mixing contemporary designs with those of all manner of past ages. However, while celebrating the vernacular tradition of colonial America, the colonial revival did not promote any reawakening of interest in the more formal aspects of English and American Palladianism. And whereas the neo-Georgian enthusiasm rekindled by the changing tastes of the 1860s – and particularly by the 1862 International Exhibition – was eclectic in its appeal, the period the revivalists looked to was the second, rather than the first, half of the eighteenth century. Adam and Sheraton were far more appealing in their delicate virtuosity than the heavy, ostentatious academicism of Kent and Channon. As is often the case today, the style of the Adam brothers was

often, and quite wrongly, taken as a shorthand for the whole of the Georgian period; thus the 1862 exhibition catalogue advised that 'the work of the Messrs Adam' should 'be considered as indicating a style of English decorative furniture of the eighteenth century'. While the architectural historian Charles Eastlake was reluctantly admitting in the 1870s that 'eighteenth-century joinery was "sound"', and *The Builder* was acknowledging that the workmanship of the early Georgian era was 'first rate', it was to Adam and Chippendale or Sheraton and Nash, rather than to Burlington and Kent, that the interior decorators on both sides of the Atlantic inevitably turned.

By 1920 the 'Queen Anne' style had evolved into the Baroque Revival, a manner sufficiently full-blooded and theatrical to mirror the social aspirations of the nouveaux riches, the corporate ambitions of the commercial world and the imperial confidence of inter-war governments. 'Queen Anne' had been lively and versatile in the hands of designers as gifted as Norman Shaw, Ernest Newton and Edwin Lutyens; however, as interpreted by more pedestrian practitioners such as Sir Herbert Baker, the buildings of the Baroque Revival – whether inserted into the heart of the City of London or erected to mark some far-flung colonial outpost – became boorish, overblown and even tedious.

On occasion, Palladianism could be adapted to serve the English country house. In 1903, for example, work started on Ernest George and Alfred Yeates' Mannerist-Palladian garden front for Lionel Dugdale's new home of Crathorne Hall in Yorkshire; even here, though, Palladianism was considered too stentorian for the whole composition, and a lively Jacobean style was chosen for the entrance front.

Palladian Revival interiors were even rarer, on either side of the Atlantic. In general, only a large country house or grand townhouse possessed rooms spacious enough to accommodate the heavy bulk of the grand, Kentian style which most decorators and designers associated with the Palladian taste. The insuperable problem for would-be Palladian revivalists was the style's strict hierarchy of form. In the early eighteenth century, smaller rooms would have been provided with relatively modest mouldings and decoration. House-owners of the nineteenth and twentieth centuries, however, invariably wanted something more pretentious and flashy. Yet the grand Palladianism of Chiswick or Houghton looked ludicrously oversized in an averagely sized room. Thus those who sought full-blown examples of Georgian style eschewed the heavily three-dimensional forms of Palladian Britain in favour of the low-relief and repetitive elegance of the Adam brothers, or the even more reticent style of the Regency era. Neither the mouldings nor the furniture of the villas of the 1720s were, it was found, suitable for the middle-class suburban interiors of the 1920s.

At the same time as Palladianism was consistently rejected by the interior designers, it was also shunned by the more myopic practitioners of the Modern Movement. By 1945 only two architects continued to work in a recognizably Palladian style: Francis Johnson and Raymond Erith. Johnson was born in 1911, and in 1934 began practising at Bridlington in East Yorkshire (appropriately, the birthplace of William Kent and the origin of Burlington's English title), where he has remained until the present day. Since 1945 he has largely specialized in the creation or remodelling of country houses for Yorkshire and the northeast. Johnson's style is not specifically Palladian: he borrows from all phases of the Georgian period. As he remarked in 1984, it is not so much a particular period which has influenced him, more the necessity that 'good manners and an attempt at harmony of character, scale and materials should be shown'. However, it is from the reticent, astylar Palladianism of the mid-eighteenth century that Johnson has derived his keenest inspiration. Calm and unhurried Palladian proportions, Georgian sashes, Venetian and Diocletian windows, and in particular a predilection for blank wall space are all found with great regularity in Johnson's compositions, particularly in houses such as Garrowby (rebuilt for the Earl of Halifax in 1981–2) and Settrington (remodelled for Samuel Storey after a fire in 1963).

Raymond Erith was born in Hackney in 1904, seven years before Johnson, and by 1938 had settled in the cosy rural environment of Dedham,

The calm, restrained neo-Georgian staircase at Francis Johnson's Garrowby, Yorkshire, of 1981–2.

in 'Constable Country' on the Essex–Suffolk border. Here he became increasingly influenced by the Palladian heritage which surrounded him. Clive Aslet has written of Erith that 'As he grew older he found that his taste was increasingly drawn further back in time and further south in geography, towards the inspiration of so much English Classicism – Palladio.' Erith studied Palladio's *Four Books* in immense detail, 'allowing himself', as his daughter and biographer Lucy Archer has written, 'an hour for each page because it was only by this method…that one could really learn anything'. As early as 1932, he was remarking that Alberti and his follower Palladio 'were obviously working towards a balanced theory; balanced truth: beauty'. By the 1950s he had come to some very definite conclusions about the superiority of real Georgian architecture over more recent shams:

> *The characteristic of the neo-Georgian style is that a regular elevation is forced on to a plan which, for convenience, is irregular; whereas in true Georgian architecture a regular elevation is the result of a regular plan…The point is that if one assumes, as one would with an old building, that the windows are at the centre of each room the eye will*

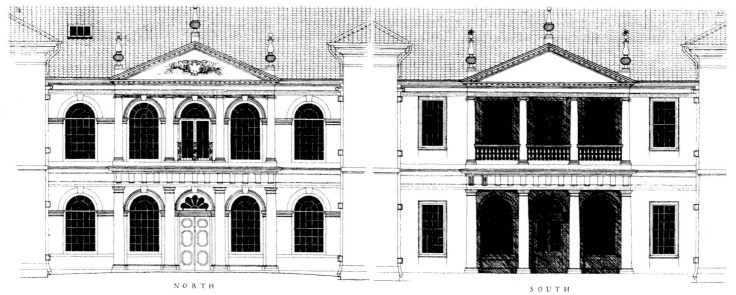

NORTH

SOUTH

Erith and Terry elevation designs for Kings Walden Bury. Begun in 1969, the central block of the south front (*right*) strongly recalls Campbell's Pembroke Lodge, Whitehall and, in its double portico, South Carolina's Drayton Hall, while the more Italianate north front (*left*) uses Roger Morris' prototypical Palladian villa of Marble Hill. The module used for this house was not the English foot but the Venetian *piede* of 14 inches. To compound the eccentricity, the bricks used here are also non-standard (even for Palladian England), being long and thin in the Tudor fashion.

understand (even if the mind may not register) the arrangement of the internal rooms by reference to the position of the windows and chimneys...

While he quoted liberally from Alberti and Palladio, many of Erith's works were unmistakably in the English Palladian tradition of Burlington, Campbell and Morris. The central portion of his 1969 villa of Kings Walden Bury in Hertfordshire, for example, bore a strong resemblance both to Campbell's Whitehall villa for the Earl of Pembroke and to Morris' Marble Hill. It was even more reminiscent of one of the most impressive and influential of all American Palladian villas, Drayton Hall in South Carolina. Inside, its bulbous stair balusters quoted the old-fashioned main staircase at Marble Hill, which itself was consciously modelled on the stair at Pratt's Coleshill – a house which in the 1720s was believed to be by Jones.

Yet perhaps Erith's greatest achievements were his more modest ones. As befitting the inheritor of the Palladian tradition, from 1959 to 1963 he comprehensively restored the London terraced home of Robert Walpole's successors, 10 Downing Street; at the same time he restored the home of the Chancellor of the Exchequer, number 11, and completely rebuilt number 12. In 1958, the year he won the commission for Downing Street, work also started on what was to become one of his most successful compositions. His Provost's House at Queen's College, Oxford is sited in the midst of the sumptuously theatrical Georgian Oxford of Nicholas Hawksmoor; yet the house neither bows to the overpowering, adjacent masonry of Queen's and All Souls Colleges nor attempts to upstage or rival the context in which it finds itself. In its use of blank wall space and isolated fenestration, the Provost's House is the most English of all Erith's Neo-Palladian works.

Erith died in 1973. For 11 years prior to his death, however, he had been training a successor. Quinlan Terry had joined Erith in Dedham in 1962, and within four years was made a partner in the firm. In 1967 Terry went

Right **Reproduction wallpaper, produced by Zoffany, based on an original eighteenth-century design found at Temple Newsam House in Leeds. Increasing numbers of genuine historic wallpaper reproductions, rather than mere reinterpretations, are now making their way onto the market; at the same time there is an encouraging revival in enthusiasm for traditional block-printed papers.**

Modern homes by Erith and
Terry in the Palladian vein.
Right, the new villa built at
Nenfield, Yorkshire, in 1979,
recalling the compositions
of the 1720s by Campbell
and Morris; *far right*, the
more eccentrically Neo-
Palladian Fawley House at
Henley, Oxfordshire,
of 1988–9.

to Rome – a journey which, as for Burlington and Kent two centuries before, was to prove hugely formative. On his return Terry not only mastered the idiom of the rural Georgian cottage and terrace, with his highly successful homes of 1967–80 in Dedham's Frog Meadow, but also that of the Neo-Palladian villa. Nenfield in West Yorkshire of 1979 is possibly his most English Palladian villa to date, bearing strong resemblances to Marble Hill and to Campbell's early essays as well as to Palladio's rural compositions.

This is not to say that Terry is wholly rooted in the language of English Palladianism. Many of his works use references from Wren and from the classicism of the second half of the seventeenth century rather than the first half of the eighteenth. His preference for steep roofs, prominent dormers and cupolas casts Terry more as the inheritor of the 'Queen Anne' movement of the late nineteenth century than as the Neo-Palladian par excellence. Terry has also been prepared to use late eighteenth-century models for his designs; thus, while his 1979 Gloucestershire villa at Waverton combines a Palladian front door with a Pratt-style elevation, the iron staircase inside is very much in the manner of the 1760s and '70s.

During the 1980s Quinlan Terry moved beyond the terrace houses and country villas that had been the mainstay of his practice into urban design. The results have not always been too successful. His Dufours Place development of 1982 in London's Soho, for example, was little more than a tediously repetitive office block, a trait also found in his unexecuted designs for the Spitalfields Market site in east London. However, Terry's massive Richmond Riverside development, begun in 1985, has found more admirers. Its varied elevations include many of the most familiar motifs of English Palladianism, especial prominence being given to that most Burlingtonian of

Quinlan Terry's Richmond Riverside development of the mid-1980s: *far left*, a courtyard dominated by sash windows and, *left*, an entrance inspired by the recurring openings at Palladio's Vicenza Basilica. The Georgian houses that originally stood on this site were demolished during the 1950s and '60s; the uncompromisingly Italianate composition of Tower House of 1858 at the southern end of the site was the only element to be reprieved from destruction, being restored in 1968. Terry's infill development is to be welcomed after years of municipal neglect. However, the muscular, asymmetrical Victorian neoclassicism of Tower House does tend to overshadow the rather pallid Neo-Palladianism of Terry's façades.

details, the Venetian window. The buildings – essentially office accommodation clad in a Palladian shell – have been criticized for the dishonest relationship between exterior and interior, and for the insipid, almost Disneyesque nature of their elevations. However, the development has won substantial praise from local residents.

For most of the postwar era, while the villa style of English Palladianism was being resurrected by Johnson, Erith and Terry, there was still a marked lack of interest in the interior decoration of the typical, middle-class Palladian home. Over the last decade, however, there has been a belated but welcome revival of interest in Palladian design. Wallpapers and fabrics from the 1720s, '30s and '40s are now available in exact reproduction, and not merely as vague reinterpretations. Domestic Palladian design is now at last being judged on its own merits, rather than as a precursor to the perennially popular style of the Adam brothers or as an eccentric antidote to the Rococo excesses of Bourbon France.

Whilst Palladianism has not enjoyed a full-blooded revival in the modern era, it has also escaped widespread censure. Indeed English Palladianism has throughout the twentieth century remained a source of fascination to the Modern Movement and its successors. With its emphasis on honesty of design and on the primacy of proportion, its appeal transcends stylistic squabbles. Palladianism is not merely a vocabulary of neoclassical elements which can be applied to any type of façade – an assumption made by many of the Post-Modern architects of the 1980s. The lessons of Palladianism – the essential role of proportion, the importance of materials, the harmony of the whole – are timeless, and as applicable to modern architecture and design as they were to the buildings of the Augustan Age.

Richard Boyle, Third Earl of Burlington (1694–1753)

Inheriting his title and estates at the tender age of ten on the death of his father, the Second Earl, within ten years Burlington was well established as one of the leading Whig aristocrats in the north of England. Soon after the accession of George I he became interested in architecture, visiting Italy in 1719 with the express intention of learning more about Palladio. His initial reliance on the architect Colen Campbell, who remodelled the Earl's Piccadilly home, was by the mid-1720s replaced by an affection for a new protégé, William Kent. Burlington's fascination with Italian opera received a major setback with the collapse in 1728 of his Royal Academy of Music. However, his interest in sixteenth- and seventeenth-century Italian architecture – and his reverence for Inigo Jones – resulted not only in lavish patronage of works such as Kent's *Designs of Inigo Jones* of 1727 and *Fabbriche Antiche*, a collection of Palladio's drawings published in 1730; Burlington also designed some of the earliest and most influential English Palladian buildings. His compositions – among them the villa at Tottenham Park, Wiltshire, begun in 1721, his house for General Wade in London's Great Burlington Street of 1723, the new Assembly Rooms in York of 1731–2 and his own home, Chiswick House, in Middlesex – were astonishingly new. They did, however, betray a rather slavish devotion to the memory of Palladio and Jones, maintained at the expense of domestic convenience. After the completion of the Assembly Rooms in 1732, Burlington designed few new buildings, but largely confined himself to advice and guidance to others. By 1740 he had wearily cast off his rôle as godfather to the Palladian movement, retiring to Chiswick and Yorkshire and living the life of a semi-recluse.

William Buckland (17?–1774)

One of the wave of British craftsmen who were enticed over to the American colonies during the 1750s, Buckland was originally trained as a carpenter and plasterer in England. Following his arrival in North America, however, he turned his attention to design as well as execution. He introduced both the latest Palladian forms and the newest 'Chinese' decoration into the interiors of Gunston Hall, Virginia in the late 1750s, and by 1770 his name was well established on America's east coast as the finest interior designer of the day. Much of his subsequent career was centred on the Maryland capital of Annapolis; it was here that his masterpiece (now known as the Hammond-Harwood House) was built in the early 1770s, being unfinished at the time of his death in 1774. Buckland's engaging, typically Palladian villa style, deceptively simple outside yet with rich plaster-work and bold mouldings inside, proved enduringly influential on North American homes of the next two centuries.

Colen Campbell (1676–1729)

Campbell, a Lowland Scot educated in Edinburgh, originally trained as a lawyer, being termed in 1702 'the best civilian that past [sic] since the Revolutione'. Possibly influenced by his fellow-Scot, the architect James Smith, Campbell soon became interested in architecture. After completing a villa at Shawfield, near Glasgow, in 1712, he moved south to London, where he was enlisted by the originators of *Vitruvius Britannicus* as a suitably learned and eloquent 'front man'. 1715 was Campbell's *annus mirabilis*: having made his name with the publication of Volume I of *Vitruvius Britannicus* (a work which included a number of Campbell's own designs) and begun work on a revolutionary Palladian house at Wanstead for the banker Sir Richard Child, he was also rapidly integrated into the rising Burlington House and Leicester House sets. His great works date from the mid-1720s: the classical Palladian villa at Stourhead, built for banker Henry Hoare and completed by 1725; Houghton Hall, the massive Norfolk mansion begun in 1722 for Robert Walpole; Mereworth Castle, the Neo-Palladian villa built for John Fane, Earl of Westmorland, in c.1722–5; Compton Place in Sussex, rebuilt for would-be Prime Minister Spencer Compton in 1726–7; and the small but influential villa erected for Henry Herbert, later Ninth Earl of Pembroke, opposite the remains of Whitehall Palace in 1724. By 1726, however, Campbell (having been saved from ignominy by Burlington seven years before, when involved in the tragi-comedy of William Benson's tenure at the Royal Works) had fallen out with Burlington. Although he secured the post of Surveyor of Greenwich Hospital on Vanbrugh's death in 1726, he designed little before his own premature death three years later.

John Channon (1711–c.1783)

Channon was born in Devon and apprenticed to an Exeter joiner, but by 1737 was trading in London. His only signed pieces are two large bookcases at Powderham Castle, near Exeter, which have brass tablets engraved 'J Channon Fecit 1740'; most of the other pieces assigned to Channon are ascribed to him for reasons of style alone. The heavy, sumptuously ornamented style of Channon's furniture owes much to William Kent and to the Baroque forms of the seventeenth century. Like Kent's furniture, Channon's works drip with dramatic, overscaled classical allusions, often finished in gilt or ormolu. As Geoffrey Beard and Christopher Gilbert have noted, his 'distinctive repertoire of flamboyant ormolu mounts include satyr and nereid masks, elaborate cartouche-shaped handle and keyhole plates and elaborate foot mounts' (although 'his decorative brass inlay work is curiously old-fashioned'). Peter Thornton and others have suggested that the Germanic style of many of Channon's earlier works was due to his reliance on German labour in his workshop. However, by 1760 both Germanic and Kentian influences had been toned down in favour of a more fashionably neoclassical but undoubtedly duller style.

James Gibbs (1682–1754)

Born near Aberdeen of Catholic parents, Gibbs began training as a candidate for the priesthood before he turned to architecture. Travelling to Italy, he became a pupil of the leading Roman architect of the day, Carlo Fontana, and returned to Britain in 1709 far better versed in current continental architecture than any of his contemporaries. However, his Catholicism and his links with Tory patrons prevented him from building a career based on official patronage after 1714, his subsequent practice being largely limited to churches and country houses for patrons outside the Palladian establishment. Partly as a result of this, Gibbs' buildings betray the influences of Hawksmoor-inspired and Italian Baroque, curiously mixed with elements of Palladian orthodoxy. His London church of St Martin-in-the-Fields of 1722–6 had an enormous influence on the ecclesiastical architecture of the period, and particularly on the new churches of the American colonies. Equally influential were the two pattern-books designed by Gibbs to provide rules and guidance for the builders of modest Georgian homes: the *Book of Architecture* of 1728 (possibly the most well-thumbed architectural work of the period) and his *Rules for Drawing the Several Parts of Architecture* of 1732.

William Kent (1685–1748)

Born at Bridlington in East Yorkshire, Kent was apprenticed to a local coach-painter before being sent to Italy in 1709 with the connoisseur John Talman. Working there as an artist, in 1719 he met the Earl of Burlington, who brought him back to live at Burlington House. As a result of Burlington's political influence, he was hired as a history painter over the head of the experienced and clearly superior Sir James Thornhill; at the same time he was commissioned to edit Burlington's pet project, *The Designs of Inigo Jones*, which appeared in 1727. By the early 1730s, having acknowledged his failure as a history painter, he turned to architecture, to landscape design and to interior decoration – proving adept at designing every element of the Palladian interior, from seat furniture to cornice. His polymath mind encompassed works as diverse as the vast Palladian mansion of Holkham Hall in Norfolk, designs for Rysbrack's Westminster Abbey monuments to Stanhope and Newton, the Gothic screen at Gloucester Cathedral, chimneypieces and furniture for the interiors of Robert Walpole's Houghton Hall and the 'natural' garden at Rousham in Oxfordshire. His political connections continued to serve him well. In 1739 he was, astonishingly, appointed Portrait Painter to the King (although George II wisely refused to sit for him), while his tenure on the Board of Works brought him the commission for the new Horse Guards block as well as a host of (ultimately unexecuted) projects for ambitious new royal and government buildings. While his furniture designs were heavy and predictably architectural in conception, his gardens represented a revolutionary break with the formalized garden planning of the seventeenth century. As Horace Walpole famously observed, Kent 'leaped a fence, and saw that all nature was a Garden'.

Batty Langley (1696–1751)

The son of a gardener in Twickenham, Middlesex, Langley was an ambitious, populist author who by 1728 was already advertising his services as a surveyor, joiner, engineer, canal-builder and gardener. A xenophobe in the mould of Hogarth, and a fierce opponent of Palladio, Jones and the prevailing Burlingtonian Palladianism of the Augustan establishment, he relied on his powerful masonic connections for the success of his books. His gardening books of the 1720s helped to foster the new enthusiasm for the 'natural' garden style. His architectural works, however, were rarely innovative and relied heavily on drawings pirated from other books; when he did attempt something novel, like his five 'Gothic' orders of 1742, the results were often ludicrous. Yet his vast output of pattern-books, from *Practical Geometry* of 1726 to *The Workman's Golden Rule* of 1750, exercised a great influence on contemporary builders and craftsmen, couching the Palladian proportions of the day in language simple enough for most literate workmen to understand.

William Linnell (c.1703–63)

By the mid-1720s Linnell, having trained with a member of the Joiners' Company, set up his own carving workshop in Long Acre, near Covent Garden in London. Before the late 1730s he concentrated largely on carving commissions, but thereafter produced increasing amounts of furniture. Like many other firms of the period, Linnell's shop was able to supply customers with most of the items for a fashionable interior: mirror-frames, picture-frames, upholstery for the seat furniture and even wooden mouldings for the cornice, dado rail and skirting. His thriving furniture workshop was taken over on his death by his eldest son John, soon to prove an even more renowned furniture-maker than his father.

Roger Morris (1695–1749)

Morris began life as a bricklayer and joiner, but was taken up first by Colen Campbell and then by Henry Herbert, who in 1733 succeeded to the title of Ninth Earl of Pembroke. With Pembroke's help, Morris won commissions for the prototypically Palladian villa of Marble Hill, begun in 1724 for the mistress of the future George II, and for Royal Lodge (now known as White Lodge) in Richmond Park, completed for George II himself in 1728. Morris' subsequent career largely comprised country villas and urban townhouses. Like Burlington, his classical style continued to be heavily reliant on Palladio and Jones, and did not develop significantly during the 25 years of his architectural practice. Like William Kent, however, Morris showed himself to be adept at accommodating himself to both academic and more fanciful Gothic styles – a versatility that was abhorred by his kinsman and one-time pupil, the architectural theorist and pattern-book author Robert Morris (1702–54).

John Wood (1704–54)

Born and raised in Bath, Wood devoted most of his career to buildings in the Ancient Roman city. After 1727 he concentrated on plans to build a 'New Town' in Bath, the first executed expression of which was his ground-breaking Queen Square, completed in 1736. His highly eccentric *Essay Towards a Description of Bath* of 1742 elaborated the architect's bizarre architectural ideology, based on what he perceived to be the historic fusion of Judaic, Druidic and Roman influences. The conclusions he arrived at are to be seen executed in stone in the frieze of his most famous work, the Circus in Bath. Begun in 1754, the year of Wood's death, the Circus was completed by his son, John Wood the Younger, who helped realize his father's grandiose schemes for Bath with the addition of the revolutionary Royal Crescent.

For comprehensive guides to the architects and furniture-makers of the Palladian era, see Howard Colvin's *Biographical Dictionary of British Architects 1600–1840* (London: John Murray, 1978) and Geoffrey Beard and Christopher Gilbert's *Dictionary of English Furniture Makers 1660–1840* (Haywards Heath: Furniture History Society/W S Maney, 1986).

Acanthus
Thick-leaved plant used as the basis for the **capitals** of the Corinthian and Composite orders (the latter a hybrid of Ionic, with its ram's horns, and Corinthian). Also widely used by the Palladians for **cornice** and **dado rail** mouldings.

Acroterion
Originally a plinth to carry an ornament placed at the summit or the corner of a **pediment**. In the eighteenth century acroteria were more usually quadrant-shaped 'ears' found at the corners of pediments or cabinet tops.

Anthemion
Ornamental motif based on the honeysuckle flower and leaves.

Architrave
Popularly, a moulded door or window surround. More strictly, the lowest part of the **entablature**, above the capital.

Arris
The sharp edge of a brick.

Ashlar
Smoothly dressed stone-work, with narrow joints.

Astragal
Small, semi-circular-profiled moulding. Also a section of window-glazing bar (called in the US a muntin).

Attic
The uppermost storey of a building, often sited above the principal external **cornice**; also the internal roof space.

Baluster
A short vertical post supporting a horizontal rail, forming a **balustrade**. In a staircase, the upright sticks supporting the handrail.

Bead
Small, semi-circular moulding, either a continuous line or resembling a string of individual beads. If the beads are alternated with narrow disks, this moulding is called bead and reel.

Bolection moulding
A heavy moulding, common in the seventeenth and early eighteenth centuries, used to hide the joint between two surfaces at different levels.

Bracket
A support designed to carry a horizontally-projecting element. A console is a bracket with a curved outline.

Buckram
Coarse hemp cloth, used by furniture-makers or decorators to stiffen upholstery and bed and curtain valances. Also, according to Peter Thornton, used in the seventeenth century for sunblinds.

Calico
Strong cotton cloth, resembling linen in texture. Its name originates from one of its principal sources: 'Calicut' (Calcutta), in what was at one time Portuguese India but which later passed into the ownership of the East India Company. Imported from India until the 1770s.

Cambric
Fine, white linen cloth, often used for bedclothes.

Canvas
Very coarse hemp or flax (linen) cloth; also known as bolting.

Capital
Decorated or moulded head of a column or **pilaster**. Its form varied according to the order used.

Caryatid
Column or **pilaster** in the shape of a female figure. The male equivalents were called Atlantes.

Casement
Traditional type of window prior to the mid-seventeenth century; side- or top-hung, opening inwards or outwards. Largely replaced by the sash window in new buildings after 1720. (See also **Scotia**.)

Cavetto
Concave moulding, a quarter circle in section.

Chintz
Printed or possibly even painted cotton. Imported from India during the Palladian era, its name derives from the Hindi 'chint', meaning 'spotted cloth'.

Coffering
Classical ceiling decoration comprising recessed panels. Much used by Inigo Jones, and thus also by the eighteenth-century Palladians.

Cornice
The upper part of the **entablature**, or the uppermost, moulded part of an internal or external wall.

Cyma recta
Double-curved moulding with a 'hollow at the top, and swelling at the bottom, so that its out-line has a waved appearance' (Isaac Ware, 1756). Also called an ogee. The reverse of this, with a swelling top and concave bottom, is termed a cyma reversa.

Dado rail
Continuous wooden or plaster interior moulding corresponding to the level of a chair back. Also called a chair rail. The section of wall below this and above the skirting is termed the dado.

Damask
Reversible patterned fabric, usually in one colour. The satin pattern is produced by exploiting the contrast

between the warp and weft of the fabric, and is most commonly executed in cotton or silk.

Deal
Cut planks of fir or pine timber. The word comes from the Low German 'dele', meaning 'plank'. Imported from the Baltic and, increasingly, from the American colonies.

Dentil
Plain, projecting moulding with a square, tooth-like profile. Often found in simple Palladian **cornices**.

Dimity
Cheap cotton fabric, sometimes striped. 'White dimity' was used as a furnishing fabric in rural cottages, particularly for curtains and bed-hangings. Originally imported from India, by the 1720s it was being made in Lancashire.

Diocletian window
A semicircular window divided into three parts by two prominent, vertical mullions. Originally found in the ancient Baths of Diocletian; for this reason also called a thermal window.

Distemper
A painted finish used for plaster, comprising (at least in the eighteenth century), chalk or 'whiting' mixed with soluble glue and water, and pigmented. Pigments which were suitable for distemper were often not

appropriate for oil paints, and vice versa.

Drugget
Thin cloth used to cover floors, carpets or furniture. Usually half-wool and half-linen, and twilled.

Egg and dart
Very common moulding in the Palladian period, resembling eggs and arrowheads and a quarter-circle or **ovolo** in profile.

Entablature
Upper part of a classical order, situated above the **capital** and comprising the **architrave**, **frieze** and **cornice**.

Festoon
Decorative swag of carved or moulded foliage. Also, by 1750, the label given to a single, vertically hung curtain.

Fillet
Small, flat band placed between more elaborate mouldings.

Frieze
Central section of the **entablature**, often decorated with mouldings or suitably classical motifs. In the textile world, the word is used to denote a stout, coarse woollen cloth often employed for simple upholstery.

Gazebo
Small yard or garden summerhouse, sometimes

attached to the house. Not to be confused with the garden privy.

Gibbs surround
Pattern of projecting **quoins** round a window or door, used in combination with a prominent keystone. Although used by the Italian architects of the sixteenth century, in Britain it was named after the architect James Gibbs, who popularized it in his executed buildings and printed guides.

Guilloche
Decorative moulding made up of interlaced Ss.

Guttae
Small, cone-like projections added below the **triglyph** of a **frieze**. (See also **Metope**.)

Holland
Linen cloth originally imported from the United Provinces (present-day Holland), but by the eighteenth century being made in Britain. Widely used for sheets and bed-hangings.

Japanning
Coloured lacquering (usually black or red) applied to imported Japanese cabinets.

Lath
A long, thin, riven or sawn piece of wood nailed to ceiling joists to give a purchase for internal plastering.

Mathematical tile
Clay tile with a large nib,

laid on a vertical wall in interlocking courses to give the appearance of brick-work.

Metope
The square space between two **triglyphs** (motifs with three vertical projections) on a Doric frieze.

Modillion
Scroll-shaped bracket, often used in Palladian cornices.

Moreen
Worsted cloth stamped with a waved or 'watered' finish, very popular for curtains and wall-hangings.

Moulding
Contour or pattern given or added to projecting surfaces in both architecture and furniture.

Muslin
Fine cotton imported from India, used for semi-transparent curtains or bed-hangings.

Newel post
Upright termination of a staircase or a flight of **balusters**.

Order
Classical architectural formula of base, column and **entablature** which constituted the most fundamental unit of Ancient Greek and Roman architecture. The five orders range from Doric and Tuscan, the plainest, to Ionic, Corinthian and the most elaborate of all,

Composite – an exuberant hybrid of the third and fourth orders.

Ormolu
Gilded alloy of copper, zinc and tin (or, in Britain by 1750, merely lacquered brass). Used for picture frames and furniture mounts.

Ovolo
Large convex moulding, a quarter-circle in profile. Also called an echinus and, by Inigo Jones, a boustell.

Patera
Flat, circular or oval ornament, often decorated with a stylized flower pattern. Commonly used at the upper corners of chimney surrounds which are not provided with either columns or **pilasters**.

Pediment
Classical architectural termination, either triangular or segmental (ie curved: a segment of a circle). A pediment with its top interrupted is called an open pediment; one which has the base moulding interrupted is called a broken pediment.

Pilaster
Flat-faced column. Not to be confused with an engaged column, a cylindrical column half-embedded in the wall behind.

Plaid
Worsted material with

interwoven stripes, used variously for bed-hangings, curtains and seat furniture. Also referred to as 'plod'.

Plush
Pile fabric, easily matted, woven from silk, wool or cotton. Frequently used for upholstery, when it was often striped.

Quirk
Sharp incision or undercutting between mouldings or adjacent surfaces, designed to throw a shadow.

Quoin
Stone or brick at the corner of a building which projects from the wall surface.

Rail
Horizontal member of a door or window, or of a piece of furniture. The meeting rails of a sash window are those rails which interlock when the sash is shut.

Reeding
Combination moulding formed from groups of beads.

Render
Plaster covering of a wall, which during the eighteenth century denoted both lime and gypsum plasters used inside and out.

Riser
The vertical element of the stair, which precedes the flat tread.

Rustication
The practice of deeply incising masonry blocks to give a strong, powerful texture. Often used to denote the basement floor of a Palladian building, and can be found simulated in stucco.

Sarcenet
Thin silk, used as a lining for curtains in grand households.

Satin
Twilled weave with a very smooth texture, designed to catch the light. Made of silk, cotton or worsted.

Scotia
Hollow moulding representing the reverse of the **ovolo**. Also called a **casement**.

Serge
Twilled cloth with a worsted warp and woollen weft, often used for upholstery, for bed- and furniture-covers and for plain curtains.

Settee
Multi-seat chair, derived directly from the design of chairs in the same suite. A sofa was originally designed independently of other seat furniture in the room.

Shag
Cheap worsted fabric with a heavy pile, used for bed-coverings and basic upholstery.

Skirting
Plain or moulded board at the bottom of the wall, corresponding to the plinth of the classical orders. (Called in North America a 'baseboard'.)

Stile
The vertical structural member of a door, window or item of furniture.

String
The side support to the risers and treads of a staircase. An open string stair has the tread ends visible, a closed string stair has the treads terminating in the rising string. Neither of these should be confused with a **string course**.

String course
Projecting horizontal band, comprising one course of brick or stonework, on the external wall of a building.

Stuff
General term referring to worsted cloths or indeed to all textiles.

Tabby
Heavy, plain silk, generally watered or waved, much used for curtains.

Term
Pedestal topped with a human or animal figure which tapers towards the bottom. Often used as a garden ornament.

Ticking
Strong linen twill woven in a herringbone pattern, and often striped. Used for mattresses and pillows, since the dense texture prevented the escape of the feathers or straw inside.

Torus
Thick, projecting moulding looking like a cable.

Tuck pointing
The technique by which inferior brickwork would, at a distance, give the impression of finely cut gauged bricks. Thin, straight lines of white mortar were tucked in to a base mortar the same colour as the bricks themselves.

Twill
Type of weave in which each weft row starts one thread further on, creating a diagonal pattern.

Velvet
Cut-pile fabric, made from cotton, wool or silk and during this period generally used for upholstery.

Venetian window
Tripartite window, of which the central opening is taller, and arched. A common motif of Palladian design.

Vitruvian scroll
Wave ornament, often used for Palladian friezes or dado rails, derived from illustrations in Vitruvius' *Ten Books of Architecture*. Also called 'running dog'.

Voussoirs
Bricks or stones radiating from the central, wedge-shaped **keystone**, which form the component parts of a window or door arch.

Warp
Strong threads arranged lengthwise in the loom to form the basis of any fabric. The weft represents the threads interlaced at right angles to these.

Worsted
Any wool yarn which is combed before spinning to produce a smoother texture.

A full glossary of historic textile terms can be found in Florence Montgomery's *Textiles in America* (New York: W W Norton, 1984) or in Pamela Clabburn's *The National Trust Book of Furnishing Textiles* (Harmondsworth: Penguin Books, 1988).

Many directories of suppliers or services which pose as authoritative and critical guides to the best sources for the subject are actually nothing of the sort. Neither are salesmen the best source of balanced information about a particular product or service area. It is thus always important to obtain the advice of an independent expert before you begin any type of repair, renovation, redecoration or research. Some of these are listed below.

Great Britain and Northern Ireland

1. Conservation Officers

In Great Britain, the Conservation Officer of your local District or Borough Council (usually part of that authority's Planning Department) can help on all aspects of renovation or repair. He or she can advise on good local suppliers and craftsmen, and provide information on any local authority grants that are available. Some county councils – principally Essex, Hertfordshire, Kent and Hampshire – also have expert conservation units which can help in a similar way. If your building is listed, the Conservation Officer can provide you with listing details of the history of the structure. In Northern Ireland, similar advice can be given by the Department of the Environment.

2. National Amenity Societies

The Georgian Group
6 Fitzroy Square
London W1
tel 020 7387 1720
(Introductory guides and general information on Georgian buildings)

The Society for the Protection of Ancient Buildings
37 Spital Square
London E1 6DY
tel 020 7377 1644
(Guides to most aspects of maintenance and repair)

3. Specialist Societies

The Brick Society
Woodside House
Winkfield
Windsor
Berkshire SL4 2DX

The Furniture History Society/The Wallpaper History Society
c/o Furniture & Interiors Department
Victoria & Albert Museum
South Kensington
London
SW7 2RL
tel 020 7938 8500

The Historical Lighting Club
23 Northcourt Drive
Abingdon
Oxon

The Men of the Stones
The Rutlands
Tinwell
Stamford
Lincolnshire
PE9 3UD

The Stone Federation
82 New Cavendish Street
London W1M 8AD
tel 020 7580 5588

The Tiles & Architectural Ceramics Society
Reabrook Lodge
8 Sutton Road
Shrewsbury
Shropshire SY2 6DD
tel 01743 236127

The UK Institute of Conservation
37 Upper Addison Gardens
London W14 8AJ
tel 020 7603 5643

4. Specialist Museums

Bristol Museum and Art Gallery (Applied Art Department)
Queens Road
Bristol BS8 1RL
tel 01272 299711
(Furnishing fabrics)

The Brooking Collection
University of Greenwich
Oakfield Lane
Dartford
Kent
DA1 2SZ
tel 020 8316 9897
(Examples of doors, windows, staircases and other elements of the house)

English Heritage
Architectural Study Centre
The Ranger's House
Chesterfield Walk
Blackheath
London SW3
tel 020 7208 8200
(Elements of the Georgian house, with a fine collection of historic wallpapers)

High Wycombe Chair Museum
Priory Avenue
High Wycombe
Buckinghamshire
tel 01494 421895

Ironbridge Gorge Museum
Ironbridge
Telford
Shropshire TF8 7AW
tel 0195 245 3522
(Examples of ironwork from the early days of the Industrial Revolution)

Queen's Park Conservation Studios
Rochdale Road
Harpurhey
Manchester M9
tel 0161 205 2645

Temple Newsam House
Temple Newsam Park
Leeds LS15 OAE
tel 01532 647321
(Floor and wall coverings, furniture and lighting)

Textile Conservation Centre
Apartment 22
Hampton Court Palace
Hampton
Middlesex
tel 020 8977 4943

Victoria & Albert Museum
(Furniture & Interiors and Metalwork Departments)
South Kensington
London SW7 2RL
tel 020 7938 8500

Whitworth Art Gallery
Oxford Road
Manchester M15 6EX
tel 0161 273 4865
(Historic wallpapers)

5. Houses Open to the Public

Abbot Hall
Kirkland
Kendal
Cumbria
tel 01539 722464

The Banqueting House
Whitehall
London
SW1
tel 020 7839 3787
(Historic Royal Palaces)

Chiswick House
Burlington Lane
Chiswick
London
W4
tel 020 8995 0508
(English Heritage)

Ebberston Hall
Ebberston
Near Scarborough
North Yorkshire
tel 01723 859516

18 Folgate Street
Spitalfields
London
E1 6BX
tel 020 7247 4013
(Evening and Sunday tours, by prior appointment only)

Holkham Hall
Holkham
Near Wells-next-the-Sea
Norfolk
tel 01828 710227

Houghton Hall
New Houghton
Near Harpley
Norfolk
tel 01485 528569

Marble Hill House
Marble Hill Park
Richmond Road
Twickenham TW1 2NL
tel 020 8892 5115
(English Heritage)

Nostell Priory
Doncaster Road
Nostell
Wakefield
West Yorkshire
WF4 1QE
tel 01924 863892
(National Trust)

Pallant House
North Pallant
Chichester
West Sussex
tel 01243 774557

Peckover House
North Brink
Wisbech
Cambridgeshire
PE13 1JR
tel 01945 583463
(National Trust)

The Queen's House
Park Row
Greenwich
London SE10
tel 020 8858 4426
(National Maritime Museum)

Rokeby Park
Near Barnard Castle
Co Durham
tel 01833 37334

Rousham
Steeple Aston
Oxon
tel 01869 47110

Saltram
Plympton

Devon PL7 3UH
tel 01752 336546
(National Trust)

Stourhead
Stourton
Warminster
Wiltshire BA12 6QH
tel 01747 840348
(National Trust)

The United States

**1. State Historic
Preservation Offices**
Each state has a designated
state historic preservation
officer (SHPO) whose
responsibilities include conducting statewide invento-
ries of cultural resources,
nominating eligible properties to the National Register
of Historic Places, administering grant and loan programmes, operating historic
museum properties, and
providing public education
and information. Your
SHPO can be an invaluable
source of guidance and
advice on proper preservation techniques, on the
National Register nomina-
tion procedure, on the
requirements for federal tax
credits for rehabilitation,
and on a number of other
subjects. A list of SHPOs
can be found in *Landmark
Yellow Pages.*

**2. Statewide and Local
Preservation
Organizations**
Local preservation organizations exist in hundreds of
communities, bringing
together preservationists for

educational programmes,
conducting tours of historic
homes and neighbourhoods,
offering advice on preservation techniques and sources
of assistance, and issuing
newsletters and other
publications. In addition,
statewide preservation
groups are to be found in
many states, linking local
groups with one another,
lobbying for state and local
legislation supportive of
preservation interests,
administering funding
programmes, and serving as
information clearinghouses.
Your National Trust
regional office (see below)
may be able to provide the
names of statewide and local
preservation organizations in
your area.

**3. Local Historic
District Commissions**
If your house has been
designated a local landmark
or is located in a locally
designated historic district,
you may be required to
obtain the permission of a
review board before making
certain alterations to the
property. Titles of these
boards vary widely as do
the provisions of the
ordinances which they
administer.
Check with city hall
for information on
whether your house or
neighbourhood is governed
by local preservation
regulations.

**4. Historic American
Buildings Survey**

Founded in the 1930s, the
Historic American Buildings
Survey (HABS) is an
invaluable collection of
photographs, measured
drawings, and documentary
research on thousands of
historic structures. To find
out whether a particular
property may have been
documented by HABS, or
to obtain copies of photos
and drawings of document-
ed structures, contact:
Historic American Buildings
Survey
Division of Prints and
Photographs
Library of Congress
Washington, DC 20540
tel 202 707 6394

**5. National Trust for
Historic Preservation**
Chartered by Congress in
1949, the National Trust is
a nationwide non-profit
organization with more
than 250,000 members. Its
mission is to foster an
appreciation of the diverse
character and meaning of
the American cultural heritage, and to lead the nation
in saving North America's
historic environments. The
National Trust publishes a
monthly newspaper, *Historic
Preservation News*, a bi-
monthly magazine, *Historic
Preservation*, and a wide variety of books and other
materials; conducts confer-
ences, workshops, and semi-
nars on a range of preserva-
tion-related topics; supports
the work of local and
statewide preservation organizations; administers a

nationwide collection of
historic museum properties;
and, through its network of
regional offices, offers
advice and information to
preservationists.

**For general member-
ship information,
contact:**
National Trust for Historic
Preservation
1785 Massachusetts Avenue,
N W
Washington, DC 20036
tel 202 588 6164

**For information or assis-
tance with a particular
subject, contact the
appropriate regional
office:**
Mid-Atlantic Regional Office
6401 Germantown Avenue
Philadelphia, PA 19144
tel 215 438 2886
(DE, DC, MD, NJ, PA,
VA, WV, Puerto Rico,
Virgin Islands)

Midwest Regional Office
53 West Jackson Boulevard,
Suite 1135
Chicago, IL 60604
tel 312 939 5547
(IL, IN, IA, MI, MN, MO,
OH, WI)

Mountains/Plains Regional
Office
910 16th Street, Suite 1100
Denver, CO 80202
tel 303 623 1504
(CO, KS, MT, NE, ND,
OK, SD, WY)

Northeast Regional Office
7 Faneuil Hall Marketplace,
5th Floor

Boston, MA 02109
tel 617 523 0885
(CT, ME, MA, NH, NY,
RI, VT)

Southern Regional Office
456 King Street
Charleston, SC 29403
tel 803 722 8552
(AL, AR, FL, GA, KY, LA,
MS, NC, SC, TN)

Texas/New Mexico Field
Office
500 Main Street, Suite 606
Fort Worth, TX 76102
tel 817 332 4398
(NM, TX)

Western Regional Office
1 Sutter Street, Suite 707
San Francisco, CA 94104
tel 415 956 0610
(AK, AZ, CA, HI, ID, NV,
OR, UT, WA, Guam,
Micronesia)

6. Old-House Journal
Published bi-monthly, the
Old-House Journal is an
excellent source of 'how-to'
advice for the do-it-your-
selfer, as well as information of interest to the
old-house aficionado. In
addition to the magazine
itself, the magazine's staff
also publishes an annual catalogue which lists sources of
traditional products for the
old home. For subscription
information, contact:
Old-House Journal
PO Box 50214
Boulder, CO 80321
tel 800 888 9070

7. Other Organizations
American Association for

State and Local History
172 2nd Avenue North,
Suite 202
Nashville, TN 37201

American Institute of
Architects
1735 New York Avenue NW
Washington, DC 20006

American Society of
Interior Designers
608 Massachusetts Avenue,
NE
Washington, DC 20002

Assocation for Preservation
Technology
PO Box 8178
Fredericksburg, VA 22404

Decorative Arts Society
c/o Brooklyn Museum
200 Eastern Parkway
Brooklyn, NY 11238

Society of Architectural
Historians
1232 Pine Street
Philadelphia, PA 19107

8. Museums
Bayou Bend Collection
1 Westcott Street
Houston, TX 77007

Cooper-Hewitt Museum
2 East 91st Street
New York, NY 10128

Daughters of the American
Revolution Museum
1776 D Street, NW
Washington, DC 20006

DeWitt Wallace Decorative
Arts Gallery
Colonial Williamsburg
Williamsburg, VA 23185

Diplomatic Reception
Rooms
US Department of State
2201 C Street, NW
Washington, DC 20520

Henry Francis du Pont
Winterthur Museum
Route 52
WinterthurDE 19735

Metropolitan Museum of
Art
4th Avenue at 82nd Street
New York
NY 10023

Museum of Fine Arts
465 Huntington Avenue
Boston, MA 02115

Philadelphia Museum of Art
26th Street and Benjamin
Franklin Parkway
Philadelphia
PA 19130

9. Houses Open to the Public
Berkeley Plantation
Route 5
Berkeley VA
tel 804 829 0618

Carlyle House
121 North Fairfax Street
Alexandria VA
tel 703 549 2997

Cliveden
6401 Germantown Avenue
Philadelphia PA
tel 215 848 1777

Codman House
Codman Road
Lincoln MA
tel 617 259 8843
(SPNEA)

Drayton Hall
3380 Ashley River Road
Charleston SC
tel 803 766 0188
(NTHP)

Oliver Ellsworth
Homestead
778 Palisado Avenue
Windsor CN
tel 203 688 8717

Hammond-Harwood House
19 Maryland Avenue
Annapolis MD
tel 301 269 1714

Moffat-Ladd House
154 Market Street
Portsmouth NH
tel 603 436 8221

Monticello
Charlottesville VA
tel 804 295 8181

Mount Clare Mansion
Carroll Park
Washington Boulevard
Baltimore MD
tel 301 837 3262

William Paca House
Prince George Street
Annapolis MD
Tel 301 263 5553

Powel House
244 South Third Street
Philadelphia PA
tel 215 627 0364

Betsy Ross House
239 Arch Street
Philadelphia PA
tel 215 627 5343

Sayward-Wheeler House
79 Barrell Lane Extension

York Harbour ME
tel 207 363 2709
(SPNEA)

Sheldon-Hawks and Wells-
Thorn Houses
Deerfield CN
tel 413 774 5581

Shirley
Route 5
Shirley VA
tel 804 829 5121

Stratford Hall
Route 214
Stratford VA
tel 804 493 8038

Webb-Deane-Stevens
Museum
211 Main Street
Wethersfield CN
tel 203 529 0612

Wentworth-Coolidge
Mansion
Little Harbor Road
Portsmouth NH
tel 603 436 6607

Wentworth-Gardner House
140 Mechanic Street
Portsmouth NH
tel 603 436 4406

Westover
Route 5
Westover VA
tel 804 829 2882

Wilton
South Wilton Road
Richmond VA
tel 804 282 5936

Chapter one
The Augustan Age

Beard, Geoffrey. *The Complete Gentleman*. New York: Rizzoli, 1993.

Black, Jeremy (ed.). *Britain in the Age of Walpole*. Basingstoke: Macmillan, 1984.

Borsay, Peter. *The English Urban Renaissance – Culture and Society in the Provincial Town 1660–1770*. Oxford: Oxford University Press, 1989.

Brownell, M R. *Alexander Pope and the Arts of Georgian England*. Oxford: Oxford University Press, 1978.

George, M Dorothy. *London Life in the Eighteenth Century*. Harmondsworth: Penguin Books/Peregrine, 1966.

Hay, Douglas, etc. *Albion's Fatal Tree – Crime and Society in Eighteenth Century England*. Harmondsworth: Penguin Books/Peregrine, 1975.

Holmes, Geoffrey. *Augustan England*. London: George Allen & Unwin, 1982.

Jarrett, Derek. *England in the Age of Hogarth*. London and New Haven: Yale University Press, 1974.

Porter, Roy. *English Society in the Eighteenth Century*. Harmondsworth: Penguin Books, 1982.

Sedgwick, Romney (ed.). *Memoirs of Lord Hervey*. London: 1952.

Speck, W A. *Stability and Strife: England 1714–1760*.

Sevenoaks: Edward Arnold, 1977.

—*Society and Literature in England 1700–60*. Dublin: Gill & Macmillan, 1983.

Thompson, E P. *Whigs & Hunters: Origin of the Black Act*. Harmondsworth: Penguin Books, 1975.

Toynbee, Philip (ed.). *The Letters of Horace Walpole*. London: 1903.

Chapter two
The Origins of Palladian Style

Ackerman, James. *Palladio*. Harmondsworth: Penguin Books/Pelican, 1966.

Harris, John. *Catalogue of the RIBA Drawings Collection: Inigo Jones and John Webb*. London: RIBA Publications, 1972.

—*The Palladians*. London: Trefoil Books, 1981.

Harris, John and Higgott, Gordon. *Inigo Jones*. London: Royal Academy of Arts, 1989.

Higgott, Gordon, 'Inigo Jones's Theory of Design' in *Architectural History*, vol. 35, 1992.

Kaufmann, Emil. *Architecture in the Age of Reason*. New York: 1955; reprinted London: Dover Publications, 1965.

Lewis, Douglas. *The Drawings of Andrea Palladio*. New York: International Exhibitions Foundation, 1981.

Mowl, Timothy. *Elizabethan and Jacobean Style*. London: Phaidon Press, 1993.

Newman, John. 'Inigo Jones's Architectural Education' in *Architectural History*. vol. 35, 1992.

Scamozzi, O B. *L'idea della architettura universale*. Venice: 1615.

Summerson, John. *Inigo Jones*. Harmondsworth: Penguin Books/Pelican, 1966.

Tavernor, Robert. *Palladio and Palladianism*. London: Thames & Hudson, 1991.

Vitruvius Pollio, Marcus, transl. M H Morgan. *The Ten Books of Architecture*. 1914; reprinted New York: Dover Publications, 1960.

Ware, Isaac. *The Four Books of Andrea Palladio's Architecture*. 1738; reprinted New York: Dover Publications, 1965.

Wittkower, Rudolf. *Architectural Principles in the Age of Humanism*. 1949; reprinted London: Academy Editions, 1973.

Chapter three
English Palladianism

Badeslade, Thomas and Rocque, John. *Vitruvius Britannicus, Volume the Fourth*. London: 1739.

Bold, John. *Wilton House and English Palladianism*. Norwich: HMSO Books, 1988.

Boyle, Richard, Third Earl of Burlington. *Fabbriche Antiche disegnate di Andrea Palladio*. London: 1730.

Bryant, Julius. *Mrs Howard*. London: English Heritage, 1988.

Campbell, Colen. *Vitruvius Britannicus, vols 1–3*. London: 1715–25.

Clark, Jane. 'For Kings and Senates Fit' in *Georgian Group Report and Journal*, 1989.

Cruickshank, Dan. 'An English Reason' in *Architectural Review*, April 1983.

Friedman, Terry. *James Gibbs*. New Haven: Yale University Press, 1984.

Hind, Charles (ed.). *New Light on English Palladianism*. London: Georgian Group, 1991.

Kent, William. *Designs of Inigo Jones, with some additional designs*. London: 1727.

Morris, Robert. *An Essay upon Harmony*. London: 1739.

Stutchbury, Howard. *The Architecture of Colen Campbell*. Manchester: Manchester University Press, 1967.

Vardy, John. *Some Designs of Mr Inigo Jones and Mr William Kent*. London: 1744.

Voitle, R. *The Third Earl of Shaftesbury*. Baton Rouge: Louisiana State University Press, 1984.

Wilson, Michael. *William Kent*. London: Routledge & Kegan Paul, 1984.

Wittkower, Rudolf. *Palladio and English Palladianism*. London: Thames & Hudson, 1974.

Chapter four
The Palladian Villa

Adams, W H. *Jefferson's Monticello*. Washington: Abbeville Press, 1983.

Architects' Emergency Committee. *Great Georgian Houses of America*. New York: Dover Publications, 1970 (reprint).

Binney, Marcus. *Sir Robert Taylor*. London: George Allen & Unwin, 1984.

Bold, John. *Wilton House and English Palladianism*. Norwich: HMSO, 1988.

Draper, Marie and Eden, W. *Marble Hill House and its Owners*. London: Greater London Council, 1970.

Hewlings, Richard. *Chiswick House and Gardens*. London: English Heritage, 1989.

Kimball, Fiske. *Thomas Jefferson, Architect*. Harmondsworth: Penguin Books/Massachusetts Historical Society, 1916.

Lees-Milne, James. *Earls of Creation*. Hamish Hamilton 1962, reprinted London: Century Hutchinson, 1986.

Morris, Robert. *Rural Architecture*. London: 1750.

—*The Architectural Remembrancer*. London: 1751.

Nichols, Frederick D. *Thomas Jefferson's Architectural Drawings*. Charlottesville: University Press of Virginia, 1984.

Chapter five
The Palladian House

Cruickshank, Dan and Burton, Neil. *Life in the Georgian City*. London: Penguin Books/Viking, 1990.

Fearn, Jacqueline. *Cast Iron*. Aylesbury: Shire Publications, 1990.

Gibbs, James. *Book of Architecture*. London: 1728.

Harris, Eileen. *British Architectural Books and Writers 1556–1785*. Cambridge: Cambridge University Press, 1990.

Mowl, Timothy and Earnshaw, Brian. *John Wood: Architect of Obsession*. Bath: Millstream, 1988.

Pierson, William H Jnr. *American Buildings and Their Architects: The Colonial and Neo-Classical Styles*. Garden City, NY: Doubleday, 1976.

Summerson, John. *Georgian London*. London: Barrie & Jenkins, 1989.

Chapter six
Fixtures and Fittings

Amery, Colin. *Period Houses and their Details*. Oxford: Butterworth Architecture, 1978.

Brunskill, R W. *Brick Building in Britain*. London: Victor Gollancz, 1990.

Beard, Geoffrey. *The National Trust Book of the English Interior*. Harmondsworth: Penguin Books, 1991.

Cruickshank, Dan and Burton, Neil. *Life in the Georgian City*. London: Penguin Books/Viking, 1990.

Edinburgh New Town Conservation Committee. *The Care and Conservation of Georgian Houses*. London: Butterworths Architecture, 1986.

Gilbert, Christopher, Lomax, James and Wells-Cole, Anthony. *Country House Floors*. Leeds: Leeds City Art Galleries, 1987.

Gilbert, Christopher, and Wells-Cole, Anthony. *The Fashionable Fireplace*. Leeds: Leeds City Art Galleries, 1985.

Lloyd, Nathaniel. *A History of English Brickwork*. 1925; reprinted London: Butterworth Architecture, 1983.

Sambrook, John. *Fanlights*. London: Chatto & Windus, 1989.

Wood, John. *An Essay Towards a Description of Bath*. Bath: 1742.

Chapter seven
Colours and Coverings

Bristow, Ian. 'Historic Town Houses: The Use of Paint and Colour' in Girouard, Mark (ed.), *The Saving of Spitalfields*. London: Spitalfields Trust, 1989.

Clabburn, Pamela. *The National Trust Book of Furnishing Textiles*. London: Penguin Books/Viking, 1988.

Fowler, John and Cornforth, John. *English Decoration in the Eighteenth Century*. London: Barrie & Jenkins, 1978.

Louw, Hentie. 'Colour Combinations' in *The Architect's Journal*, 4 July 1990.

Montgomery, Florence. *Printed Textiles: English and American Cottons and Linens 1700–1850*. London: Thames & Hudson, 1970.

—*Textiles in America*. New York: W W Norton, 1984.

Oman, Charles and Hamilton, Jean. *Wallpapers*. London: Sotheby's Publications, 1982.

Nylander, Jane C. *Fabrics for Historic Buildings*. Washington: Preservation Press, 1990.

Nylander, Richard C. *Wallpapers for Historic Buildings*. Washington: Preservation Press, 1992.

Priestley, Ursula. *The Fabric of Stuffs: The Norwich Textile Industry from 1565*. Norwich: University of East Anglia, 1990.

Rosoman, Treve. *London Wallpapers: Their Manufacture and Use 1690–1840*. London: English Heritage, 1992.

Thornton, Peter. *Authentic Decor: The Domestic Interior 1620–1920*. London: Weidenfeld & Nicolson, 1984.

Von Rosenstiel, Helene and Gail Casey, Winkler. *Floor Coverings*. Washington: Preservation Press, 1988.

Walton, Karin. *An Inventory of 1710 from Dyrham Park*. London: Furniture History Society, 1986.

Wells-Cole, Anthony. *Historic Paper Hangings*. Leeds: Leeds City Art Galleries, 1983.

Chapter eight
Using the House

Bickerton, L M. *English Drinking Glasses 1625–1825*. Aylesbury: Shire Publications, 1984.

Bold, John. 'The Design of a House for a Merchant, 1724' in *Architectural History*, 1990, pp.75–82.

Cooke, Lawrence S (ed.). *Lighting in America*. Main Street Press, 1984.

Cruickshank, Dan and Burton, Neil. *Life in the Georgian City*. London: Penguin/Viking, 1990.

Drummond, J C and Wilbraham, Anne. *The Englishman's Food*. 1939; reprinted London: Pimlico, 1991.

Gilbert, Christopher, etc. *Country House Lighting*. Leeds: Leeds City Art Galleries, 1992.

Girouard, Mark (ed.). *The Saving of Spitalfields*. London: Spitalfields Trust, 1989.

Laing, Alistair. *Lighting*. London: V&A Museum, 1982.

Moss, Roger. *Lighting for Historic Buildings*. Washington: Preservation Press, 1988.

Sparkes, Ivan. *English Windsor Chairs*. Aylesbury: Shire Publications, 1981.

Stead, Jennifer. *Food and Cooking in 18th Century Britain*. London: English Heritage, 1985.

Chapter nine
Revivals

Archer, Lucy. *Raymond Erith*. London: The Cygnet Press, 1985.

Aslet, Clive. *Quinlan Terry*. London: Penguin Books/Viking, 1986.

Banham, Joanna, McDonald, Sally and Porter, Julia. *Victorian Interior Design*. London: Cassell, 1991.

Cornforth, John. 'In the Yorkshire Tradition: The Country Houses of Francis Johnson' in *Country Life*, 8–22 October 1984.

Author's acknowledgements

I would like to thank all those who have helped in the gestation and production of the text, most notably Patrick Baty, Joanna Bush, Howard Colvin, Ivan Hall, John Harris, Richard Riddell, Dwight Young and, of course, Valerie Parissien. Thanks also to those who have helped in obtaining the illustrations for the book, particularly Baer and Ingram, Michael Blake, David Coke, Dan Cruickshank, Philippa Lewis and Gillian Darley at Edifice, The Irish Architectural Archive, The Irish Georgian Society and John Redmill. And especial thanks go to Kit Wedd for her patient and painstaking proofreading, her innumerable and always helpful suggestions, and for her continual support.

Photographic acknowledgements

r: right   l: left
t: top   b: bottom
Bridgeman Art Library/ John Bethell: 102; BAL/Bonhams, London: 207(br & cl); BAL/British Library: 69; BAL/Christies, London: 8, 132; BAL/Cinzano, London: 212 (l & r); BAL/Coram Foundation: 26; BAL/Goodwood House, Sussex: 122; BAL/Guildhall Art Gallery, Corporation of London: 16; BAL/Lennox Money Antiques Ltd: 205 (cl); BAL/Mallet & Sons Antiques: 203(l), 205(tr); BAL/Roy Miles Gallery, London: 65; BAL/National Gallery, London: 47, 187; BAL/Philadelphia Museum of Art (John H McFadden Collection): 171; BAL/Private Collection: 178, 212(c); BAL/Royal Albert Memorial Museum, Exeter: 13, 204; BAL/Royal Naval College, Greenwich: 11; BAL/Sir John Soane's Museum: 146; BAL/Sotheby's, London: 205(bl & r); BAL/Stourhead, Wiltshire: 200(r); BAL/Temple Newsam House: 203(r); BAL/Towner Art Gallery, Eastbourne: 56; BAL/V&A Museum, London, courtesy of the Board of Trustees; 34, 99, 181(t), 213; BAL/Wilton House, Wiltshire: 52; BAL/City of York Art Gallery: 62; Peter Aprahamian, Photographer: 144, 150; Arcaid/Mark Fiennes: 222, 223(l & r);

Baer & Ingram Ltd: 221; Patrick Baty (Papers and Paints, London): 175; Birmingham City Museum and Art Gallery: 185; Michael Blake, Photographer (Dublin): 153, 191(r); Buckinghamshire County Museum: 1(half-title page); Carlyle House Historic Park, Alexandria, Virginia. Courtesy of the Northern Virginia Regional Park Authority: 119; Martin Charles, Photographer: 2, 6, 78(tl), 80(l & r), 81, 87, 89, 90, 108, 136(l & r), 137(l & r), 141, 143, 148, 152(tl & r), 153(l), 154(l & r), 156(l & r), 159, 164(r), 166(l & r), 174(l & r), 185(r), 188, 201(l), 214; Coram Foundation, London: 29; Country Life Picture Library: 219; Dan Cruickshank: 133(r), 134; Courtesy of Drayton Hall, Charleston, South Carolina (A property of the National Trust for Historic Preservation): 116, 155; Edifice, London (Lewis/Darley): 44(bl/Drury), 61, 95, 105, 117, 126, 131, 133(tl), 139(l & r), 142; English Heritage Photographic Library: 109, 208, Endpapers; English Life Publications Ltd, Derby: 74(l & r), 75; Angelo Hornak, Photographer: 41; Houghton Hall, Norfolk: 70(l & r), 71; Anthony Kersting, Photographer: 44; Ken Kirkwood, Photographer: 96, 100, 101, 103(l & r), 110(l & r);

Robert Llewellyn, Photographer (Virginia): 100; The Mansell Collection, London: 14, 18, 22, 23, 35(l & r), 48, 58; Museum of Early Southern Decorative Arts, Salem, North Carolina: 205(tl), 207(t & bl); Musée Historique des Tissus, Lyons: 181; National Gallery, London: 31, 190; National Portrait Gallery, London: 161; National Trust Photographic Library/John Blake, London: 107(b); Ian Parry, Photographer: 91; Private Collection: 205 (cr); Quinlan Terry Architects: 215, 220; RIBA Drawings Collection: 3(title page), 68, 83, 138, 157; The Royal Collection © 1994 Her Majesty the Queen: 51; Eddie Ryle-Hodges, Photographer: 88, 107(t), 140; SCALA, Florence: 44(tl & br); Charles Schoffner, Photographer (Virginia): 118; Tate Gallery, London, by kind permission of the Andrew Lloyd Webber Foundation: 76; Brian Vanden Brink, Photographer (Maine): 120, 164(l); V & A Museum, London, courtesy of the Board of Trustees: 103(c), 163, 168, 179, 181(bl), 182, 183, 200(l), 207(tr); Winterthur Museum, Delaware: 207(cr), 210; Yale Center for British Art, Paul Mellon Collection: 149, 162; City of York Art Gallery: 73; York Castle Museum: 191.

The publishers would especially like to thank the following for their kind assistance and co-operation in the preparation of this book:

The Administrators at Abbot Hall, Kendal; Michael Blake, Photographer; Charles Brooking (The Charles Brooking Collection); Baer & Ingram Ltd; Paul Bancroft Architects; The Clermont Club, London; David Coke at Pallant House; Mr C Cottrell-Dormer; Dr Bill Cotton; Dan Cruickshank; Philippa Lewis, Edifice; Sebastian Edwards, The Iveagh Bequest, Kenwood; Sylvester Groves, Bath; Joanna Hartley at BAL; Mr and Mrs Feeney, Ballymahon; Sir Andrew Morritt; The National Trust for Historic Preservation, Washington; Penny Hawes and Peter Isaac at Peckover House; Eddie Ryle-Hodges, Photographer; Mr Swinburn, Eaglestar; Mr and Mrs de Wend Fenton at Ebberston Hall.